THE
MILITARY-
INDUSTRIAL
COMPLEX

THE MILITARY-INDUSTRIAL COMPLEX

A Historical Perspective

Paul A.C. Koistinen

Foreword by
Congressman Les Aspin

Introduction by
Major Robert K. Griffith, Jr.

PRAEGER SPECIAL STUDIES • PRAEGER SCIENTIFIC

Library of Congress Cataloging in Publication Data

Koistinen, Paul A   C
    The military-industrial complex.

    Bibliography: p.
    Includes index.
    1. War--Economic aspects--United States. 2. In-
dustry and state--United States. I. Title.
HC110.D4K64   330.9'73'09   79-20569
ISBN 0-03-055766-6

Published in 1980 by Praeger Publishers
CBS Educational and Professional Publishing
A Division of CBS, Inc.
521 Fifth Avenue, New York, New York 10017 U.S.A.

Printed in the United States of America

For my mother, father,
and seven siblings

FOREWORD
by Congressman Les Aspin

The Military-Industrial Complex! We even capitalize the words now, as if it were incorporated and had a board of directors, a chief executive officer, and a phalanx of vice presidents.

Even many citizens who hold no truck with conspiracy theories tend to see some sort of formalized structure to the Military-Industrial Complex (MIC). It's viewed as a kind of confederation of business firms and military services.

But in truth there is no structure there—which actually makes the MIC more interesting. The ends of MIC Uninc. are achieved through 1001 individual and basically unrelated decisions, which taken together have the effect of a conspiracy without there ever being one. The decisions are taken not only by the services and their contractors, but also by labor unions, local politicians, and a press inflicted with community boosterism. These factotums, who might otherwise be brawling with one another, rarely link arms in pursuit of the ends of the MIC, but the decisions they take in the pursuit of their perceived self-interest have the same result.

On the other side, there is no other side. The power of a labor union or of a big business is circumscribed by the fact that there are opposite (if not equal) pressures working against it. But the MIC has long functioned in an atmosphere of at best inchoate countervailing pressures. Even the Soviet equivalent of our MIC promotes our Military-Industrial Complex. The two are mutually supporting, as the alleged achievements of one urge the other on to greater heights.

Until C. Wright Mills and Dwight D. Eisenhower pointed their fingers at the MIC two decades ago, the system had the added benefit of functioning without anyone realizing it existed—including those who benefited from it. In more recent years the might of the MIC has been restrained as attention has focused on it. One might say the Military-Industrial Complex is allergic to light. For as the light shed by economists, sociologists, and irate politicians have shone down upon the MIC the Complex has found the going gets more complex.

In a society as intricate as ours, with so many centers of power, light focused on a dark corner of power helps to break down the concentration of authority, or at least to trim the more vile abuses of it.

Paul Koistinen's study adds a whole new dimension to our knowledge of the American MIC. Until now we have tended to think of the Military-Industrial Complex as a by-product of the Cold War. This has led to the not unnatural conclusion that if the MIC waxed when the Cold War waxed, then the MIC will wane as the Cold War wanes. Professor Koistinen, with his original historical approach to the MIC, has burst that bubble. The MIC was there in Philadelphia while the Continental Congress sought to win a revolution, and the MIC will be with us long after the Cold War has been laid to rest.

Broadly speaking the Military-Industrial Complex is one more special interest group seeking special attention from our government—a contract here, a tax benefit there, a rewriting of the regulations to make the pursuit of the golden bough easier, cheaper and, in the end, more profitable. Our first line of defense against these special interests is an understanding of how they came about and how they function. There have been a number of analyses of how the MIC functions; Professor Koistinen adds the knowledge of how it came about.

The passage of time makes it all too easy to assume that things are done in a particular way because that is the natural order of things. We have tended to see the uniformed military as the chief plotter of the Military-Industrial Complex, since if there is any corporate headquarters of the MIC, it would have to be the Pentagon.

Professor Koistinen explodes that myth and shows that the army had to be dragged kicking and screaming into the bed it now finds so comforting. The institution of the army—like the other institutions of nonprofit making government—have historically looked on business disdainfully and shied away from it as from a slime-covered eel. From the Revolution through the nineteenth century one of the constants of the army was to put great distance between itself and private business and to get control of its own supply system. Even the modern complex of military commissaries (supermarkets), which the taxpayer subsidizes to the tune of three-quarters of a billion dollars a year, originated a century ago as the army's reaction to the shoddy goods being foisted on servicemen by sutlers whose sole interest was the fast buck. Yet now the commissary system is one of the nation's biggest food retailers with an intricate web of special interest groups tied to its suppliers. The cure has become a new disease. The Military-Industrial Complex goes far beyond the purchase of weaponry.

Professor Koistinen touches briefly upon an institution with which I like to think I have some familiarity, the United States Congress. He notes in Chapter six that the Committee on the Conduct of the [Civil] War "refused to suspend its judgment in deference to asserted military expertise, and it rejected any assertion of executive privilege in the area of national security."

This, of course, has not been true of the post-World War II era. Since Watergate, however, Congress has reasserted itself in many areas. Regrettably this has not been true in the defense area. The House Armed Services Committee may be a weaker legislative institution today than it was before the Vietnam War. The committee rarely poses fundamental policy questions. It loves to tinker with weapons systems, but tinker only. Several years ago when it saw fit to grapple with a fundamental policy question of whether the army, air force, or Marine Corps should be charged with the mission of close air support, it decided after months of hearings to let all three services go right on doing what they were doing. On commissaries the committee has spent a decade ducking the basic issue of the degree to which the taxpayer should be expected to subsidize the system while spending endless time deciding whether post exchanges should be allowed to sell tires or childrens' wear. In this instance the committee is acting as a referee between the MIC and the private retail interests that view the military retail system as unfair, subsidized competition.

The members of Congress who do not sit on the committee feel they are at a great disadvantage when it comes to judging the military. In their districts they deal every day with issues of education and health policy, with questions of land use and pollution abatement. They feel at home with these issues. But national security and military issues are something else, so on the floor of Congress the membership rarely challenges the judgment of the Armed Services Committee. But since the committee rarely makes judgments in fundamental policy areas, the failure of floor challenges doesn't matter all that much.

The point here is that we ought not to look to Congress—even the post-Watergate and post-Vietnam Congresses that are supposed to be so assertive—to provide true oversight of the Military-Industrial Complex. Oversight will have to originate with an aware and aroused public. Professor Koistinen's work is a major contribution to our increased awareness.

PREFACE

Ever since the publication of C. Wright Mills' classic volume, *The Power Elite* (New York: Oxford University Press, 1956) and President Eisenhower's 1961 farewell address, the Military-Industrial Complex (MIC) has been the subject of spirited and often highly ideological debate. Surprisingly, historians have contributed little directly in the way of analysis of this phenomenon.* They have left the field to sociologists, economists, political scientists, other scholars, public officials or ex-officials, military officers, and journalists. While these analysts have offered many rich insights, the topic suffers from historians' neglect. Without the time dimension which constitutes the historian's framework, the MIC is denied its proper depth and breadth.

One of the major reasons historians have had little to say about the MIC stems, no doubt, from their general unwillingness to confront and deal forthrightly with the operations of power in American society.† This tendency probably results from two related trends prevalent among American historians: first, the dismissal of radical thought as unimportant for or even irrelevant to understanding the nation's past and, second, the assumed, but seldom stated, conviction that the United States is a truly pluralist society. Most so-called New Left historians are an exception to these observations. Defining and examining the operations and consequences of power is admittedly elusive and frustrating, and the historian's narrative or narrative-analytical approach does not lend itself readily to focusing upon concepts such as power. However, without explicitly joining the social scientists' ongoing and heated controversy over whether power is concentrated or fluid in the United States no historian can get very far in analyzing whether an MIC exists or how it operates. For whatever reasons, as long as historians avoid facing the issues of power head on, subjects like the MIC will be denied the time perspective, which can so enrich social scientists' concepts, whose theories and models tend to be restricted by their belief that they need go

---

*Historians have produced valuable edited volumes on the MIC. Particularly important because of its historical framework is Carroll W. Pursell, Jr., ed., *The Military-Industrial Complex* (New York: Harper & Row, 1972).

†An outstanding exception is the prodigious and exciting work of Edward Pessen on the nineteenth-century United States. Pessen cites and summarizes many of his findings in "Who Rules America? Power and Politics in the Democratic Era, 1825–1975," *Prologue* 9 (1977): 5–26.

back no further than World War II to understand the present-day MIC. By training and instinct, the historian knows better.

Of course, many historians deal with power functions, but they do so principally in a tangential and/or peripheral rather than a central manner. The same holds true for their treatment of the MIC. Numerous monographs, biographies, and more general work do contribute to our understanding of the complex. Again, however, the insights gained have frequently been expressed indireclty rather than by outright statement or forthright analysis. Interestingly enough, this was not the case between the wars. As shown in Chapter Six of this volume, a number of historians directed their research and writing toward what we would today call the Military-Industrial Complex, even though they never used that precise designation. This attention grew out of reflections on World War I, the growth of the peace and isolationist movements in the 1920s and 1930s, and the prospect of another war. In Chapter Six, I hypothesize why this interwar ferment among historians ended so abruptly.

By itself, the failure to grapple with power is an inadequate explanation for historians' silence about the MIC. Even New Left historians have contributed little to our knowledge of the complex, the "warfare state," the "national security state," or whatever name is used. Something else must be inhibiting historians. What might be involved is the paucity and mediocrity of written history about the military not immediately associated with combat. A new generation of first-rate historians, such as Russell F. Weigley, Edward M. Coffman, John Shy, Peter Karsten, and Richard H. Kohn, has focused on the armed services. These historians, however, have had to concentrate so much time and effort on mastering subjects previously ignored or parochially treated that they have not yet had the opportunity for producing, either singly or collectively, a full-scale, sophisticated study of the military as a total institution within the entire context of American life. Without such a volume or series of volumes, any historical study of the MIC becomes enormously, almost impossibly, difficult.

I have been grappling with the immensely broad and very weighty, yet maddeningly elusive, topic of the Military-Industrial Complex since writing my doctoral dissertation, which was completed in 1964 and which examined the 1920-45 period. Once completing the dissertation, I extended my research back to World War I in order to understand better what I had already written about in the dissertation. This work resulted in three articles, published between 1967 and 1973.

The next step was to push my research back even further, to the colonial period, in order to explicate more fully my subject matter. As explained in Chapter One, some aspects of the institutional interaction over time which has produced the MIC simply cannot be fully grasped without starting with the colonial years. Additionally, gauging twentieth-century warfare against that of the eighteenth and nineteenth centuries lends a significant richness to the study of the political economy of warfare.

My backward trek proved fruitful in that it allowed me to formulate a theoretical framework for analyzing the institutional interaction which over time has produced the MIC of today. This theoretical construction is presented in Chapter One and is applied generally—and for some periods specifically—in that chapter and Chapter Six.

Before being able to formulate this analytical model, I had to work my way through an enormous amount of the relevant secondary literature and selective primary sources as well. In extending my historical reach from the twentieth century to the colonial period, I inevitably pursued more than one wrong avenue or cul-de-sac. Quite often, I felt overwhelmed both by the ambitious nature of the project and by the quantity of sources involved. Nonetheless, the effort, I believe, was fully worthwhile.

My decision to publish this volume stemmed from an invitation to deliver an address and conduct seminars at the United States Military Academy on the historical evolution of the MIC. Over a period of three days in late February and early March 1979, I met with a class of graduating cadets and faculty members of the American Institutions course. This new, interdisciplinary offering was created at the instigation of the Military Academy's superintendent, General Andrew J. Goodpaster, in order to help break down the "fortress" mentality the army had assumed towards civilian institutions in the wake of the Vietnamese debacle. In my address, I traced the MIC's historical growth and argued that the complex had eroded "military professionalism" rather thoroughly. My speech and the discussion in the seminars created, to the great satisfaction of the faculty, a literal furor among the cadets. In spite of—indeed, because of— their intense response to what I had to say, the cadets were forced to contemplate some hard and unavoidable truths about themselves, the institution they had joined, and American society. In every way, the West Point visit was both revealing and gratifying. The interdisciplinary faculty is most impressive in attitude and training, and the cadets are generally bright, informed, and concerned.

I used the opportunity of the Military Academy address to pull together in a relatively brief statement many of my thoughts about the MIC. Since the address had such a dramatic impact at West Point, I decided that I should publish it now, together with my articles and other essays. In this way, I would have the opportunity to gather in one place my written analyses and conclusions concerning a study which, I believe, says something important and fresh about a subject that is vital to the existence and survival of our society. It is my sincere desire that this volume will cast new light upon the MIC and its origins and that it will be helpful to other scholars, students, government officials, the military, and the public.

Chapter One is based on the West Point address. Chapters Two through Four are published articles. Chapter Five is a critique presented at the Annual Meeting of the Organization of American Historians in 1974 of a paper which proposed that the MIC was declining in importance and power. The last chapter is from a seminar report delivered in January 1975 at the Charles Warren Center for Studies in American History, Harvard University. That report constitutes my fullest statement to date on the political economy of warfare in the United

States. The first chapter is only sparsely footnoted except for the post-World War II period. Some of the sources I have drawn upon for analyzing economic mobilization from the colonial times through the early twentieth century are included in a bibliography which is part of Chapter Six. Elaborate documentation for the period from World War I through World War II is contained in the reprinted articles.

As with any collection of essays on a single theme, which were written over a period of time and for different purposes, this collection includes varying styles and structures and involves some overlapping and repetition. Nevertheless, all of the essays are distinct in that they say something new, address a common theme from a different perspective, or use a different approach.

These essays have benefited from the criticism of several colleagues at Northridge, especially John J. Broesamle, Jr., Ronald L. F. Davis, Sheldon H. Harris, Leonard Pitt, Ronald Schaffer, Morris Schonbach, James E. Sefton, John N. Shaeffer, Reba N. Soffer, and Rena L. Vassar, and Joseph A. Ernst of York University. The superb and demanding editing of Martin Ridge, of the *Journal of American History*; Norris Hundley, Jr., of the *Pacific Historical Review*; and James P. Baughman, of the *Business History Review*, proved extremely helpful in the articles I published in those journals. I already owe such a great debt of gratitude to numerous librarians and archivists whose services I inevitably will call upon yet again in further research that I have decided to delay extending my appreciation to them until later publication. To Robert Soman, David Greenstate, and H. Lee Meyerhoff I can only say thanks for their friendship and valuable support over the years. Without the broad range of secretarial assistance of Judy St. George and Nancy Meadows and the research assistance of Teena Stern-Fagan and Francine Bloom, this book certainly would have been delayed. Finally, the constant support and assistance of my wife, Carolyn Epstein Koistinen, has been indispensable to the completion of this work.

Numerous grants and fellowships from the California State University, Northridge Foundation, from 1964 to the present, and Research Fellowships from Harvard's Charles Warren Center for Studies in American History and the American Council of Learned Societies in 1974–75 have facilitated my research and writing. I am grateful for that assistance.

Of course, I, not those advising me, am responsible for what is and is not said in this study.

The dedication of this volume is not my obeisance to the current fascination about ethnic origins. Instead, it is meant to acknowledge and pay respect to those from whom I received my values.

CONTENTS

LIST OF ABBREVIATIONS

AEF	American Expeditionary Force
AFL	American Federation of Labor
ATC	Army Transportation Corps
BLS	Bureau of Labor Statistics
CIO	Congress of Industrial Organizations
GOPO	Government-Owned, Privately-Operated
ILA	International Longshoremen's Association
MIC	Military-Industrial Complex
MLPC	Management-Labor Policy Committee
NDAC	National Defense Advisory Commission
NIRA	National Industrial Recovery Act
NLRB	National Labor Relations Board
NRA	National Recovery Administration
NSC-68	National Security Council Document Sixty-Eight
OASW	Office of the Assistant Secretary of War
OPM	Office of Production Management
OWM	Office of War Mobilization
OWMR	Office of War Mobilization and Reconversion
PEC	Production Executive Committee
UAW	United Automobile Workers of America
USSR	Union of Soviet Socialist Republics
WDLB	War Department Labor Branch
WIB	War Industries Board
WLB	War Labor Board
WMC	War Manpower Commission
WPB	War Production Board
WPC	War Policies Commission
WRB	War Resources Board

THE
MILITARY-
INDUSTRIAL
COMPLEX

INTRODUCTION
by Major Robert K. Griffith, Jr.

The Military-Industrial Complex (MIC) is more than an issue. It is an American institution. As Professor Paul Koistinen demonstrates in the first essay of this collection, the MIC evolved over a number of years to become, in the words of sociologist Robert Bierstedt, "a formal, recognized, established and stabilized way of pursuing some activity in society."[1] In terms of Bierstedt's definition, the MIC is the accepted process by which other institutions—notably the military, business, and government—work together to provide the nation with the sinews of war.

Koistinen first presented this innovative essay to cadets enrolled in the American Institutions course of the United States Military Academy at West Point in February 1979. In his essay Koistinen does three things. First, he traces the evolution of the MIC from colonial times to the present, Next, he analyzes the impact of the MIC on civil-military relations in the United States. Finally, he comments on the MIC's corrosive effect on the American military.

Unlike those sociologists and political scientists who see the MIC as a relatively recent by-product of the enlarged post-World War II military establishment, Koistinen, one of the few historians to deal systematically with the subject, argues that all of American history is relevant for understanding how and why the MIC of today evolved and operates. Even in colonial society the need for common defense required the coordination of pre-industrial economic, military, and political resources. In this pre-industrial period the principal roles of businessmen-merchants, soldiers, and politicians were often combined in a single individual with the result that efforts to prevent private contractors from taking advantage of public responsibilities depended largely on the personal integrity of the individuals concerned. As the nation matured the industrial revolution vastly complicated both the technology and methods of waging war, and the means by which the economy supported a military establishment. By

1

World War I the scope of the warfare economy had widened to such an extent that the federal government was forced to assume a permanent role as arbitrator in the mobilization process. Since both the military and the government continued to depend heavily on business expertise, the various institutions involved in mobilization remained interdependent, much as they had been in colonial times. Thus the prevention of abuses of public power for personal gain continued to depend largely on the integrity of the business experts and military and political decision makers.

Koistinen argues that the effects of the Military-Industrial Complex on civil-military relations and military professionalism are profound and dangerous. Memories of the chicanery by civilian supply agents and contractors in the eighteenth and early nineteenth centuries were partly responsible for the armed forces insisting on military control of weapons and material procurement. But by the early twentieth century the increasing complexity of war eventually forced the military to integrate its planning and procurement specialists into government regulatory boards established to coordinate mobilization. These government boards—typified by the War Industries Board (WIB) of World War I—also, in part, reflected popular fears that the industrial community required government oversight in time of war lest it place its own interests above those of the nation. But businessmen dominated the WIB and its successors, and the military found itself in a partnership with industry that it had once sought to avoid.

Koistinen maintains that this business-military partnership destroys military professionalism. Proceeding from an elitist model of American society, Koistinen contends that a power elite made up of business, banking, and industrial leaders, dominates the government and thus controls the military. This elite, which relies "upon economic growth to solve most problems," has sought to maintain an American economic empire abroad in order to insure growth at home. Koistinen charges that as a result of its close association with and increased dependence on the business sector since World War II, the military has unwittingly accepted expanded roles for itself as well as weapons that are "useless, inappropriate, or even hazardous to their users." The military has supported business interests as opposed to those truly involving national security. The end result is that the military ethic of selfless devotion to the nation has given way to slavish devotion to a business ethic that has changed little since the colonial period.

It is Koistinen's last point that distinguishes his work from the sizable and by now familiar New Left literature on the Cold War and the MIC. By suggesting that the armed forces' role in the MIC is self-destructive of the military professional ethic, Koistinen joins a small but growing number of scholars in and out of the uniformed services who are deeply troubled about the values and ethics of our military establishment. For example, Charles Moskos, a professor of sociology at Northwestern University, argues that the shift to an all-volunteer armed force has transformed military service. When motivation to serve is defined largely in economic terms the military becomes more and more just another job, and men and women no longer join out of a devotion to a higher order.[2] Richard Gabriel and Paul Savage, professors of politics at Saint Anselm's College and both former army officers, contend that efforts to apply business management techniques to military leadership in the 1960s created a generation of "corporate executives in uniform" who became more concerned with advancing their own careers than with traditional devotion to duty, honor, and country. Gabriel and Savage point to the failure of the army in Vietnam, increased desertion rates, and the recent cheating scandal at West Point as evidence of the military's moral bankruptcy.[3] Captain Andrew Bacevich, assistant professor of history at West Point, sees much deeper roots to the problem. Bacevich suggests that the shift away from the professional ethic of selfless service ironically had its origin in the reorganization of the army begun in the early twentieth century by military reformers like Elihu Root and Leonard Wood. The unintended result of the creation of the General Staff system was the emergence of a larger bureaucracy increasingly concerned with its own self-perpetuation.[4]

In his essay Koistinen urges the military to "participate in the fundamental reordering of its own system for the purpose of reestablishing the professionalism that both it and the nation vitally require." Again, he is not alone. Moskos and his colleague Morris Janowitz, professor of sociology at the University of Chicago, recently proposed specific changes in the system of recruiting the volunteer force aimed at fostering "a civic norm of the importance of national service," which, by implication, would help to purge military service of its drift toward occupational tendencies.[5] Gabriel and Savage urge the establishment of a formal code of ethics for the officer corps and the creation of an independent agency to administer and police it. They also propose several structural reforms, in the nature and duration of service for officers, designed to reduce individual preoccupation with career advancement.[6]

The army itself is seeking to strengthen the commitment to traditional values of service among those now in uniform. At West Point, the addition of both the American Institutions course and a new philosophy course to the curriculum endeavors to acquaint the army's future leaders with the bases of different ethical and value systems. The American Institutions program, an experimental multidisciplinary elective, examines the evolution, structure and function, and value systems of selected national institutions and analyzes how those value systems determine each institution's response to problems confronting American society. At Fort Benjamin Harrison, Indiana, the army's Human Resources Development Division is currently studying systems for ethical and professional development which will be of potential use in future training programs.

There are risks associated with these efforts to define and reinforce professional military values in the armed forces of a democratic society. On the eve of his retirement from the army after 43 years of service, General Walter T. Kerwin, Jr. observed, "The values necessary to defend the society are often at odds with the values of the society itself." American society today is increasingly self-oriented—some would argue selfish and hedonistic. The military, in Kerwin's words, "must concentrate, not on the values of our liberal society, but on the hard values of the battlefield. Those values are simple: Live or Die—Win or Lose."[7] The dilemma is clear. If the military is to be representative of the society it serves, it will acquire perforce norms and values of that society—norms and values that may be destructive to the military function. Yet to preserve the military ethic from such inroads, the armed forces must isolate themselves from the society they are supposed to serve. The resultant divergence of values could one day lead to an unwillingness to defend societal norms and values no longer shared by both soldiers and civilians.

NOTES

1. Robert Bierstedt, *The Social Order* (New York: McGraw-Hill, 1974), pp. 328–329.

2. Charles Moskos, Jr., "From Institution to Organization: Trends in Military Organization," *Armed Forces and Society* 4 (1977): 44–50.

3. Richard Gabriel and Paul Savage, *Crisis in Command: Mismanagement in the Army* (New York: Hill and Wang, 1978), p. 19.

4. Captain Andrew Bacevich, Jr., "Progressivism, Professionalism, and Reform," *Parameters* 9 (1979): 66–71.

5. Morris Janowitz and Charles Moskos, Jr., "Five Years of the All-Volunteer Force: 1973-1978," *Armed Forces and Society* 5 (1979): 171–218.

6. Gabriel and Savage, *Crisis in Command*, pp. 127–143.

7. Walter T. Kerwin, Jr., as quoted in "Values of Today's Army," *Soldiers* (September 1978), p. 4.

1

THE MILITARY-INDUSTRIAL COMPLEX IN HISTORICAL PERSPECTIVE

Addressing the issue of the Military-Industrial Complex at the United States Military Academy has a very special meaning. After all, it was President Eisenhower, a West Point alumnus and a long time soldier, who coined the phrase "Military-Industrial Complex" and used the opportunity of his farewell address in 1961 to warn the nation against its many dangers.[1] For our purposes, it is essential that we establish some working definition of this complex. Let me begin by summarizing the arguments others have presented.

The exponents of the MIC theory take the position that prolonged international conflict since 1945 has produced high levels of military expenditures which have created powerful domestic interest groups who require a Cold War ideology in order to guard their power and prestige within the state's political and economic structure. These interest groups include the military services, corporations, high government officials, various members of Congress, and lesser groups, such as labor unions, scientists and scholars, and defense societies. These groups occupy powerful positions within the state; they are mutually supportive, and, on defense-related matters, their influence exceeds that of any existing countervailing coalitions or interests.

Since most MIC theorists regard this Cold War ideology as either false or exaggerated, they maintain that its adherents either deliberately engage in deception in order to further their own interests, falsely believe themselves to be acting in the broader public or national interest, or some combination of the two. Whatever the case, proponents of arms without end, so-called hawks, serve to perpetuate Cold War tensions. Some MIC theorists also maintain that

---

The following is based on an address delivered at the United States Military Academy, February 27, 1979.

capitalism has no monopoly on defense and war complexes, that the Soviet Union has its own complex, and MICs within the two countries interact to continue a mutually advantageous but actually enormously dangerous and ultimately destructive state of heightened competition.[2]

Historians have used this MIC model but have played little direct part in developing it. That this is so is, I think, unfortunate. I have no wish to denigrate the work of the MIC theory's authors and its detractors, but it seems to me that we lack a historical perspective on the subject and so many questions necessarily are left unanswered and even unaddressed. It is imperative that we address certain basic and important historical issues. First, can we ignore all of U.S. history and still understand fully the present-day Military-Industrial Complex? Second, are there unique aspects distinguishing the U.S. MIC from the MICs of other nations? To answer these questions reliably, we need a comprehensive study of the political economy of warfare in the United States and a comparative study involving the major nations of the world over time. A comparative study is far off, but a comprehensive study of the political economy of warfare in the United States is something this author has been engaged in for many years.

By the political economy of warfare I mean the method a nation has employed to mobilize its economic resources for defense and hostilities. Several key conditions have influenced the mobilization process significantly. While the magnitude and duration of the war have dictated *what* the nation must do to harness its economic power, prewar trends have largely determined *how* it would do so. Of particular importance in determining the method of mobilization are the maturity of the economy; the size, strength, and scope of the federal government; the character and structure of the military services and their relationship to civil society and authority; and, finally, the state of military technology.

From the time of the American Revolution to the present, three major stages are discernible in the American economic mobilization process. The War for American Independence, the Civil War, and twentieth-century warfare best characterize these stages. (I have labeled them pre-industrial, transitional, and industrial. I purposefully have avoided the term "post-industrial" because it seems to make little sense to me.)

During the Revolution, that is, the pre-industrial stage, economic, governmental, and military institutions were all in an embryonic state and were not clearly distinguished one from the other.[3] Additionally, military technology was rather primitive and varied little from what was produced in the peacetime economy. Hence, economic mobilization involved increasing civilian output and diverting products from civilian to military use in order to supply the armed forces without converting the economy. Nonetheless, because the economy's potential was so limited, comprehensive regulation of the nation's economic life became essential. The undeveloped nature of economic, political, and military institutions, however, not only prevented such regulation from ever working well but also resulted in private and public, civil and military activities becoming inextricably intertwined. Merchants simultaneously served as public officials and military officers while they continued to conduct their private business matters with an extraordinary mixing of financial accounts taking place. This state of affairs produced a level of malfeasance, misfeasance, peculation, and corruption so high that it can only be described as treasonable. The colonial business community had developed an ethic in which absolute honesty was insisted upon among merchants themselves but the larger public was largely considered fair game. As discussed below, the attitudes and the practices they spawned had a critical impact upon the future political economy of warfare in the United States.

By 1861, the nation had entered the second, or transitional, mobilization stage. The Union's economy by now had enormous production capacity; it was diversified and quite industrialized. In addition, specialized functions existed in banking, marketing, manufacturing, and the like, although the size of firms was comparatively small. Even though the federal government was limited in size, scope, and activity, it was capable of expanding its existing structure in order to handle the emergency effectively and efficiently. On their part, both military services had become professionalized to the point where they had definable structures and missions. But military technology had progressed little since the revolutionary years. Consequently, economic mobilization again required only expanding and diverting civilian production, not economic conversion. The means employed for accomplishing that end varied significantly from those in the first stage. Now, market forces in a strong competitive economy, not elaborate regulation, were relied upon without intolerable inflation. Moreover, the separation of institutions remained intact. In the economic realm, there was little mixing of activities and personnel among private and public, civilian and military affairs. The only major exception involved the railroads, which had begun to organize themselves as modern corporations before hostilities began.

Union success in economic mobilization contrasted sharply with the Confederacy's failure. Weak economic and political systems consistently undermined the South's economic mobilization effort. Like the colonies/states during the Revolution, the Confederacy experimented with comprehensive economic regulation without much success under increasing, and ultimately devastating, inflationary conditions.

Modern warfare in the twentieth century represents the third, and final, economic mobilization stage. By 1900, the United States had become a mature industrialized nation with a modified capitalist system. While market forces remained significant in the production and distribution of goods, the administered decisions of several hundred modern corporations exercised a strong and at times dominant influence over the economy's direction. In order to make concentrated and consolidated economic power more responsible to the public and also to stabilize an enormously complex economy, the federal government began to act as economic regulator. The growth of huge bureaucracies in the corporate and governmental spheres began to blur the institutional lines between the two. Businessmen often staffed the government's regulatory agencies, and the affairs of government and business touched or merged at many points. A government-business regulatory alliance had begun to emerge during the Progressive Era.

For a time during the late nineteenth century, the military services were in literal isolation in the United States. This isolation can be explained by the fact that the nation had become absorbed in industrialization, that the threat of war had receded, and that the army and navy had become intensely involved in professionalizing their functions. However, among other developments, a technological revolution in weaponry in the later years of the nineteenth century drew the civilian and military worlds back together. The consequences of this revolution were first manifest in the navy. In order to build a new fleet of steel, armor, steam, propeller, and modern ordnance, a production team of political leaders, naval officers, and businessmen had to be put together. Although the composition, responsibilities, and operations of this team have varied, it exists to the present day. The army was slower to feel technology's impact upon its functions, but it eventually experienced the same needs and a similar relationship to industry and civil authorities as had the navy.

It is clear that on the eve of World War I the federal government, the business community, and the military services had all developed complex, modern, and professionalized structures, with each dependent upon the others for national defense. Economic mobilization for World War I forcefully demonstrated this institutional interdependence. The quantity and sophistication of military demand meant that increasing and diverting civilian production was no longer adequate; large sectors of the nation's economic machine had to be converted in order to produce the often specialized military hardware. Market forces could not be relied upon to achieve that purpose. Allocation, priority, price, and rationing controls all had to be introduced, and, unlike conditions during the Civil War, existing governmental departments and agencies were unequal to the task. New mobilization bodies had to be created, the most important of which was the War Industries Board (WIB). Through the WIB, centralized control over a planned economy was established and carried out by representatives of the government, the business community, and the military. In so doing, institutional lines were obliterated. Civilian and military, private and public activities had once again become almost indistinguishable. For very different reasons and with very different results, the first and third, or pre-industrial and industrial, mobilization stages are strikingly similar and both differ from the second, or transitional, stage.

The World War I mobilization experience left an indelible imprint on national life. Between the wars, direct and indirect economic planning patterned after the WIB was tried. Additionally, close ties linking the civil and military sectors of the government, the industrial community, and other new and old interest groups were maintained in order to design, produce, and procure specialized munitions and to plan for industrial mobilization. During World War II, a modified form of the World War I model was used to mobilize the economy. With the Cold War conflict following World War II, the nation, for the first time in its peacetime history, supported a massive military establishment which became inordinately expensive because of a continuing transformation of weaponry through scientific and technological advancement. The result has been a defense and war "complex" that includes and affects most private and public institutions in American life.

The nature of civil-military relations has been vitally affected by the various mobilization stages. Fearful of executive tyranny, the authors of the Constitution divided authority over the military between the executive and legislative branches of government. In historical perspective, this division has proven to be flawed. Before and immediately after the adoption of the Constitution, from 1783 through 1800, the intense nationalists, led by Alexander Hamilton, consistently and almost successfully sought to use the military to subvert the constitutional forms of government. At a time when all institutions were weak and without clear definition, the military, because of the machinations of civilians, constituted a real threat to the nation's constitutional system. Once the various civilian institutions gained strength as separate entities, civilian control of the military was secure during most of the pre-industrial and all of the transitional stages, principally because in peacetime the military remained small, its structure and technology uncomplicated, and its relations with various levels of civilian society casual. During these earlier stages, however, neither the executive, the legislative, nor the two combined ever devised adequate systems for commanding and monitoring the military on a day-to-day basis. Hence, in war, it was the quality of civilian and military leadership, much more than the system, that made the military function properly.

As the military entered the third, industrial stage, it began to grow in size and complexity and also to establish intricate relations with civilian subsections of the federal government, the business community, and other civilian institutions. Although the civil side of the government matured, the basic system for regulating the armed services has remained the same. This regulatory system, which did not work adequately in the first and second stages, has not worked in the third, particularly when civil-military relations have become so intertwined that distinctions between the two in many areas are almost impossible to make. Therefore, as with the political economy of warfare, civil-military relations in the third stage resembles the early first phase, with control over the military being uncertain.

An ongoing analysis of the political economy of warfare in the United States has several virtues, the most important being the opportunity it presents for studying the emergence of American society and the relative strength of various institutions. Since warfare exaggerates prewar conditions, locating the focus of power, determining how and why institutions interact with one another, and assessing the overall maturity of the nation are all facilitated. What remains obscure in times of peace is often made obvious under the strain and demands of war. That being the case, we can draw upon and supplement, where necessary, the information and analysis I have provided up to this point in order to clarify some aspects of the so-called MIC that remain obscure.

In terms of the political economy of warfare, the United States is unique among twentieth-century industrial nations in allowing the armed services to do their own procuring. Why it does so involves the operations of the entire social system and specifically includes; first, when and under what circumstances the armed services achieved control of their own procurement; second, the emergence of a government-business regulatory alliance as the principal mode of twentieth-century political economy; and, finally, the public's long-term reverence for, yet suspicion of, the industrial community.

The armed services did not achieve full control of their own procurement until after the War of 1812, when permanent bureaus like the Quartermaster Corps and the Ordnance Department were created for the army, and similar developments took place in the Navy Department. Up until then, the military services were subjected to varying forms of civilian supply agents and/or contractors who were most unreliable and often thoroughly corrupt. So bad was the system that military commanders frequently considered their services of supply behind the lines a greater threat than the enemy to the front. Consequently, once gaining control of supply, the military was determined never to lose it again. One hundred years later, this attitude had produced such rigidity that the services almost lost control of procurement during World War I.

Between 1915 and 1918, American businessmen fashioned the War Industries Board as the agency for mobilizing the economy for World War I. The WIB was actually no more than an extension and elaboration of the regulatory mechanism the state had built up to monitor the large corporations since the late nineteenth century. It was staffed by industrialists who served largely without compensation and who generally maintained both their positions and incomes as private citizens. As a result, conflicts of interest were rife, and few safeguards existed to insure that the board operated for the larger public interests. Within the Woodrow Wilson administration, Congress, and the public, grave reservations were held about such a vast and blatant surrender of power and responsibility to private interests, who had rather consistently demonstrated a greater capacity for greed than for trust. However, since government lacked the personnel, information, or expertise for mobilizing the economy on its own, no viable alternative method existed.

The nature of the civilian mobilization agency ultimately acted to protect military procurement prerogatives. Paralyzed by the fear of losing control of supply and failing to appreciate the imperatives of modern warfare, the War Department refused to cooperate with the WIB, thus creating a situation that threatened the entire economy. In the face of military recalcitrance, business-men insisted, in effect, that all procurement be turned over to the WIB. This solution was rejected because it would have placed billions of dollars of con-tracts directly in the hands of industry, which few Americans trusted. Instead, the Wilson administration literally forced the War Department to reform its structure and operations and, along with the Navy Department and other buying agents, integrate its personnel into the WIB. With World War I, therefore, we can find the real roots of the current MIC, which, themselves grew out of deep-seated historical trends.[4]

To insure that the armed services remained prepared for modern warfare, Congress in the National Defense Act of 1920 authorized the War Department not only to plan its own operations for economic mobilization but also to plan for the entire economy in wartime. This last charge stemmed in part from Congress's conviction that such planning was safer in military than industrial hands. Although reluctant to undertake what were believed to be civilian re-sponsibilities, the War Department commenced industrial mobilization planning in the early 1920s with several significant results. First, the army planners be-came among the most knowledgeable individuals on World War I mobilization. Second, after a long and bitter conflict, the planners finally succeeded in con-vincing the General Staff that its war plans had to be based on the economy's potential. Only then had the army as a whole fully accepted the radical changes wrought by twentieth century warfare on its operations; industrial production had become at least as important as tactics or strategy to military success. Relat-ing its entire operations to a mobilized economy had become part of the modern military mission. Third, the army planners produced an Industrial Mobilization Plan in 1930, which was repeatedly revised throughout the 1930s and which proposed using a refined version of the WIB to mobilize the economy in a future emergency.

In a curious way, the army's economic mobilization planners aligned themselves with the Special Senate Committee to Investigate the Munitions In-dustry (the famous or infamous, depending upon your point of view, Nye Com-mittee). Between 1934 and 1936, the committee conducted a most comprehen-sive and sophisticated review of the imperatives and consequences of modern warfare. Its most impressive contribution shattered industry's carefully culti-vated image of the WIB as a collection of selfless businessmen sacrificing per-sonal and institutional interests in order to marshall all their ingenuity for the higher purposes of the nation. Although there were numerous instances of true patriotism and sacrifice in economic mobilization, the committee demonstrated that the rampant conflicts of interest in the WIB also left a record of uncon-scionable profiteering and other questionable practices which placed considera-tions of power and the ledger book ahead of those of the nation. If the World War I model was used in another major war, the committee insisted, there would be another round of flagrant profiteering, further consolidation of economic power, and, most seriously, rampant inflation and huge debt, which would gravely distort the foundations of the economy, perhaps permanently.

To avoid such a calamity, the Nye Committee supported legislation which, in the event of war, would prohibit any conflicts of interest in all mobilization agencies, severely tax all sources of income so that the nation could pay for the war largely without borrowing, and draft into federal service any owner or manager of business or industry who proved obstreperous. The committee quickly backed away from this legislation shortly after recommending it. The army's planners, who had worked closely with the Nye Committee throughout its investigations and knew even more than the committee investigators about World War I mobilization, convinced the committee that its legislation would not work. It would take a social revolution and dictatorial forms of government to implement the bill, the army planners maintained. No nation would engage in such a suicidal venture when threatened by or engaged in war. The nation was stuck with all of the virtues and liabilities of its economic system when it went to war; industrialists would run the mobilization show and would insure that their own welfare was, thus, not only protected but also, in all likelihood, furthered. That the interests of industry coincided with those of the nation as a whole was by no means certain. Once embracing those truths, most members of the Nye Committee concluded that the only way to guard against the untoward consequences of modern warfare was to avoid war and even heavy peacetime defense spending. Consequently, committee members became arch-advocates of stringent neutrality legislation and a popular referendum on war as well. The logic of insight had driven the committee to desperation.

Actually, the army planners had gone through an experience very similar to that of the Nye Committee. Once familiar with what had transpired during World War I, they began drafting plans not unlike those that the Nye Committee first proposed and then rejected. These plans brought forth outraged cries from the ex-chairman of the WIB, Bernard M. Baruch, and other former war mobilizers that the army was proposing to take over the civilian economy in the event of war. Quickly retreating, the army planners rewrote their Industrial Mobilization Plans to reflect the World War pattern from 1930 on. However, the planners were most uncomfortable with their handiwork. Circumstances were forcing the armed services into a partnership with industry which, while providing all sorts of advantages, could also sully the military by associating it with industry's too prevalent rapacity and could even distort the military mission. The army planners faced a Hobson's choice. In the face of modern warfare they could not say that they wanted no part of industry; nor could they propose that if war came the nation legislate a revolution. Instead, they suppressed their doubts and went on perfecting their plans.[5]

Principally because of the interwar planning, few problems in industrial-military relations were encountered during World War II compared with World

War I. Nonetheless, economic mobilization for World War II was every bit as tumultuous as it had been for World War I because New Dealers, labor, small business, and public advocates were constantly challenging the industrial-military hold on the economy. For that reason, in addition to the greater sophistication and expertise of government inflation rates were less than in World War I, taxation produced more revenue and was more equitable, and profit rates were more modest. Still and for all, on every key issue, industry and the military engaged in a practice of mutual support which reached proportions of irresponsibility for the nation as a whole.[6] The trepidations of the Nye Committee—and even the army planners—proved fully justified.

Despite World War II developments, the interwar economic mobilization planning left a deep imprint upon the army. Throughout the war years, all services engaged in extensive planning for their postwar combat roles. Born of technology and without deep roots in the U.S. past, Army Air Force planning was aimed at furthering its own parochial interests regardless of those of the nation. The Navy Department was more circumspect but still far from responsible. At the insistence of General George C. Marshall, chief of staff, however, all army plans were geared to what was considered reasonably feasible for the economy.[7] This same proclivity on the part of the army again manifested itself during the heated debate set off in the Truman administration in 1949-50 by National Security Council Document Sixty-Eight (NCS-68), written under the guidance of Secretary of State Dean Acheson and Chairman of the State Department Policy Planning Staff Paul H. Nitze. This document proposed that, to be effective, the nation's containment policy had to be backed up by extensive expansion of the military establishment. State Department planners estimated that the current defense budgets of about $13 billion would have to be increased to at least $35 billion (actually, with the added burden of the Korean War, expenditures rose from $13 to $50.4 billion in fiscal years 1950-54). Echoing General Marshall's dictums, the chairman of the Joint Chiefs of Staff, General Omar Bradley, dissented and maintained that such lavish spending would threaten the nation's economic system and could constitute as great a threat as the Soviet Union itself.[8]

Years later, Eisenhower, who had served in the army's economic planning branch during the interwar years, put the case even more eloquently:

> *No matter how much we spend for arms, there is no safety in arms alone. Our security is the total product of our economic, intellectual, moral, and military strengths.*
>
> Let me elaborate on this great truth. It happens that defense is a field in which I have had varied experience over a lifetime, and if I have learned anything, it is that there is no way in which a country can satisfy the craving for absolute security—but it easily can bankrupt itself, morally and economically, in attempting to reach that illusory goal through arms alone. The military establishment, not

productive of itself, necessarily must feed on the energy, productivity and brainpower of the country, and if it takes too much,
our total strength declines.[9]

The soldier-statesman was tapping a source of wisdom the Nye Committee and
the interwar army planners fully shared: the MIC and its policies may actually
exacerbate international tensions and thus threaten to extinguish civilization as
we know it, as well as the nation's economic strength through wrongheaded
priorities, waste, and corruption. What Eisenhower left unsaid, however, was
something the army's interwar planners only dimly perceived: Military spending
without restraints could also wreak havoc on military professionalism. This
theme will be addressed later within the larger context of the nation's warfare
complex.

In analyzing the contemporary MIC, I will refer to Charles C. Moskos, Jr.'s
article on the concept of the Military-Industrial Complex.[10] As the above discussion makes clear, it is my conviction that such a complex does exist, although
it is a rather amorphous, loosely structured entity. Moreover, its origins are to
be found in the evolutionary nature of U.S. institutions, and its massive growth
has been dictated by the nation's foreign policy. In other words, this complex
grew out of the needs of foreign policy, and not vice versa. Once fully developed, however, this MIC has helped to perpetuate Cold War tensions because,
over time, intricate institutional arrangements, like warfare itself, can begin to
take on a life of their own. Additionally, I believe that this MIC is not con-
spiratorial and is only in part based upon "false consciousness." What has occurred since 1945 is that foreign policy "ends" have generated "means" not
anticipated by and beyond the absolute control of their authors.

This MIC is an outgrowth of a "power elite," which has emerged in this
nation since the latter part of the nineteenth century.[11] The elite is made up of
a core of about 200 corporations, largely in the heavy and high-technology industrial sector, and the federal executive branch, particularly the president, his
chief advisers, and the most important cabinet departments. These two com-
ponents of the elite have a separate, though hardly unrelated, power base which
reflects a very definite middle-to-upper class bias. Although both share a common capitalist ideology, significant differences exist over means within and between the corporate and governmental spheres. Moskos proposes that the "Administrative Bureaucracy" and "Corporate Wealth" fall into entirely separate
spheres. This analysis is untenable. In order to make it consistent, Moskos must
assume—since he only alludes to the subject both in his text and footnotes—the
interpretation set forth by Adolf A. Berle, Jr. and Gardiner C. Means in 1932,
and later developed more explicitly by Berle. This interpretation proposes that
a separation has occurred between ownership and management in the corporate
world. In whole or in part, such an analysis is questionable. Most of top management reflect owner values and become substantially invested in the corpora-

tions they direct. Where such is not the case, since ownership (broadly defined to include financial institutions as well as individual and family stockholders) is highly concentrated, the owners and their associates usually can set the major strategies for their corporations and hire and fire managers according to their will. Control of all of the intricacies of the so-called technostructure of a corporation is not essential for determining its larger policies even though elaborate bureaucracies tend to possess a rather intractable quality.[12]

Consistently throughout the twentieth century, this corporate structure, along with its financial and legal allies, has staffed the most important offices of the federal executive.[13] Whenever the nation explicitly planned its economy— during World War I, with the National Recovery Administration during the Great Depression, and during World War II—the power of corporate America within the government was made blatantly clear. Perhaps this is one of the reasons that formal rather than informal planning has been the exception, not the rule, in the United States; the corporate elite has never wanted its control to be too visible. However, this does not mean that the government is merely the puppet, patsy, or "executive committee" of the corporate world. Contrary to Marxian analysis, the federal government does have an independent power base and constantly exercises it. Once again, it is in exaggerated situations similar to warfare when this assertion's obvious truth is made manifest. In the whole pattern of events leading up to Watergate, the Nixon administration was blackmailing corporations to make political contributions, and they allowed themselves to be "shaken down" because they realized the state could dramatically harm them just as dramatically as it could help them.[14]

America's elite power system possesses a unique quality. The United States is the only major industrial nation that, for very complex reasons, has never experienced the growth of a widespread, truly radical movement based upon lower-class consciousness.[15] Thus, unlike the elite of similar nations, the U.S. elite has never faced a significant challenge to its power, and so elite leadership has been and is rather consistently shortsighted in terms of its own and the nation's larger interests. The use of power tends to be most responsible only when a meaningful challenge exists which threatens to remove power from those exercising it. This shortsightedness has been rather consistently evident throughout the twentieth century in what C. Wright Mills characterized as "socialism for the rich; free enterprise for the poor." The result has been reform movements that make the minimal changes necessary to protect existing power relations with a legacy of high levels of poverty, the crudest social welfare systems in the developed world, with basic services, such as medicine, all but denied to large sectors of the population, transportation and communication systems which are at best inadequate, at worst destructive, an economic system which is incredibly wasteful in terms of energy sources, and, most importantly, an economy which, in general, performs rather badly.

The U.S. elite generally has relied upon economic growth to solve most problems, with the result that domestic affairs have become fully fused with world events. Moskos makes reference in his article to a "revisionist" school of U.S. diplomatic history which he labels as Marxist and caricatures through a brief discussion of William Appleman Williams. Here Moskos is on shaky ground. While much of this New Left pursues an economic interpretation, most are no more Marxist than was Charles A. Beard, one of the true giants of American historical thought. Moreover, many of the salient points of the New Left have been incorporated into liberal and even some conservative historiography, principally because they make more sense in explaining twentieth-century U.S. foreign policy than does the analysis of traditionalists, who look upon the nation's expanding abroad as designed primarily to check the aggressive intentions of other nations.[16]

What the New Left posits—and I largely accept this interpretation—is that the United States, fully consistent with an expansionist past reaching back to the colonial period, has been an imperialist nation throughout the twentieth century. In pursuing this course, it adopted the nineteenth-century British strategy of forging formal for informal empire. That empire was acquired by the spread of U.S. economic might throughout the world community under the aegis of the Open Door policy, a policy designed to end colonialism and other "closed doors," which inhibited or kept in exclusive circles the free flow of trade, investment, and raw materials. U.S. dollars abroad were intended to insure prosperity at home and spread U.S. influence and its democratic-capitalist ideology abroad. While the Open Door policy has had a mixed record as a means for exporting and supporting capitalism and democracy, it certainly aided in enriching the nation and gave the United States a global reach. So committed did the United States become to this policy that it was central to the nation's participation in two world wars. The destruction of those wars, however, left havoc in their wake, helping to make possible totalitarian socialism in Russia and fascism in Germany and elsewhere, putting an end to traditional colonialism everywhere, and accelerating modern revolution throughout the developing world.

Up through World War II and continuing until 1950, the U.S. leadership believed that it could pursue its Open Door policy successfully principally through diplomacy and the overwhelming weight of its economic power, once power relations were corrected through war. From 1950 on, however, the nation's statesmen concluded that since international conditions had become so desperate, they had to employ continuing force in order to maintain the world they wanted. For the first time in its history, the nation began to build a massive peacetime military establishment designed to police the world. Those policies made the nation the most massively counterrevolutionary nation of all times, with disastrous consequences at home and abroad that only the Vietnamese debacle made fully and agonizingly evident.

Where do the armed forces fit into this scheme of things? Here my answers are much more tentative because the secondary literature leaves much to be desired, and I have done only preliminary work in primary sources. Moreover, and before continuing, I should note that the military is no more monolithic than business or government, although, as with the latter two, differences within and between the armed services tend to be more over means than ends.[17] With these caveats in mind and, once again, drawing upon the moskos paradigm, it is a gross exaggeration to view the military as either beyond the reach of civilians or irrelevant to power considerations. Reality lies somewhere between these two extremes. The military always has been and, despite post-World War II trends, remains in U.S. society a derivative or secondary, not a primary, power grouping. While an essential service group for the elite, it is not of the elite itself. Hence, the armed forces are a power to contend with, but, without aberrational developments, they are manageable by civilians. Post-World War II trends make this point clear. Although the nation's most prominent military spokesmen expressed doubts about the wisdom of NSC-68, they were ignored in the massive military build-up that took place after 1950. Since then, military influence has grown along with the military budgets but within a context set by civilian hardliners. The rapid escalation of U.S. involvement in Vietnam beginning in 1965, however, divided the elite into hawks, doves, and those in between. That condition continues to the present. If, miraculously, the elite tomorrow were to unite on a more circumscribed role for the nation in world affairs, on arms control and limitations, and on a military establishment to match such policies, these decisions would be implemented regardless of dissent from the armed forces and, if the past is any guide to the future, without any military threat to U.S. constitutional processes. The military moon reflects the light from the elite sun, not vice versa. Since the elite is divided, however, matters are much more complex, and military power is increased to the degree that civilians lack unity on fundamental issues.

Many signs point to the fact that the more modest foreign and defense policies sketched briefly above are favored by a substantial portion of the elite. However, such policies are and will be difficult to implement for two related reasons. One, too many interests, as the MIC theory suggests, have a stake in continued international militancy and the military spending that militancy involves. Two, since Vietnam split the elite for the first time on an extended basis since the interwar years, the public and its representatives in Congress have joined the debate over U.S. foreign and defense policies, with unpredictable results.

To take up the first point: A prominent example of elite irresponsibility is the fact that no significant planning on either the public or private levels has taken place for reduced or reordered military spending despite the existence of sophisticated techniques for doing so.[18] As long as corporations, communities, unions, and the like are not presented with alternatives to defense expenditures, on which they depend wholly or partly, they will continue to oppose modifica-

tion in defense spending. The same holds true for the public and its concerns
for the general state of the economy. As far as the military is concerned, its era
of freewheeling appropriations is over. Congress is in the process of working out
methods for scrutinizing the nearly impenetrable military budgets which have
given the armed forces such wide latitude in the past. Additionally, the growing
taxpayers' revolt, which is presently squeezing the welfare area, will ultimately
reach the armed forces, and the effects will be salubrious. Even the military's
friends admit that about 25 percent of defense budgets is pure fat, to say nothing
of the conflicts of interest and corruption involved.[19] Worse yet, the weapons
the armed services get too often are useless, inappropriate, or even hazardous to
their users. Root and branch change is desperately needed in the whole military
weapons development and acquisition process, which has become thoroughly
corroded with the debilitating corporate ethic which ends up robbing the military and the public and has undermined military professionalism. Current military leaders face a much greater challenge than their World War I and interwar
predecesors who had to adjust the armed forces to the dictates of modern warfare, for the officers of the past were trusted while those of today suffer from
the same tarnished, Madison Avenue image as do government and business.

As to the second point, which complicates reordered foreign and defense
policies because of divisions within the elite opening up the debate to the
public: this condition is much more volatile than the first. The establishment's
schism over Vietnam created a near-vacuum at the very apex of our society
which was filled by Nixon and his marginal elements, who almost succeeded in
subverting the U.S. constitutional system. The Watergate scandal and the Vietnamese War laid bare to the public the fact that all the policies, techniques, and
even violence of the Cold War abroad had come home to debauch and defile
practically every institution in American life.

As a result, since 1968 the nation has been lurching about erratically,
without apparent direction. On one level, this painful wrenching is inevitable as
the elite attempts to regroup its forces and reestablish its authority and credi-
bility and an angry, confused, and distrustful public attempts to assimilate the
truth and consequences of the dishonesty, deceit, and dissembling to which it
was subjected and to which it too easily acquiesced. On a higher level, however,
the U.S. imperial system is in a period of major transition, with the final outcome yet unrevealed. On both levels, uncertainty prevails, and this uncertainty
is a state of affairs that not many can tolerate with equanimity. Few nations
accept diminished power gracefully, least of all Americans with our deeply en-
grained sense of superiority, duty, and destiny. Never before in U.S. history has
the nation's power structure required more time and latitude to establish that
the U.S. system is worth saving; never before has time been so dear or latitude
so narrow. It would seem that conditions are propitious for the zealots, op-
portunists, and demagogues either to divide the nation to the point of paralysis

or to gather unto themselves sufficient power in order to rip the society away from its democratic moorings.*

As a secondary power group, the military can aid the nation's power elite by beginning to put its own house in order. Stuart H. Loory, in his volume, *Defeated: Inside America's Military Machine* (1973), has proposed that Clemenceau's epigram that "War is much too serious a matter to be entrusted to the military" be supplemented by another: "War is much too serious a matter to be used indiscriminately by civilians." Loory argues that the leaders of the armed forces thoroughly undermined military professionalism by first passively and then enthusiastically endorsing the civilian hawks in their conviction that military power strengthened by the vaunted U.S. technology could meet any and all challenges abroad.[21] Vietnam exposed for all the world to see the impotence of misapplied military power and the military bankruptcy that went with it. The end result was a gargantuan military machine in shambles: the officer corps demoralized, the enlisted men exploited, and the armed forces as a whole confused and bewildered about their mission. In desperation, some parts of the military flirt with counterinsurgency (a euphemism for counterrevolution) as the military's principal goal for the future. Such a mission creates trends and proposals that logically lead to the advocacy of military supremacy over civilian authority.

Without forthright civilian leadership, no limited or comprehensive reform on the part of the military services is possible. With proper civilian guidance, the military essentially faces two choices. Looking backwards, it can attempt to thwart change by engaging in bureaucratic infighting in order to preserve the status quo. Worse yet, the armed forces could align themselves with elite or peripheral fanatics intent upon pursuing even more vigorously the disastrous policies of the past to the point of grievously, if not mortally, wounding the nation. Looking forward, however, the military could participate in the fundamental reordering of its own system for the purpose of reestablishing the professionalism that both it and the nation vitally require.

---

*Between November 30 and December 10, 1978, the Louis Harris Organization conducted a national public opinion survey which probed issues involving "The Dimensions of Privacy." In analyzing the results of this poll, Alan F. Westin, a professor of public law and government at Columbia University who helped develop the survey, concluded:

the American public today remains deeply skeptical. The message it is sending is that our political institutions are not working as well, [sic] as they ought to, and that more courageous and enterprising policies may be required.

For the next decade, this warns that unless society finds a blend of leadership styles, new policies and institutional reforms that build public confidence, one can expect to see an increasing erosion of the support on which effective democratic government ultimately rests.[20]

Together the nation's power elite and its armed forces have amply demonstrated since 1945 their capacity as architects of illusion and self-delusion. Unless they can now muster the ingenuity and the will to extricate the nation from the all-pervasive crisis to which they have delivered it, the future is indeed bleak.

NOTES

1. Dwight D. Eisenhower, "Farewell Radio and Television Address to the American People, January 17, 1961," in *U.S. Presidents, Public Papers of the President of the United States: Dwight D. Eisenhower, 1960-61* (Washington, D.C.: Government Printing Office, 1961), pp. 1035-40.

2. In the above definition of the MIC, I am relying heavily upon Steven Rose, ed., *Testing the Theory of the Military-Industrial Complex* (Lexington, Mass.: D. C. Heath, 1973), pp. 1-25. Rosen's volume is the one best source on the whole subject of the MIC.

3. Sources for the period from colonial times to the early twentieth century are cited in a bibliography included with Chapter Six.

4. For fuller development and documentation concerning World War I, see Chapter Two.

5. For fuller development and documentation concerning the interwar years, see Chapter Three. General Embick was a highly placed general officer who shared some of the attitudes of the army economic planners and was a model of professionalism. See Ronald Schaffer, "General Stanley D. Embick: Military Dissenter," *Military Affairs* 37 (October 1973): 89-95.

6. For a fuller development and documentation concerning World War II, see Chapter Four.

7. Michael S. Sherry, *Preparing for the Next War: American Plans for Postwar Defense, 1941-45* (New Haven: Yale University Press, 1977); Perry McCoy Smith, *The Air Force Plans for Peace, 1943-45* (Baltimore: The Johns Hopkins Press, 1970); and Vincent Davis, *Postwar Defense Policy and the U.S. Navy, 1943-1946* (Chapel Hill: University of North Carolina Press, 1966).

8. Russell F. Weigley, *The American Way of War: A History of United States Military Strategy and Policy* (New York: Macmillan, 1973), pp. 378-81, 394.

9. Dwight D. Eisenhower, "Spending Into Trouble," *Saturday Evening Post*, May 18, 1963, p. 18.

10. Charles C. Moskos, Jr., "The Concept of the Military-Industrial Complex: Radical Critique or Liberal Bogey?" *Social Problems* 21 (April 1977): 498-512.

11. The literature on power in the United States, much of which deals with the MIC, is enormous. Moskos cites many of the relevant sources. Good introductions to the subject are available in Richard Gillam, ed., *Power in Postwar America* (Boston: Little, Brown, 1971); and Norman L. Crockett, ed., *The Power Elite in America* (Lexington, Mass.: D. C. Heath, 1970).

12. Berle and Means, *The Modern Corporation and Private Property* (New York: Macmillan, 1932); Berle, *The 20th Century Capitalist Revolution* (New York: Harcourt, Brace, 1954); Berle, *Power without Property: A New Development in American Political Economy* (New York: Harcourt, Brace, 1959); and other works by Berle.

The issue of ownership and control of large corporations is, of course, addressed in any question of power in the United States. Hence, footnote 11, above, is relevant to the discussion. G. William Domhoff, *Who Rules America?* (Englewood Cliffs, N.J.: Prentice-Hall, 1967) is a good introduction. John Kenneth Galbraith, in a period of about 20 years, has gone from a pluralist to something resembling an elitist critique of U.S. political economy, see: *American Capitalism: The Concept of Countervailing Power* (Boston: Houghton Mifflin, 1952); and *Economics and the Public Purpose* (Boston: Houghton Mifflin, 1973). For some of the more recent and differing literature on the subject of corporations and power, see David M. Kotz, *Bank Control of Large Corporations in the United States* (Berkeley: University of California Press, 1978); Irving Kristol, *Two Cheers for Capitalism* (New York: Basic Books, 1978); Alfred D. Chandler, Jr., *The Visible Hand: The Managerial Revolution in American Business* (Cambridge, Mass.: Belknap Press, 1977); Samuel Richardson Reid, *The New Industrial Order: Concentration, Regulation, and Public Policy* (New York: McGraw-Hill, 1976); Michael Harrington, *The Twilight of Capitalism* (New York: Simon and Schuster, 1976); Arthur Selwyn Miller, *The Modern Corporate State: Private Governments and the American Constitution* (Westport, Conn.: Greenwood Press, 1976); Robert Sobel, *The Age of the Giant Corporations: A Microeconomic History of American Business 1914-1970* (Westport, Conn.: Greenwood Press, 1972); and Robert J. Larner, *Management Control and the Large Corporation* (New York: Dunellen, 1970). Any list of publications on U.S. political economy would be incomplete without mentioning the numerous and always provocative volumes of Robert L. Heilbroner.

Kotz, *Bank Control*, chapter 1, provides an excellent discussion of the varying theses involving who determines corporate policies.

13. Richard J. Barnet, *Roots of War: The Men and Institutions Behind U.S. Foreign Policy* (New York: Atheneum, 1972), chaps. 3, 7; Gabriel Kolko, *The Roots of American Foreign Policy: An Analysis of Power and Purpose* (Boston: Beacon Press, 1969), chap. 1; David T. Stanley, Dean E. Mann, and Jameson W. Doig, *Men Who Govern: A Biographical Profile of Federal Political Executives* (Washington, D.C.: Brookings Institution, 1967); and John C. Donovan, *The Cold Warriors: A Policy-Making Elite* (Lexington, Mass.: D. C. Heath, 1974).

14. The crucial issue of government versus corporate power is basic to the analyses in Chapters Two, Three, and Four and is addressed most directly in Chapter Six.

15. The very best brief discussion of this vital subject, including bibliographic references, is Jerome Karabel's review of Werner Sombart, *Why Is There No Socialism in the United States?* in *New York Review of Books* 26 (February 8, 1979): 22-27.

16. Williams, *The Tragedy of American Diplomacy*, 2d rev. ed. (New York: Dell, 1972) remains the best New Left statement. However, the multi-volume work of Gabriel and Joyce Kolko is indispensable. Good bibliographic discussions of U.S. foreign policy can be found in William H. Cartwright and Richard L. Watson, Jr., eds., *The Reinterpretation of American History and Culture* (Washington, D.C.: National Council for the Social Studies, 1973); Thomas G. Patterson, ed., *The Origins of the Cold War*, 2d rev. ed. (Lexington, Mass.: D. C. Heath, 1974); and Lloyd C. Gardner, *Architects of Illusion: Men and Ideas in American Foreign Policy 1941-1949* (Chicago: Quadrangle, 1970), chap. 11. For liberal and conservative authors who have assimilated much of the revisionist critique see Daniel Yergin, *Shattered Peace: The Origins of the Cold War and the National Security State* (Boston: Houghton Mifflin, 1977); Sherry, *Preparing for Next War*; Stephen E. Ambrose, *Rise to Globalism: American Foreign Policy, 1938-1976*, rev. ed. (New York: Penguin, 1976); and Ronald Radosh and Murray N. Rothbard, eds., *A New History of Leviathan: Essays on the Rise of the American Corporate State* (New York: E.P. Dutton, 1972).

17. Richard K. Betts, *Soldiers, Statesmen, and Cold War Crises* (Cambridge: Harvard University Press, 1977) examines in elaborate detail the shared and differing outlook of the armed services and military officers. Betts draws heavily upon the pioneering work of Samuel Huntington and Morris Janowitz. For my observations about these two authors, see Chapter Six.

18. Emile Benoit and Kenneth E. Boulding, eds., *Disarmament and the Economy* (New York: Harper & Row, 1963), particularly important in which is the pioneering work of Wassily W. Leontief involving input-output analysis, pp. 89–98. For a collective assessment of that type of analysis, see National Bureau of Economic Research, Conference on Research in Income and Wealth, *Input-Output Analysis: An Appraisal* (Princeton, N.J.: Princeton University Press, 1955).

19. For one of the prominent examples, see J. A. Stockfish, *Plowshares into Swords: Managing the Defense Establishment* (New York: Mason and Lipscomb, 1973).

20. Westin's summary and appraisal of this poll appear in Los Angeles *Times*, April 29, 1979.

21. Loory, *Defeated* (New York: Random House), pp. 373–86. An intensive scrutiny of the military began and continued with the Vietnamese crisis. Some of these volumes include James A. Donovan, *Militarism, U.S.A.* (New York: Charles Scribner's Sons, 1970); Ward Just, *Military Man* (New York: Alfred A. Knopf, 1970); Adam Yarmolinsky, *The Military Establishment: Its Impact on American Society* (New York: Harper & Row, 1971); Edward L. King, *The Death of the Army: A Pre-Mortem* (New York: Saturday Review Press, 1972); Michael T. Klare, *War without End: American Planning for the Next Vietnams* (New York: Vintage, 1972); Zeb B. Bradford, Jr. and Frederic J. Brown, *The United States Army in Transition* (Beverly Hills, Calif.: Sage, 1973); William L. Hauser, *America's Army in Crisis: A Study in Civil-Military Relations* (Baltimore: The Johns Hopkins University Press, 1973); David Cortwright, *Soldiers in Revolt: The American Military Today* (New York: Anchor Press, 1975); Drew Middleton, *Can America Win the Next War?* (New York: Charles Scribner's Sons, 1975); and Richard A. Gabriel and Paul L. Savage, *Crisis in Command: Mismanagement in the Army* (New York: Hill and Wang, 1978). No study of military institutions and society is complete without a careful reading of John U. Nef, *War and Human Progress: An Essay on the Rise of Industrial Civilization* (Cambridge: Harvard University Press, 1950).

2

WORLD WAR I

The rubric "military-industrial complex" has gained widespread currency in the United States since being coined by President Dwight D. Eisenhower in 1961. Though imprecise, the term usually refers to the partial integration of economic and military institutions for the purpose of national security. The nature and consequences of the "complex" remain matters of dispute, but few contest that modern, industrialized warfare has had far-reaching effects upon American life at all levels. Scientific and technological advances have dictated a revolution in weaponry—a revolution which has broken down the distinction between both the civilian and military worlds and the private and public economic functions. Massive spending for war and defense has spread the influence of the "managers of violence" far and wide.

Numerous studies treating the Military-Industrial Complex directly and indirectly already exist. Almost without exception, all have concentrated upon the World War II and Cold War years. To focus on those years is quite natural, for it is then that the most blatant manifestations of the "complex" are evident. Nevertheless, to neglect the years before 1940 greatly limits our understanding of the subject for several reasons. In the first place, the so-called complex is more difficult to penetrate after 1940 than before. So comprehensive are the effects of twentieth-century warfare that it is often difficult to distinguish the central from the peripheral. Moreover, in many instances essential documents are still denied the scholar. In the second place, and more importantly, the

The following is a reprint of an article which originally appeared as "The 'Industrial-Military Complex' in Historical Perspective: World War I," *Business History Review* 41 (Winter 1967): 378–403. Permission from the editor to reproduce this essay is gratefully acknowledged.

years after 1940 mark not a start but rather a culmination in the process of partially integrating economic and military institutions.

World War I is the watershed. In 1917, the United States had to mobilize its economy totally for the first time. Since a large share of the nation's industrial productivity went to the armed services, their supply and procurement systems had to be integrated into civilian mobilization agencies. The means for doing so were determined by a very chaotic interaction of the federal government as a whole, the industrial community, and the military services. From the wartime experience, the foundations for the so-called complex were laid. But the armistice ended the experiment in industrialized warfare before it was complete. What began with the war, however, did not end with it. Directly and indirectly, the 1920s and 1930s were years of consolidation for the government, for industry, and for the armed services in terms of fighting a war under modern conditions. The present article deals with these processes during World War I; the interwar years will be the subject of a future essay.

According to Professor Ellis W. Hawley, three schools have dominated American thinking about what should be the government's policy toward the concentration of economic power: maintaining competition through the antitrust laws; economic regulation and planning by the federal government; and industrial self-regulation through cooperation within business and between it and the government.[1] Of course, the three schools have never been mutually exclusive; numerous shadings within and among them exist. Industrial self-regulation as the middle way probably best characterizes the political economy of twentieth-century America. The antitrust impulse has had widespread appeal but inadequate political support. Economic planning and regulation has lacked both popularity and sustained backing. For a nation torn between its competitive, laissez faire ideology and the massive problems of consolidated economic power, the drift towards industrial self-regulation was quite natural. To varying degrees it found favor in the business community. For the nation at large, cooperation, or a "new competition" as it was often called, had the attraction of meeting the dictates of ideology while still solving some practical economic problems.

In theory and practice, industrial self-rule, policed by the federal government, made impressive gains during the Progressive Era.[2] But its hold was far from absolute. Antitrust sentiments were still strong; numerous divisions still existed within business and the government over matters of political economy. Despite various attempts, industry was not granted immunity from the antitrust laws by having the federal government determine in advance the legality of business practices.

What was not possible during peace became imperative during war. Even if it was politically possible, the federal government lacked the personnel, the information, or the experience necessary for the massive economic regulation World War I demanded. Under the auspices of the government, businessmen had to do it themselves. War created the ideal conditions for industrial self-regulation. The demand for maximum munitions production and the lavish prosperity federal spending brought about, quieted temporarily antitrust and anti-business dissent. Wartime opportunities for rationalizing the economy, however, were matched by grave risks. Converting the huge American economic machine to war production could end disastrously unless exactly the right means were employed.

Neither the Wilson administration, Congress, nor prominent American industrialists, financiers, and the firms they represented appeared excessively concerned about the economics of warfare between 1914 and 1917. Less prominent members of the business community led in the drive for economic preparedness. The Chamber of Commerce of the United States was in the vanguard. Since its organization in 1912, the Chamber was an outstanding advocate for government-policed industrial self-regulation. Backed by the nearly unanimous vote of its membership, the Chamber was consistently far ahead of the administration, the Congress, and the general public in policies it supported for industrial mobilization between 1915 and 1918.[3] Legitimately concerned about the economic effects of war, the Chamber also perceived that a state of hostility would further its peacetime goal. A mobilized economy "will make individual manufacturers and business men and the Government share equally in responsibility for the safety of the nation," declared *The Nation's Business* in mid-1916.[4] Chamber spokesmen never tired of reiterating that the national emergency was the perfect opportunity for businessmen to prove their new morality and patriotism to the country. Writing to the DuPonts in December 1916, the chairman of the Chamber's Executive Committee on National Defense stated:

> The Chamber of Commerce of the United States has been keenly interested in the attempt to create an entirely new relationship between the Government of the United States and the industries of the United States. It is hoped that the atmosphere of confidence and cooperation which is beginning in this country, as shown by the Federal Trade Commission, the Federal Reserve Board and other points of contact which are now in existence, may be further developed, and this munitions question would seem to be the greatest opportunity to foster the new spirit.[5]

Though the Chamber of Commerce was the prominent advocate of economic preparedness, other members of the commercial world initiated the specific action in behalf of industrial preparedness. Their first opportunity came in mid-1915, when Secretary of the Navy Josephus Daniels called upon members of leading engineering and industrial societies to serve as unofficial industrial consultants for the expanding navy. Called the Naval Consulting Board, this group ultimately organized down to the local level.

The most dynamic accomplishments of the Naval Consulting Board were performed by a subdivision called the Industrial Preparedness Committee, Discovering that neither the army nor the navy had adequate information about the nation's industrial potential, the committee during 1916 inventoried thousands of industrial facilities for the services. The detailed work was done by voluntary effort and private financing under the direction of the then virtually unknown Walter S. Gifford, chief statistician for the American Telephone and Telegraph Company. But the real moving spirit behind the project was Howard E. Coffin, vice-president of the Hudson Motor Car Company.[6]

For Coffin, efforts in behalf of preparedness were only an extension of his peacetime endeavors. In 1910, as president of the Society of Automotive Engineers, he had, with the help of others, transformed the society and the auto industry by bringing about the standardization of specifications and materials.[7] Rationalizing the productive process and promoting industrial organization were continuing interests of this restless individual. As few others, he foresaw the threats as well as the possibilities of industrial mobilization.

"Twentieth century warfare," Coffin insisted, "demands that the blood of the soldier must be mingled with from three to five parts of the sweat of the man in the factories, mills, mines, and fields of the nation in arms."[8] World War I was "the greatest business proposition since time began."[9] In the Progressive rhetoric, he and other industrialists were moved by "patriotism." Just as important, however, was the "cold-blooded" desire to protect their own interests.[10] Only industrialists and engineers were qualified to run a mobilized economy, Coffin averred. Under such leadership, war could be fought without untoward damage to the economy.

Coffin and his colleagues had plans for gradually expanding the activities of the Industrial Preparedness Committee as an agency for industrial mobilization. But a committee of unofficial industrial consultants was unsuited for such grandiose responsibilities. In August 1916, the Council of National Defense was created; the council ultimately absorbed the Naval Consulting Board.

The Council of National Defense was the brain child of Dr. Hollis Godfrey, president of the Drexel Institute of Philadelphis—an industrial training and management education institution. As early as 1899, Godfrey was nearly obsessed with the idea of management education as the high road to industrial efficiency and progress. Even before 1914, Godfrey reasoned that his ideas concerning management could serve the nation in war as well as in peace.

Early in 1916, unable to sit by while the nation drifted unprepared into war, Godfrey outlined to General Leonard Wood a plan for applying the principles of management to the economy in order to achieve optimum performance. The two sketched out a proposal for a council of national defense. Over a period of weeks, Godfrey then consulted with numerous industrial colleagues, influential friends, and administrative officials.[11] The final legislation was drafted in the War Department under Secretary Newton D. Baker's instructions. It was shepherded through Congress by the respective chairmen and influential members of the two Military Affaris committees. No meaningful congressional debate took place.

Passed in August 1916, as part of the Army Appropriations Act, the legislation provided for a Council of National Defense consisting of six cabinet officers. Council members would nominate and the president appoint seven experts in various fields to act as a National Defense Advisory Commission (NDAC) to the council. Together with the NDAC, the council would serve as the president's advisory body on all aspects of industrial mobilization.

The creation of the NDAC was actually a formalization of the procedures adopted by the Naval Consulting Board: industrial experts voluntarily donated their talents as public officials without surrendering their positions or incomes as private citizens. The precedent was an important one. It provided the wherewithal for industrialists to guide the process of mobilizing the economy. Moreover, the personnel selected for the National Defense Advisory Commission revealed that it was more an expansion of the Naval Consulting Board than a new agency. Walter S. Gifford was selected as director, and Grosvenor B. Clarkson, a journalist, advertising executive, and former civil servant who had handled publicity for the board, was ultimately to become secretary. Both Coffin and Godfrey were chosen as members along with Bernard M. Baruch and others.

The legislation for the Council of National Defense was predicated on the assumption that private industry would be the primary source of munitions supply in the event of war. Nevertheless, opponents of preparedness zeroed in on the munitions makers in an effort to discredit the drive for an enlarged military force. War mongering, profiteering at the nation's expense, it was charged, would be reduced if the government alone produced munitions. Almost to a man, military personnel opposed the proposition as impractical. It would be prohibitively expensive and would not provide the armed forces the quantity of munitions needed once war was fought, they maintained.[12] Industry, of course, took a similar stand, especially since the armaments industry was threatened as Allied orders were cut back.

To settle the issue, the National Defense Act of 1916 authorized a board of three military officers and two civilians to study the matter and make recommendations. They met in November-December 1916, under the direction of Colonel Francis J. Kernan. Benedict Crowell, chairman of Crowell and Little Construction Company of Cleveland and later assistant secretary of war, and R. Goodwyn Rhett, former mayor of Charleston, S.C., president of the People's National Bank of Charleston, and president of the Chamber of Commerce of the United States, served as the civilian members. In its study, the Kernan Board relied heavily on the work of the Naval Consulting Board. Coffin, along with others involved in industrial preparedness, lent his advice.

After inspecting government arsenals and consulting with some leading industrialists, the board reported that it was "not desirable for the Government to undertake, unaided by private plants, to provide for its needs in arms, munitions, and equipment." In the event of war the government should depend "largely upon private plants for war material." But the board did not stop there. Reading like an editorial from *The Nation's Business*, its report praised business-men for their patriotism in helping to prepare for an emergency and assured the nation that industry would continue to cooperate in the future. Concerning more immediate problems, the board recommended that plants producing muni-tions for the Allies not be permitted to remain idle when orders were terminated. It concluded by calling for a comprehensive plan for industrial mobilization.[13]

Though only beginning steps in the long trek toward a mobilized economy, the work of the Naval Consulting Board, the organization of the Council of Na-tional Defense and its National Defense Advisory Commission, and the conclu-sions of the Kernan Board were of the greatest significance. They signaled the beginning of a government-industry partnership for the purpose of national security. The initiative came from industry, but, out of necessity, the federal government, and specifically the military services, appeared willing to go along. When announcing the appointment of the NDAC members in October 1916, President Wilson observed: "The organization of the Council [of National De-fense] . . . opens up a new and direct channel of communication and coopera-tion between business and scientific men and all departments of the Govern-ment"[14] Howard E. Coffin had ambitious plans for the Council of National Defense. He wrote to the DuPonts in December 1916:

> Private industry in all the varied lines of Governmental supply must be encouraged and not discouraged. It must be educated, organized, and trained for the national emergency service. A closer and more mutually satisfactory business relation [sic] must be established be-tween the industrial lines and every Department of the Government, and the work of the newly created Council of National Defense must be directed to this end.
>
> The first meeting of the Council of National Defense and its Advisory Commission will be held in the office of the Secretary of War, December 6th, and within six months thereafter it is our hope that we may lay the foundation for that closely knit structure, in-dustrial, civil and military, which every thinking American has come to realize is vital to the future life of this country, in peace and in commerce, no less than in possible war.[15]

Organized in December 1916, the Council of National Defense and its National Defense Advisory Commission did not actively function until March. When war was declared, the council and the NDAC, authorized only to investi-gate, advise, and recommend policies to the president and his administration, also assumed responsibilities for mobilizing the economy.

Lack of experience explains in part the failure to create a better, more powerful agency. No one was fully able to anticipate what was required. The nation had to go through the pragmatic process of working out solutions as problems arose. More importantly, there was the widespread desire to avoid permanent political and economic change during the war. Hopefully, a makeshift organization like the Council of National Defense, without clearly defined authority and consisting mainly of existing department heads, would be sufficient to meet war needs. When hostilities ceased, it could easily be disbanded.[16] Moreover, vital issues of political economy were central to any scheme for industrial mobilization. With Progressive divisions still great over the government's role in the economy, any attempt to set up new, powerful mobilization machinery could end in paralyzing debate in Congress and in the nation. Consistently, the president and the Congress avoided facing issues of economic mobilization whenever possible. Not until the mobilization program was on the verge of collapse during the winter of 1917-18 did President Wilson strengthen the nation's industrial mobilization apparatus. Even then, only the minimal changes essential to the continued operation of the economy were made.

Consistent with prewar precedents, business representatives of the NDAC, not the cabinet members of the Council of National Defense, led in mobilizing the economy. Haltingly, the commissioners groped their way in search of the proper means. At the outset, they chose to create the most efficient organization possible with the least disturbance to the status quo. That meant the federal government would accept, use, and adjust itself to the configuration of power in and the basic pattern of the private sector of the economy.[17]

Several months after its creation, the NDAC divided itself into semi-autonomous committees corresponding to the natural subdivisions of the economy: the most important were transportation, raw materials, munitions and manufacturing, and general supplies. In order to relate commission activities to those of the economy as a whole, the commissioners selected or had various industries choose members to represent their interests on committees within the commission. Over 100 such committees were ultimately organized. Almost inevitably, major firms were dominant. Where a trade association like the American Iron and Steel Institute was supreme in its field, it provided the representatives. The Cooperative Committee on Canned Goods, for example, consisted of individuals from the California Packing Corporation, Libby, McNeill & Libby, the H. J. Heinz Company, and others; the steel committee included Elbert H. Gary as chairman and other members from Bethlehem Steel Corporation, Jones and Laughlin Steel Company, Republic Iron and Steel Company, and Lackawanna Steel Company.

The "dollar-a-year" man system was devised to provide the government with the services of experts without undue sacrifice on their part. Because appropriations were limited, businessmen often paid for their own expenses, clerical help, and even office space. Though far from a perfect solution, the system worked for awhile. It assured industry's cooperation at a time when the nation's mobilization agency was without authority. Industrialists and merchandizers worked hand in hand with the commissioners. Information on the capacity of the essential industries was collected, the means for curtailing production for civilian uses and converting industry to meet governmental needs were considered, and rudimentary price, priority, and other controls were developed.[18]

Quite early in the war, therefore, the NDAC devised the means for organizing and controlling the private sector of the economy. The methods were often crude and piecemeal, but they could be perfected. Rapid progress was possible because the cooperative efforts of industry and the federal government in behalf of economic regulation during the Progressive Era prepared them to a degree for wartime conditions. Nevertheless, the economic mobilization program floundered for almost a year. Organizing supply—the civilian economy—was not enough. Demand—the multiple needs of claimant agencies like the army and navy—also had to be controlled. Throughout the war, demand exceeded supply. Consequently, unless war contracts were distributed with care and in order of precedence, the equilibrium of the economy could not be maintained. The NDAC, however, had no authority over the procurement agencies. They were free to do as they liked. A crisis was avoidable as long as claimant agencies procured in an orderly manner and cooperated with the NDAC. To a degree, most did. The Navy Department adjusted to hostilities without major difficulty. That was possible because it was always in a state of semi-preparedness and had an efficient supply system dating back to the late nineteenth century. Other private and public civilian agencies like the American Red Cross, the Emergency Fleet Corporation, and the Fuel and Food Administration also proved to be sufficiently flexible. But not the War Department. The flagrant inadequacies of its supply apparatus undermined the efforts of the NDAC.

When war broke out, five, and later eight, bureaus—the Quartermaster Corps, the Ordnance Department, and the like—independently procured for the army. Each had its own purchasing staff, handled its own funds, stored its own goods, and transported its own supplies. Determined to meet their own needs, the bureaus competed with one another and other claimant agencies. Contracts were let indiscriminantly, facilities commandeered without plan, and equipment transported without regard to need. With such a system, it was virtually impossible for the War Department to come up with reliable statistics concerning requirements.

War Department difficulties did not start with the war. The politics of supply had been a constant source of aggravation within the department for decades.[19] The strife became especially intense around the turn of the century when the Chief of Staff-General Staff system was created by the reforms of Elihu Root (Secretary of War, 1899–1904). Supervising the bureaus and bringing them under some centralized control were part of the responsibility of the chief of staff. But the tenaciously independent bureaus successfully resisted control. The staff-bureau conflict continued into the war years. Secretary of War Baker would not move forcefully to resolve it. A Progressive dedicated to applying local solutions to modern problems, Baker opposed temporary changes in the federal government during the war out of fear they might become permanent. Moreover, the former mayor of Cleveland consistently avoided controversy. Attempting to compromise nearly irreconcilable differences between the General Staff and the bureaus, Baker allowed the War Department to drift hopelessly toward disaster.[20]

The General Staff-bureau controversy in part was responsible for the army failing to anticipate the nature of twentieth-century warfare. Industrial production was as important, or more important, to military success as tactics or strategy. Relating its supply and procurement apparatus to a mobilized economy had to be part of the military mission in modern times.[21] Had the staff-bureau conflict ended with the war and an efficient supply system been fashioned, the army could have adjusted to emergency conditions with relative ease. Since neither took place, the army came close to losing its control of supply by threatening the entire civilian economy.

Out of war costs approximating $32,000,000,000, the army spent $14,500,000,000 between April 1916 and June 1919.[22] Pouring such vast amounts of money into the economy through the department's antiquated supply system unavoidably produced havoc.

To mitigate the effect, the National Defense Advisory Commission, while still organizing supply and attempting to perfect wartime economic controls, was forced to assume responsibility for coordinating supply and demand. No other agency existed for the purpose. Its task was almost impossible. The procurement agencies had the statutory authority; the NDAC had no more than advisory powers. They were not enough to hold the largest of the procurement agencies in line.

The NDAC's difficulties with the War Department stemmed from two sources. In the first place, according to military dictum, those who controlled strategy must also control supply. The army looked upon civilian mobilization agencies as a threat to its supply prerogatives. The very weakness of the army supply system served only to strengthen the suspicion. Secondly, the War Department's supply network did not correspond with that of the civilian economy. The bureaus were organized along functional lines—ordnance, quartermaster, and the like; the economy was informally structured according to commodities— raw materials, industrial products, and so forth.[23] With the NDAC patterned after the economy, effectively coordinating supply and demand was out of the question. Logically, the army had not only to reform its supply system but also restructure it along commodity lines. It stubbornly resisted until early in 1918.

The army was able to resist not only because of its statutory authority, but also because Baker was selected as chairman of the Council of National Defense and served as President Wilson's chief adviser on industrial mobilization. Unable to bring order out of confusion in the War Department, Baker failed to rise above departmental interests as chairman of the council. He used his position to maintain the army's prerogatives undiminished.[24] For almost a year after the outbreak of war, therefore, the War Department insisted that the civilian economy adjust to its decentralized, inefficient, functional supply system rather than vice versa. The tail was attempting to wag the dog.

At first the NDAC accepted the War Department terms. It attempted to make the War Department system work by serving more or less as a bridge between the industrial and military worlds. With the army bureaus unable to keep up, the recently organized Cooperative Committees of the NDAC performed procurement activities. Individuals and committees aided the army in distributing contracts within the industries they represented. In the case of the Quartermaster Corps, the Committee on Supplies literally built a procurement system around the corps and assumed many of its functions. NDAC aid unquestionably kept the army bureaus from being totally swamped. But, as worked out, the system was not an unmixed blessing. Indeed, commission operations were often illegal. Actually, if not nominally, industrialists awarded contracts to themselves and their colleagues. Small groups of businessmen admittedly engaged in collusive activity—activity sanctioned by the government. Army regulations and the antitrust laws were being violated.

The expediency, not the legality, of the NDAC's operations was what bothered its members. Out of need, the NDAC was forced to assume the responsibilities of a general mobilization agency without that authority. The army, and the navy as well, used or ignored the NDAC to suit its own purposes. Frustrated, the commissioners began pressing the Council of National Defense to sanction a more effective organization. The latter yielded to NDAC entreaties only reluctantly. At first, a Munitions Standards Board, later a General Munitions Board, was created. Both were intended to facilitate military procurement; neither had much effect. As creatures of the Council of National Defense, they lacked authority. Technically independent of the NDAC, they were really only extensions of it. After months of turmoil, the hopelessly inadequate NDAC still remained the principal mobilization agency.[25] As spring gave way to summer in 1917, confusion was rife and the efforts to harness the economy were bogging down.

By July 1917, change was essential. The NDAC structure could not maintain economic balance. Backed by influential members of the administration like William G. McAdoo, the secretary of the treasury and President Wilson's son-in-law, the commissioners made a plea for the creation of a mobilization agency freed from military control and able to centralize and enforce its decisions.[26]

The impetus for change was strengthened by the first extended debate in Congress involving economic mobilization. NDAC operations, where favored businessmen could serve simultaneously as government agents and contractors, took on the proportions of a national scandal when publicized. The agitation was triggered by those business interests who found themselves excluded from a decision-making process which affected their interests. After acrimonious debate, Congress included in the Lever Act a provision restricting individuals from serving or acting in a capacity to influence the awarding of contracts beneficial to themselves or their firms.[27]

The drive for a more effective mobilization agency combined with congressional criticism led to a general reorganization in July 1917. The Council of National Defense replaced the NDAC structure with the War Industries Board (WIB). As its name implied, the board was to regulate the entire industrial might of the nation, not simply to expedite munitions production. The WIB absorbed the various committees and boards that had proliferated over the months under the Council of National Defense. For the first time, the federal government had one centralized organization for controlling industry.

In order to meet congressional and business criticism, the WIB between August and December 1918, disbanded the Cooperative Committees of Industries. It then turned to the Chamber of Commerce of the United States to supervise and certify the formation of new industrial committees. Industries with trade associations or similar societies "democratically" elected members to represent them before the WIB. Precautions were exercised to insure that non-member firms had a voice. For unorganized industries, the Chamber facilitated organization. The elected bodies were called War Service Committees. Unlike the NDAC committees, their members were private, not public, representatives; industry financed their operations. Many of the committees were new, some, such as steel, were the old group with a new name and only minor changes. The Chamber of Commerce had been advocating such a system since before the war. In part it was based on the English mobilization experience.[28]

The War Service Committees granted business far more immunity from the antitrust laws than even the most sanguine advocates of industrial cooperation espoused during the Progressive years. A private, commercial body, not the federal government, certified committees to represent the collective interests of business. As a result, the modern trade association movement began to come of age. Associations grew rapidly in number and importance during the war years.[29]

The change from the informal, legally tenuous NDAC Cooperative Committees, reminiscent of the ambiguous relations between the government and industry during the Progressive years, was essential. Without the full support of all industrial elements, economic mobilization was difficult, if not impossible. Out of need, the federal government dropped its reservations about trade associations. Indeed, industry could treat with the government only on an organized basis. Writing in *The Nation's Business* in August 1918, Chamber of Commerce President Harry A. Wheeler (vice-president, Union Trust Company of Chicago) declared:

> Creation of the War Service Committees promises to furnish the basis for a truly national organization of industry whose proportions and opportunities are unlimited. . . .

> The integration of business, the expressed aim of the National Chamber, is in sight. War is the stern teacher that is driving home the lesson of cooperative effort.[30]

Representing private interests, the War Service Committees were not officially a part of the WIB. Subdivisions of the board, called Commodity Committees, determined policy for and administered the various industries. The committees were usually staffed with industrialists on a "dollar-a-year" basis but allegedly free from conflicts of interest. Claimant agencies such as the army and navy also had representatives on the committees. To maintain a clear line of demarcation between the public and private domains, War Service Committees only "advised" the Commodity Committees. Some 57 Commodity Committees and over 300 War Service Committees were ultimately organized. The former were grouped according to the natural patterns of the economy: chemicals, textiles, finished products, and so forth. The latter operated with the Commodity Committee to which they corresponded.

The WIB never really got under way until early in 1918. By then it was clear that the distinction between public and private interests within the board was more apparent than real. The chief of the Agricultural Implements and Wood Products Section had been manager of the John Deere Wagon Company; at the head of Automotive Products was the former treasurer of the Studebaker Corporation; the former president of the Fisk Rubber Company was chief of the Rubber and Rubber Goods Section.[31] Serving in such capacities, industrialists were supposed to "dissociate" themselves from their firms. But in November, 1918, the acting chairman of the WIB observed that individuals could absent themselves from negotiations if their own firms were involved. Not until mid-1918 did the board begin to institute precautionary policies against compromising appointments.[32]

Even if no conflict of interest existed, the Commodity Committee-War Service Committee system was not the neat separation of private and public interests that is proponents maintained. At best, the decision-making process was organic. Grosvenor B. Clarkson described it as follows:

> Through the commodity sections on the side of Government and the war service committees on the side of business, all industry was merged in the War Industries Board. Subject to the veto of the chairman of the Board, as the supreme interpreter of the national good, industry imposed its own emergency laws and regulations and assumed nine tenths of the burden and responsibility of enforcing them.

Clarkson went on to say that the Commodity Committee-War Service Committee system was the very nerve center and major source of policy for the WIB.[33]

The board was a form of industrial self-regulation writ large. Nonetheless, the organization of the WIB was a giant step forward. Effective industrial control was possible. Private industry was organized, an agency capable of coordinating mobilization existed, and trained personnel were available.

Regardless of the progress, the reorganization did not deal with the fundamental flaw. The WIB was without authority. Created by the Council of National Defense, it had only advisory powers. Actually the board's creation was a victory for Secretary Baker and the War Department. They had resisted the concerted drive for an agency independent of and superior to the military services. Wilson upheld them.[34] The army still had the authority to force its methods on the economy. The WIB stood by helplessly. An impasse had been reached. Either the army had to give way or the mobilization program would halt. The latter occurred before the former.

Chaired by Frank A. Scott, president of Warner and Swasey Company, a Cleveland precision equipment manufacturer, the WIB first faltered and then stumbled. Deterioration was rapid after October 1917, when Scott resigned, his health broken through agonizing months spent in government service. Daniel Willard, president of the Baltimore and Ohio Railroad Company, was practically drafted to replace him. But on January 11, 1918, he also quit in disgust over the board's impotence. A crippled WIB simply could not fulfill its functions. Various sections remained active but without over-all direction. Like a convulsed person, the WIB's limbs twitched without central motor control. For a time, a so-called War Council, made up of representatives from leading war agencies and others, tried without much success to provide leadership. The crisis was at hand. A new chairman for the WIB was not appointed until March. No one who was considered qualified would take the job without sweeping changes.[35]

The paralysis that gripped the board was matched by that of the economy. Uncontrolled procurement overloaded the Northeast with contracts far beyond its capacity to produce. With the unusually severe winter of 1917–18, fuel was critically short and the railroad and shipping industries virtually halted in some sections of the nation. The mobilization effort, indeed the entire economy, appeared on the brink of collapse. To remedy the crisis, the administration was forced to bring the railroads under national control in December 1917. But over-all coordination of procurement and production was essential to resolve the critical economic conditions. On that crucial issue the administration was stalemated.[36]

In the absence of executive leadership, the Senate Military Affairs Committee, under the leadership of a Democratic maverick, Senator George E. Chamberlain of Oregon, moved on its own. The committee conducted an investigation of the War Department from December 12, 1917, until the end of March. It established beyond question the chaos in army supply and highlighted its effects on the economy.

The Chamberlain Committee was greatly influenced by Waddill Catchings, formerly of J. P. Morgan and Company, now chairman of the War Committee of the Chamber of Commerce of the United States, and president of ironworks in New York and Ohio. For months, argued Catchings, Chamber members had devoted full-time effort to perfecting the nation's mobilization machinery only to have conditions deteriorate rather than improve. Businessmen found their economic fortunes threatened not by government regulation but by government chaos. With a united Chamber behind him, Catchings recommended that the United States follow the British experience: separate procurement from the military and place it under a civilian-controlled ministry of munitions; and create a War Cabinet to direct the over-all national war effort.[37]

In January 1918, the Chamberlain Committee presented two bills to Congress incorporating the Chamber of Commerce recommendations.[38] The proposed legislation led to the most extended and knowledgeable debate on economic mobilization heard in the halls of Congress during World War I. Legislation for a ministry of munitions, but not the war cabinet, was seriously considered. In order to circumvent it, the army began to reform its supply system, and the administration came forth with the Overman Act: a sweeping grant of authority for the president to reshuffle his administration to meet the demands of warfare. With the full weight of the administration behind the compromise proposal, the Chamberlain Committee legislation never stood a chance. In May 1918, the Overman bill passed with only slight opposition.[39]

The compromise succeeded only because Wilson ended the War Department's domination of the mobilization program in March. Under his general powers as president and commander in chief, Wilson separated the WIB from the Council of National Defense and placed it directly under himself. After the passage of the Overman Act, the president confirmed his action with an executive order. To chair the strengthened board, Wilson selected Bernard M. Baruch. According to the latter's instructions, the WIB's specific and general powers were great indeed. They included general coordinating authority over procurement. Without *statutory* authority, much of the board's action remained legally tenuous. Moreover, the president's directive was vaguely qualified at many points. Nevertheless, with Wilson's full backing, the nearly complete support of business, and the critical conditions the nation faced, the WIB was able to enforce its decisions in most instances. The winter crisis, therefore, was resolved with the military services maintaining control of supply but not of the economy.

Probably without anyone being fully aware of its consequences, the Overman Act set a most important precedent for twentieth-century warfare. Unlike most belligerent nations, in the United States the military services continued to procure their own munitions and, therefore, remained in a position to affect the economy most directly and vitally during war as well as peace. To varying degrees Great Britain and France separated procurement from the services and placed it under civilian-controlled munitions ministries. Even in pre-revolutionary Russia the armed services did not maintain unqualified control of their own purchasing. In Germany, quite a different pattern emerged. The economy was largely mobilized under military authorities in league with large industrial elements.[40]

Maintaining procurement in the hands of the armed services was dictated more by political economy than military necessity. Businessmen had directed economic mobilization since April 1917, because they were the only ones qualified to do so. Yet, Wilson, members of his administration, and the public at large, doubted the ability of business to place the interests of the nation above its own.[41] Such attitudes, combined with the desire to avoid political and economic changes during the war, led to granting industry a great deal of latitude for perfecting the mobilization machinery, while ultimate authority was continued with the traditional procurement agencies. Only when that expedient failed did the business-dominated WIB gain some authority under the Overman Act.

To many government officials, going further than the Overman legislation by separating supply from the armed services was both undesirable and politically hazardous. It would have meant turning over to industry directly billions of dollars of contracts. The ministry of munitions legislation supported by the Chamberlain Committee was no more than a general grant of authority for a director of munitions to perform procurement functions. Out of necessity, the director would have to use the WIB or a similar agency controlled by businessmen to fulfill his responsibilities. Of course, under WIB operations, contracts were virtually in industry's hand anyway. Nonetheless, as long as the armed services maintained the legal right of contracting, ceremonial distinctions between government and business operations were preserved.

Since the Commodity Committee-War Service Committee system nominally separated private and public interests, Congress appeared satisfied with the WIB. Nevertheless, the "dollar-a-year" man and War Service Committee practices—the very life blood of the WIB—were vulnerable. During 1917 they came under repeated attack; in January 1918, legislation was introduced to prohibit the use of industrial advisory committees and government officials serving on a nominal salary. Instead, the wartime economy would be run by paid employees free of compromising affiliations.[42] For the most part, critics of the NDAC and WIB were conveniently ignored. Had Congress moved to place procurement in the hands of the WIB or attempted to write detailed legislation as to how civilians would perform procurement functions, WIB methods at least would have been in jeopardy.

The Overman Act allowed the administration and the Congress to dodge the vexacious problems of industrial mobilization. The WIB was strengthened without in any way disturbing its operations or clearly defining its authority. Moreover, the War Department—the major obstacle to successful mobilization—was forced into line. Issues almost too complex for direct resolution were, thereby, avoided.

Business representatives had every reason to support the Overman compromise and did so. Before the Chamberlain Committee, no one from among the business members on the Council of National Defense or on the WIB favored a ministry of munitions.[43] As members of the Wilson administration they could not have done otherwise. But as long as the president was willing to strengthen the WIB they had no reason to press for the ministry idea. Furthermore, businessmen within government were not unconscious of the threat of a ministry of munitions to the existing mobilization machinery. While still chairman of the crippled and helpless WIB during the winter crisis of 1917–18, Daniel Willard pleaded with business not to support a supply ministry. It was a risky experiment requiring legislation, he argued. Such legislation, Willard implied, was undesirable.[44] Both Grosvenor B. Clarkson and General Hugh S. Johnson, intimately involved with the wartime economic experience, concluded that the flexibility granted the NDAC and the WIB by the lack of specific statutes was a decided advantage, if not imperative.[45] The attitude of businessmen within the administration apparently influenced the business community. In February 1918, the Chamber of Commerce of the United States, largely responsible for the Senate Military Affairs Committee's legislation, not only switched its support to the Overman Act but also defended the bill against its critics. "Those in charge of the administrative machinery of the Government" were opposed to more extended legislation, announced a Chamber member. Through the Overman Act, the desired ends could be achieved without weathering the cumbersome legislative process.[46]

Baruch's selection as chairman was as important to the WIB as its new grant of authority. From the day the NDAC was organized, Baruch was a prominent figure. His intimate but detached knowledge and understanding of the U.S. economy and the men who ran it was central to his success. Long before war was declared, Baruch reasoned that successful mobilization depended upon winning industry's voluntary cooperation and maintaining the existing power structure. That meant industry would virtually have to be incorporated into the government. While a member of the NDAC, Baruch was instrumental in devising what ultimately became the Commodity Committee-War Service Committee system.[47]

The nature of the WIB demanded that its chairman have the confidence of industry and yet be above charges of conflict of interests or of favoring private over public welfare. Ironically, Baruch, the "Wolf of Wall Street," was tailor-made for the job. Before joining the NDAC, he divested himself of any connections that could compromise his activities. His speculative career raised opposition to his appointment in some circles, but a congressional committee gave Baruch a clean bill of health. Henceforth, his public image improved. For a time industrialists and financiers approached him with reservation because of his unorthodox occupation. However, uncertainty gradually gave way to trust as Baruch proved his abilities. Because he was largely above suspicion in the eyes of the public and the business community, Baruch could guide the risky process of incorporating industry into government while mostly giving industry its way. A more suspect individual would have met impossible obstacles.

When appointed chairman of the WIB, Baruch instituted policies which he had successfully applied in private business. He selected knowledgeable, competent young men to direct the major subdivisions of the WIB and gave them maximum freedom for carrying out their responsibilities. Authority was centralized, administration decentralized. The Commodity Committees were enlarged and strengthened. In effect they became small war industries boards for the various industries of the nation.[48]

By early 1918, then, a mobilization agency with authority had been perfected. Organized supply was integrated into its structure. But the system would not operate unless demand, and particularly the War Department, was fitted into it. The prospect for a successful merger was better in March 1918, than ever before.

Actually, Baker began patchwork reform of the army supply network in late summer 1917. When it became clear, during the winter crisis of 1917-18, that fundamental change was essential to prevent complete severance of supply from the War Department, the General Staff was reorganized to establish more effective supervision of the bureaus and to better coordinate the army's operations with those of the WIB.[49]

The more radical reforms Baker initiated did not produce the desired results until March 1918, when General Peyton C. March was appointed first acting, and later chief of staff. In record time, the dynamic, aggressive March fashioned a powerful agency out of the withered General Staff he inherited.[50]

General George W. Goethals became March's chief lieutenant for supply and procurement. Basing his authority on the Overman Act, he directed a near-revolution by managing to break down the old bureau structure and replacing it with a centralized supply system. It was a herculean task that met with intense resistance from the bureaus. At the time of the armistice the job was incomplete.

Ultimately Goethals became an assistant chief of staff and directed supply through a subdivision of the General Staff called the Division of Purchase, Storage, and Traffic. All of the Quartermaster Corps and the supply functions of the other bureaus, including purchase, storage, transportation, and finance were incorporated into the division. In the process, army supply operations were reorganized along commodity, instead of functional, lines. The War Department's system now paralleled that of the WIB. At last, the army was adjusting to the civilian economy. Reforms also included methods for obtaining reliable requirements information, centralized procurement of common items, and the standardization of contract forms and procedures.[51]

War Department reforms were originally intended to head off a strengthened civilian agency in order to safeguard army supply independence.[52] Nevertheless, army and navy operations were slowly integrated into those of the WIB.

For the army, that was possible because of new vitality and new personnel. When selected to work with the WIB, officers like General Hugh S. Johnson at first approached the board with typical military suspicion. Soon they came to appreciate that the civilian agency helped secure rather than threaten military prerogatives by aiding the army in fulfilling its responsibilities.[53] Antagonism gradually gave way to harmony. Flexibility within the WIB helped. At the outset, authority in the Commodity Committees rested exclusively with the civilian section chief. Army members on various committees felt that under the circumstances they were unable to protect War Department interests. Upon the plea of General Johnson, the entire committee was made the source of authority.[54] With similar organization, with a spirit of cooperation, the civilian mobilization agency and the War Department had finally reached a *modus operandi*. From March 1918 forward, the crisis of the economy was resolved.

That is not to say that the mobilization machinery ran without flaws or that the munitions picture was bright at war's end. Procurement agencies still set their own requirements; the WIB only determined how they were met. The board lacked the authority, and often the information, for working out a production program that was feasible for the economy. When hostilities ceased, the WIB faced the need to limit demand in order to avoid another crisis.[55]

All of the claimant agencies affected WIB operations, but none as greatly as the War Department. Chief of Staff March looked upon the board as no better than the War Department's equal, perhaps its inferior. As shifts in military requirements took place, March refused to inform the WIB. Only a major showdown between Baruch and March resolved the matter in favor of the board. Realizing that the services tenaciously guarded the right to determine their needs, the WIB never even attempted to institute review procedures. Had the war continued with demand multiplying faster than supply, the explosive military requirements riddle would have become a major devisive issue. The 30-division American Expeditionary Force program for 1918 was to be increased to 80 for 1919; General John J. Pershing was holding out for even more. Throughout 1918, Pershing's forces were critically short of needed supplies, including ordnance, signal equipment, motor vehicles, and medical provisions; by fall conditions were becoming desperate. Only the armistice saved the day.[56]

Nonetheless, when hostilities ceased, there existed a mobilization scheme that worked. The armed services had preserved control of supply; the business community had experienced a return to stability despite the exigencies of war. The basic pattern was sound even if the mechanics needed perfecting and the lines of authority required clarification.

Scholars and other writers have generally interpreted the War Department's encounter with the WIB and predecessor agencies as a struggle between civilian and military elements over domination of economic mobilization.[57] That is a misconception. The conflict arose as civilian and military institutions were going through the throes of adjusting to modern warfare where economically the rigid lines of demarkation between them were no longer possible.

Civilian administrations adapted with greater ease to the new conditions. The War Department, however, resisted the minimum changes essential for the successful mobilization of the economy.

Throughout a good part of World War I, the War Department was barely able to manage its own affairs, let alone extend its control over the economy. Its resistance to civilian mobilization agencies was more a result of isolation from, suspicion of, and ignorance about the civilian economy than a desire to dominate it. The army supply bureaus, really more civilian than military with their close congressional ties and detachment from the line, and Baker's fear of bringing them under control, were a central cause of the friction. Even Chief of Staff March's arrogant attitude toward civilian institutions reflected a failure to grasp the fact that it was no longer possible to compartmentalize civilian and military functions with finality.

Civilians were not anxious to take over military roles. The business community and its representatives were largely responsible for industrial mobilization. Their first concern was finding the means for mobilizing the economy without endangering the status quo. Some saw the war as an opportunity for strengthening the Progressive ties between government and industry. From the beginning, however, circumstances made the military services central to any mobilization scheme. While perfecting their own institutions, therefore, members of the NDAC and WIB and private businessmen worked hand in hand with army personnel to modernize military supply procedures.* Ultimately the War Industries Board proved to be the right means for harnessing the economy. Civilians in general, but businessmen in particular, would not permit the War Department to ruin what they had carefully worked out to protect their own and the nation's interests. Either the army had to adjust to the WIB or lose its procurement prerogatives. Since separating procurement from the armed services was politically undesirable, the former rather than the latter solution was adopted with the Overman Act. Wartime industrial self-rule was possible because of the emergency, but only when left undefined. Severing supply from the army and navy could have threatened the entire enterprise. Out of those conditions, economic and military institutions were integrated for the duration of the war and the foundation for the Military-Industrial Complex was laid.

---

*Businessmen, in and out of government service, before and after the winter crisis of 1917-1918, devoted many hours to War Department supply problems. Before war was declared, the Chamber of Commerce organized advisory boards to facilitate the operations of local quartermasters. The following were among those who aided the Army in setting up the Purchase, Storage, and Traffic Division of the General Staff: Otto H. Kahn, of Kuhn, Loeb & Company; C. D. Norton, president of the First National Bank of New York; R. J. Thorne, president of Montgomery Ward & Company, Inc.; H. H. Lehman of Lehman Brothers; Girard Swope, president of Western Electric Company, Inc.; and F. C. Weems, of J. P. Morgan & Company.[58]

NOTES

1. *The New Deal and the Problem of Monopoly: A Study in Economic Ambivalence* (Princeton, 1966).

2. Robert Wiebe, *Businessmen and Reform: A Study of the Progressive Movement* (Cambridge, 1962); Gabriel Kolko, *The Triumph of Conservatism: A Reinterpretation of American History, 1900-1916* (New York, 1963); Arthur M. Johnson, "Anti-trust Policy in Transition, 1908: Ideal and Reality," *Mississippi Valley Historical Review*, XLVIII (Dec., 1961), 415-34.

3. Galen R. Fisher, "The Chamber of Commerce of the United States and the Laissez-Faire Rationale, 1912-1919," (Ph.D. dissertation, University of California, Berkeley, 1960).

4. *The Nation's Business*, June, 1916, 4.

5. Reproduced in U.S. Congress, Senate, Special Committee Investigating the Munitions Industry, *Hearings, Munitions Industry*, 73rd Cong., 1935, Part 15, 3661—hereafter cited as Nye Committee, *Hearings*.

6. Lloyd N. Scott, *Naval Consulting Board of the United States* (Washington, 1920), 7-37, 220-23.

7. George V. Thompson, "Intercompany Technical Standardization in the Early American Automobile Industry," *Journal of Economic History*, XIV (Winter, 1954), 1-12.

8. Quoted in, Franklin H. Martin, *Digest of the Proceedings of the Council of National Defense during the World War*, U.S. Congress, Senate, 73rd Cong., 2nd Sess., Document No. 193 (Washington, 1934), 512.

9. U.S. Congress, Senate, Committee on Military Affairs, *Hearings, Investigation of the War Department*, 65th Cong., 2nd Sess., 1917-1918, 2281—hereafter cited as Chamberlain Committee, *Hearings*.

10. U.S. Congress, House, Committee on Naval Affairs, *Hearings, Estimates Submitted by the Secretary of the Navy—1916*, 64th Cong., 1st Sess., 1916, 3360.

11. U.S. Congress, House, Subcommittee No. 2 (Camps), Select Committee on Expenditures in the War Department, *Hearings, War Expenditures*, Serial 3, 66th Cong., 1st Sess., 1920, 880-90—hereafter cited as Graham Committee, *Hearings*.

12. Arthur A. Ekirch, Jr., *The Civilian and the Military* (New York, 1956), 160; U.S. Congress, House, Committee on Military Affairs, *Hearings, To Increase the Efficiency of the Military Establishment of the United States*, 64th Cong., 1st Sess., 1916, 62-64, 342, 347, 498-513, 518-20, 532-35, 550-51, 738-39—hereafter cited as HMAC, *Hearings*, 1916; U.S. Congress, Senate, Committee on Military Affairs, *Hearings, Preparedness for National Defense*, 64th Cong., 1st Sess., 1916, 84-85, 519-20, 524-30—hereafter cited as SMAC, *Hearings*, 1916; Marvin A. Kreidberg and Merton G. Henry, *History of Military Mobilization in the United States Army, 1775-1945*, U.S. Dept. of Army Pamphlet No. 20-212 (Washington, 1955), 336-37.

13. U.S. Congress, Senate, *Government Manufacture of Arms, Munitions, and Equipment*, 64th Cong., 2nd Sess., 1917, Document 664, 5-17.

14. New York *Times*, Oct. 12, 1916, 10.

15. Reproduced in Nye Committee, *Hearings*, Part 16, 4056-57.

16. For the best expression of this sentiment see: U.S. Congress, Subcommittee of the House Committee on Appropriations, *Hearings, Council of National Defense*, 65th Cong., 1st Sess., 1917, 37-38, 42-43—hereafter cited as Appropriations Subcommittee, *Hearings*. See also, Daniel R. Beaver, *Newton D. Baker and the American War Effort, 1917-1919* (Lincoln, 1966), 51-52, 71-76.

17. Preserving the economic *status quo* during wartime was a central idea of Coffin and was a basic assumption of the Kernan Board. See the discussion of Baruch below and

also: Nye Committee, *Minutes of the General Munitions Board From April 4 to August 9, 1917*, 74th Cong., 2nd Sess., 1936, Senate Committee Print No. 6, 1, 2, 4, 6, 39; Nye Committee, *Final Report of the Chairman of the United States War Industries Board to the President of the United States, February, 1919*, 74th Cong., 1st Sess., 1935, Senate Committee Print No. 3, 43–44; Fisher, "Chamber of Commerce," 435–36.

18. For a complete list of NDAC committees see: U.S. Council of National Defense, *First Annual Report* (Washington, 1917), 97-127. See also, Nye Committee, *Minutes of the Council of National Defense*, 11-14, 18-19, 30, and *Minutes of the Advisory Commission of the Council of National Defense and Minutes of the Munitions Standard Board*, 3, 11, 28, 30-32, 74th Cong., 2nd Sess., 1936, Senate Committee Prints 7 and 8; Appropriations Subcommittee, *Hearings*, 3-157; Grosvenor B. Clarkson, *Industrial America in the World War: The Strategy Behind the Line, 1917-1918* (New York, 1923), 26-29.

19. Testimony of military and other witnesses before congressional committees is the best source for military supply operation immediately before and during World War I. See the relevant portions of: HMAC, *Hearings*, 1916; SMAC, *Hearings*, 1916; Graham Committee, *Hearings*, Serial 1 and 3; Chamberlain Committee, *Hearings*; U.S. Congress, Senate Subcommittee of the Committee on Military Affairs, *Hearings, Reorganization of the Army*, 66th Cong., 2nd Sess., 1919; U.S. Congress, House, Committee on Military Affairs, *Hearings, Army Reorganization*, 66th Cong., 1st Sess., 1919-1920–hereafter cited as HMAC, *Hearings*, 1920.

Secondary sources on the Army are legion. None of them treat adequately with supply factors. The better ones include: John Dickinson, *The Building of an Army: A Detailed Account of Legislation, Administration and Opinion in the United States, 1915-1920* (New York, 1922); J. Franklin Crowell, *Government War Contracts* (New York, 1920); Paul Y. Hammond, *Organizing for Defense: The American Military Establishment in the Twentieth Century* (Princeton, 1961); Samuel P. Huntington, *The Soldier and the State: The Theory and Politics of Civil-Military Relations* (New York, 1964); Otto L. Nelson, Jr., *National Security and the General Staff* (Washington, 1946); Kreidberg and Henry, *Military Mobilization*; Erna Risch, *The Quartermaster Corps: Organization, Supply, and Services* (Washington, 1953); Constance McLaughlin Green, Harry C. Thomson, and Peter C. Roots, *The Ordnance Department: Planning Munitions for War* (Washington, 1955).

20. Beaver, *Baker*, 5-7, 51-52, 71-72, 80-81, 108-109, 152, 178, 210-11, 215-17, 243-46; C. H. Cramer, *Newton D. Baker: A Biography* (New York, 1961), 136-37.

21. Industrial Mobilization Plan, 1933–contained in U.S. War Policies Commission, *Hearings*, 72nd Cong., 1st Sess., House Document No. 163, 401–402.

22. John M. Clark, *The Cost of the World War to the American People* (New Haven, 1931), 30; Crowell, *War Contracts*, 63. For comparative purposes, the War Department figure would be slightly lower if estimated normal expenses for the war years were subtracted.

23. U.S. War Department, Purchase, Storage, and Traffic Division, General Staff, Supply Bulletin, No. 29, Nov. 7, 1918–reproduced in, Graham Committee, *Hearings*, Serial 1, 128-32.

24. Cramer, *Baker*, 122-23; Frederick Palmer, *Newton D. Baker: America at War* (2 vols., New York, 1931), I, 372; Beaver, *Baker*, 71-76; Clarkson, *Industrial America*, 41-42.

25. Testimony of various members of the NDAC before Congressional Committees is one of the best sources on Commission activities: Chamberlain Committee, *Hearings*, 1850-1884–Gifford; Graham Committee, *Hearings*, Serial 3, 869-79, 987-1019–Gifford and Frank A. Scott; Graham Committee, *Hearings*, Serial 1, 333-447, 1793-1857–Clarkson, Charles Eiseman, and Baruch; Appropriations Subcommittee, *Hearings*, 3-157. The day to day evolution of the Council of National Defense and its Advisory Commission are traced out in; *Council of National Defesne Minutes; NDAC Minutes; General Munitions Board*

Minutes; Nye Committee, *Minutes of the War Industries Board from August 1, 1917, to December 19, 1918,* 74th Cong., 1st Sess., 1935, Senate Committee Print No. 4; Council of National Defense, *First Annual Report,* and *Second Annual Report* (Washington, 1918).

26. *Council of National Defense Minutes,* 140; *NDAC Minutes,* 75–78, 80–81; Martin, *Digest,* 234; Beaver, *Baker,* 71.

27. *Cong. Rec.,* 65th Cong., 1st Sess., Vol. 55, Part 4, 3335–41, Part 5, 4590–4610, 4651–79, 4814–15, 5001–5049 (intermittent), 5169–89 (intermittent), 5214–25; *Cong. Rec.,* 66th Cong., 2nd Sess., Vol. 59, Part 4, 4089–4091; *Council of National Defense Minutes,* 129; *NDAC Minutes,* 80, 82, 85; *General Munitions Board Minutes,* 131, 142–43, 208–209. For an extended investigation of NDAC committees involving alleged conflict of interest in general and the Committee on Supplies in particular, see: Chamberlain Committee, *Hearings,* 593–1604 (intermittent), 1791–98. See also, Seward W. Livermore, *Politics is Adjourned: Woodrow Wilson and the War Congress, 1916–1918* (Middletown, 1966), 52–57.

28. For the creation of the WIB and its War Service Committees, see: *Council of National Defense Minutes,* 151–52, 170–71, 196–97, 215–16; *WIB Minutes,* 31, 38, 50, 69, 78, 93, 111–12, 208, 504–505; Chamberlain Committee, *Hearings,* 1850–84–Gifford testimony; Fisher, "Chamber of Commerce," 335–40, 343–461; William F. Willoughby, *Government Organization in War Time and After: A Survey of the Federal Civil Agencies Created for the Prosecution of the War* (New York, 1919), 80–91; Bernard M. Baruch, *American Industry in the War: A Report of the War Industries Board* (March, 1921), ed. by Richard H. Hippelheuser (New York, 1941), 20–23, 109–116; Clarkson, *Industrial America,* 240, 300–314; Benedict Crowell and Robert F. Wilson, *The Giant Hand: Our Mobilization and Control of Industry and Natural Resources, 1917–1918* (New Haven, 1921), 24–27, 99–103; *Final Report of the WIB,* 13–15, 40–41, 50–51.

29. There is no one outstanding comprehensive work on trade associations. Several of the better volumes include: Joseph H. Foth, *Trade Associations: Their Service to Industry* (New York, 1930); National Industrial Conference Board, *Trade Associations: Their Economic Significance and Legal Status* (New York, 1925); U.S. Department of Commerce, *Trade Association Activities* (Washington, 1927).

30. *The Nation's Business,* August, 1918, 9–10.

31. Principal WIB officials, their affiliations, and sources of income, are given in Nye Committee, *Hearings,* Part 16, 4142–45. Complete lists of WIB personnel and members of the War Service Committees are conveniently available in Clarkson, *Industrial America,* 501–543.

32. Michael D. Reagen, "Serving Two Masters: Problems in the Employment of Dollar-A-Year and Without Compensation Personnel" (Ph.D. dissertation, Princeton University, 1959), 7–8, 17.

33. Clarkson, *Industrial America,* 98, 303–311.

34. Beaver, *Baker,* 71–75.

35. *Ibid.,* 75–78; *WIB Minutes,* 2, 6, 13–15, 94, 146; *Council of National Defense Minutes,* 200; Chamberlain Committee, *Hearings,* 2282–83–Coffin testimony; War Policies Commission, *Hearings,* 169–70, 177–78–Daniel Willard testimony; Palmer, *Baker,* I, 378–79; Clarkson, *Industrial America,* 36–49, 83–84, 202–203; Crowell and Wilson, *The Giant Hand,* 22–27.

36. See the following secondary sources for the winter crisis and its resolution: Beaver, *Baker,* 79–109; Alexander D. Noyes, *The War Period of American Finance, 1908–1925* (New York, 1926), 244–78; L. C. Marshall, "A Nation of Economic Amateurs," *Readings in the Economics of War,* eds. by J. Maurice Clark, Walton H. Hamilton, and Harold G. Moulton (Chicago, 1918), 221–24; Clarkson, *Industrial America,* 42–45, 51–59, 138–39, 199–200, 234–35, 453; Benedict Crowell and Forrest Wilson, *The Armies of Industry,* I. (New Haven, 1921), 4–6; Livermore, *Politics is Adjourned,* 62–104; Palmer,

Baker, II, 66–84; Frederic L. Paxson, *America at War: 1917-1918* (Boston, 1939), 210–228, 250–53.

37. Chamberlain Committee, *Hearings*, 1885–1924.

38. *Cong. Rec.*, 65th Cong., 2nd Sess., Vol. 56, Part I, 557, 1004, Part 2, 1077–78; U.S. Congress, Senate, Committee on Military Affairs, *Director of Munitions*, 65th Cong., 2nd Sess., 1918, Senate Report No. 200 to accompany S. 3311, 1–2.

39. *Cong., Rec.*, 65th Cong., 2nd Sess., Vol. 56, Part 1, 977–79, 980–83, Part 2, 1194–1211, 1242–44, 1607–21, 1686–95, 1747, 1819–32, 1842–52, 2095–2105, Part 3, 2136–49, Part 4, 3815, 4504–26, 4572–83, 4945–73, 5013–23, 5551–71, 5739–66, Part 9, 8616.

40. E. M. H. Lloyd, *Experiments in State Control at the War Office and the Ministry of Food* (London, 1924); John A. Fairle, *British War Administration* (New York, 1919); Pierre Renouvin, *The Forms of War Government in France* (New Haven, 1927); S. O. Zagorsky, *State Control of Industry in Russia during the War* (New Haven, 1928); Robert B. Armeson, *Total Warfare and Compulsory Labor: A Study of the Military-Industrial Complex in Germany during World War I* (The Hague, 1964).

41. Beaver, *Baker*, 52, 96 (and footnote 64), 105–106. Revering, yet suspecting, the business community has been a long-run trend in American life. See: Thomas C. Cochran, *The American Business System: A Historical Perspective, 1900-1955* (New York, 1962), 2–10, 194–205.

42. *Cong. Rec.*, 65th Cong., 2nd Sess., Vol. 56, Part 1, 558; New York *Times*, January 5, 1918, 3. See also citations for the *Cong. Rec.* in footnotes 27 and 39.

43. See the testimony of Willard, Baruch, Gifford, and Coffin, Chamberlain Committee, *Hearings*, 1799–1847, 1850–84, 2253–89.

44. *The Nation's Business*, Feb., 1918, 7–9.

45. Clarkson, *Industrial America*, 5–9, 20, 215–16; *Final Report of the WIB*, 3–4 – for authorship of the *Report* see Nye Committee, *Hearings*, Part 22, 6393–95, 6642.

46. New York *Times*, Feb. 27, 1918, 4; Fisher, "Chamber of Commerce," 378–80.

47. Concerning Baruch, the NDAC, and his qualifications for the WIB chairmanship, see: sources cited in footnote No. 18; Bernard M. Baruch, *My Own Story* (New York, 1957); 308–312; Bernard M. Baruch, *Baruch, The Public Years* (New York, 1960), 20–25, 28–33, 48–49; Clarkson, *Industrial America*, 66–73, 89, 301–302; Crowell and Wilson, *The Giant Hand*, 24–25, 27–31; Palmer, *Baker*, II, 201–202; Hugh S. Johnson, *The Blue Eagle From Egg to Earth* (New York, 1935), 113–14; Margaret L. Coit, *Mr. Baruch* (Boston, 1957), 147–52, 167–76; Beaver, *Baker*, 104–108.

48. The *WIB Minutes* are helpful in tracing the board's development, as are Crowell and Wilson's volumes, *The Giant Hand and The Armies of Industry: I*. The 52-page introductory essay to the *Final Report of the WIB* is the one best source on the board. Clarkson, *Industrial America* and Baruch, *American Industry* are indispensable despite their very numerous limitations.

49. Graham Committee, *Hearings*, Serial 1, 518–20–Geothals testimony; Nelson, *National Security and the General Staff*, 242–43; Beaver, *Baker*, 93–97.

50. The quality of March's leadership is a main theme of Edward M. Coffman, *The Hilt of the Sword: The Career of Peyton C. March* (Madison, 1966)–see especially, 67–68, 76–77, 149, 151, 247–49. See also, Peyton C. March, *The Nation at War* (New York, 1932), 56.

51. The one best secondary source for analyzing and describing the modernization of the Army's supply structure is, Dickinson, *Building of an Army*, 284–307. For primary sources and other secondary sources, see citations in footnote 19.

52. Clarkson, *Industrial America*, 42, 54, 84–85, 128–31; Beaver, *Baker*, 95, 97.

53. Johnson, *Blue Eagle*, 90–93; Clarkson, *Industrial America*, 128–32. Not only did Johnson become an enthusiastic supporter of the WIB, but he was also instrumental in

drafting the proposals for restructuring the Army supply system to parallel that of the WIB. See Goethals testimony, Graham Committee, *Hearings*, Serial 1, 529.

54. *WIB Minutes,* 427–28; *Final Report of the WIB*, 14–15; Baruch, *American Industry*, 111–12.

55. David Novick, Melvin Anshen, and W. C. Truppner, *Wartime Production Controls* (New York, 1949), 28–30; Beaver, *Baker*, 172–73.

56. *Ibid.*, 156–61, 165–69, 171–79, 186–88; Baruch, *Public Years*, 56–58; Clarkson, *Industrial America*, 100–102, 128, 132–135; Johnson, *Blue Eagle*, 91; Coffman, *Hilt of the Sword*, 73–74, 76, 84–94, 104–110, 136–41.

57. For the most recent example, see: Beaver, *Baker*, 76.

58. See: Fisher, "Chamber of Commerce," 331–34; HMAC, *Hearings*, 1920, 447; Graham Committee, *Hearings*, Serial 1, 293; Dickinson, *Building of an Army*, 305–306.

3

THE INTERWAR YEARS

Scholars and journalists have limited their analyses of the "Military-Industrial Complex" to the years of World War II and the Cold War.[1] This focus is quite natural, for it is during this period that the multibillion-dollar war and defense budgets have had the most dramatic effects upon the nation's institutional structure. Nevertheless, to neglect the years prior to 1940 greatly limits an understanding of the "complex" which has resulted from the military's expanded role in the federal government and its elaborate ties with the industrial community.

The "Military-Industrial Complex" of World War II and after is an outgrowth of economic mobilization for World War I, of interwar planning by the armed forces and the business community for future emergencies, and of defense spending during the 1920s and 1930s. Almost all practices currently ascribed to the "complex" arose before 1940.

During World War I, as during World War II, federal agencies, largely controlled by industry and the military, regulated the economy. World War I differed from World War II, however, in that the army, the largest wartime military service, was a reluctant participant in the civilian mobilization agencies. Relatively isolated within the federal government and the nation before hostilities, the army was suspicious of, and hostile toward, civilian institutions. It was also unprepared for the enormous wartime responsibilities. Congress and the Wilson

The following is a reprint of an article which originally appeared as "The 'Industrial-Military Complex' in Historical Perspective: The InterWar Years," *The Journal of American History* 56 (March 1970): 819–39. Permission from the editor to reproduce this essay is gratefully acknowledged.

administration had to force the army to integrate its personnel into the War industries Board (WIB). This integration was essential for coordinating army procurement with the board's regulatory functions in order to maintain a stable economy.

After the war, Congress authorized the army to plan for procurement and economic mobilization in order to insure its preparation for future hostilities. The navy also joined the planning process. The interwar planning was guided by thousands of industrialists, and by the late 1930s the armed services were not only prepared for wartime operations but also in full agreement with prominent industrial elements on plans for economic mobilization. Those plans, based on World War I mobilization, provided the guidelines for regulating the World War II economy.

Interwar planning was inseparable from defense spending. Many of the businessmen who participated in the planning were associated with firms that were actual or potential military contractors. Despite the relatively small defense budgets of the 1920s and 1930s, the pattern of industrial-military relations during those years foreshadows in many striking ways what developed after World War II.

The U.S. economy was mobilized for World War I by federal agencies devised and staffed primarily by businessmen.[2] In the Army Appropriations Act of August 1916, Congress provided for a Council of National Defense, which consisted of six cabinet members, to serve as the president's advisory body on industrial mobilization. It was assisted by a National Defense Advisory Commission (NDAC), composed largely of businessmen serving for a dollar-a-year or without compensation; most of the members surrendered neither their positions nor incomes as private citizens. When the nation declared war, NDAC assumed responsibility for mobilizing the economy. In July 1917 a more effective mobilization agency, WIB, took over NDAC functions; the former agency, like the latter, was controlled by business elements. Until March 1918, neither NDAC nor WIB had legal authority to enforce its decisions; both were subordinate to the Council of National Defense, and it could only advise the president.

During 1917, businessmen perfected the mobilization agencies and devised the means for curtailing civilian production and converting industry to meet governmental needs. In addition, they developed price, priority, allocation, and other economic controls. By the end of the year, WIB had created the organization and the controls essential for regulating a wartime economy.

Through WIB, industry largely regulated itself during World War I. Key to WIB's operations were major subdivisions called Commodity Committees, which served under the chairman and his lieutenants. These committees, which made policy for and administered the various industries, were staffed by businessmen who often came from the industries they directed. Assisting the Commodity Committees were War Service Committees, which were trade associations or councils elected by the national industries. Since the War Service Committees were neither organized nor financed by the government, they officially only "advised" the Commodity Committees. But in practice the Commodity Committees relied heavily upon industry representatives to formulate and execute all policy decisions.

Even without legal authority to enforce its decisions, WIB had industry's cooperation becasue businessmen dominated it. Industry's cooperation, however, was not enough to maintain a stable wartime economy. WIB required some control over procurement by the War and Navy Departments and other agencies. Throughout 1917 it attempted to coordinate procurement with its own operations in order to prevent the various departments and agencies from competing among themselves and to insure uniform prices and the distribution of contracts according to availability of facilities, resources, and transportation. Economic stability depended upon such coordination, since wartime demand always exceeded supply. With only advisory powers. WIB relied upon the procurement agencies' voluntary cooperation. While most of these proved to be reasonably cooperative, the War Department—the largest, most powerful procurement agency—undermined WIB's regulatory efforts by acting independently and purchasing billions of dollars worth of munitions. As a result, industrial plants in the Northeast were overloaded with contracts; prices skyrocketed; critical shortages of fuel, power, and raw materials developed; and the railway and shipping systems became hopelessly congested.

The War Department was both unwilling and unable to cooperate with WIB—unwilling, because it feared that the civilian agency would try to take over army procurement functions; unable, because the department could not control its own supply operations, let alone coordinate them with WIB. As many as eight supply bureaus, such as the Quartermaster Corps and the Ordnance Department, purchased independently for the army. Competing with one another and other purchasing agencies, the bureaus let contracts indiscriminately, commandeered facilities without plan, and hoarded supplies. Cooperation between WIB and the War Department was also thwarted by the fact that WIB was organized along commodity lines, while the army's supply network was structured by function (such as ordnance and quartermaster). Before army procurement could be coordinated with WIB, the War Department had first to accept the need for cooperating with the civilian mobilization agency and then to centralize its supply network along commodity lines. For months, the department would do neither, not only because it was suspicious of WIB but also because it was torn by internal dissension.

In theory, the War Department was under the centralized control of the chief of staff, aided by the General Staff. Serving as the secretary of war's principal military adviser, the chief of staff supervised the entire army, including the supply bureaus as well as the combat troops. This system never worked in practice. The bureaus resisted control by the chief of staff. Conflict between the General Staff and the bureaus rent the War Department before the war; it paralyzed the department during hostilities.

Unable to regulate the economy without War Department cooperation, WIB during 1917 sought the authority to impose its will on the department. But Secretary of War Newton D. Baker, reflecting army suspicion of the board, squelched the efforts to give it more than advisory powers. He managed to do so because he served as chairman of the Council of National Defense, under which WIB functioned, and as Woodrow Wilson's chief adviser on industrial mobilization.

By the winter of 1917-18, with WIB stalemated by the War Department and the latter virtually collapsing under burgeoning munitions requirements, the economy had become critically dislocated. The business community and Congress demanded that the crisis should be resolved by placing military procurement under a civilian munitions ministry. Adamantly opposed to such a drastic remedy, Wilson headed off the critics in March 1918 by separating WIB from the Council of National Defense and placing it directly under his control. He granted it broad powers for regulating the economy, including a measure of authority over the procurement agencies. To avoid losing control of procurement and to facilitate coordination with WIB, the War Department also began reforming its supply system. In December 1917, the department began to consolidate the bureaus into one agency under General Staff control. The new organization was structured to match WIB's Commodity Committee system.

From March 1918, the strengthened WIB, under the chairmanship of Bernard M. Baruch, effectively used the organization and economic controls developed over the past year to regulate the economy. Procurement was coordinated with WIB activities by integrating War Department representatives and those of the other purchasing agencies into WIB. Once the department reorganized its system and adopted a cooperative attitude, members of the army commodity committees joined WIB committees and shared equally in making decisions. Working together, industrial and military personnel learned that WIB could function for their mutual interests. Through WIB's operations, the foundation for the Military-Industrial Complex was laid.

The collaboration of industry and the military continued during the 1920s and 1930s and took the form of procurement and economic planning for future wars. This planning was authorized by Congress in the National Defense Act of 1920, which reorganized the War Department's system of supply and procurement. To insure that the army did not disrupt economic mobilization in a future emergency, the act placed the supply bureaus under an assistant secretary of war. It was assumed that he would be an industrialist. The assistant secretary would supervise the bureaus and, through planning, prepare them for wartime procurement. Since the assistant secretary was made the chief of staff's equal, the secretary of war had two principal advisers instead of one, as had been the case before 1920.[3]

Congress based the legislation upon the recommendations of Assistant Secretary of War Benedict Crowell, various industrial consultants, several bureau chiefs, and other military personnel. Crowell, a Cleveland businessman who had been involved in military procurement since 1916, believed that World War I demonstrated that industrial production was as important to military success as were tactics and strategy. He felt that supply and procurement must receive the same emphasis in War Department affairs as did the traditional military functions. That would not take place, he maintained, under the old system in which the chief of staff, aided by the General Staff, served as the secretary of war's principal adviser. The General Staff would neglect supply and procurement because it knew little about those subjects. Only by placing the bureaus under a qualified civilian who was equal to the chief of staff, he argued, would the army be prepared for future hostilities.[4] Crowell and his associates intended that the assistant secretary of war should plan only for army procurement. Congress went further. The National Defense Act empowered the assistant secretary, though in an ambiguous way, to plan for an entire wartime economy. Why Congress authorized the more comprehensive planning is obscure.

J. Mayhew Wainwright, the first assistant secretary of war under the act, set up an Office of the Assistant Secretary of War (OASW) with personnel drawn from the bureaus. In 1922 an Army-Navy Munitions Board was created in order to include the navy in the planning and to coordinate the supply systems of the two services. And, in 1924 the War Department supply planners organized an Army Industrial College to facilitate their work.[5]

At first, OASW concentrated upon wartime military procurement, but it soon became obvious that this planning was futile without also planning for economic mobilization.[6] Though authorized to draft such plans, War Department officials, civilian and military alike, hesitated to assume what they considered to be civilian responsibilities. It took the influence of Baruch to convince the War Department that economic planning was not exclusively a civilian matter. After World War I, he and other architects of wartime mobilization insisted that the nation's security depended upon constant preparation for war. They favored joint industry-military planning for economic mobilization in order to avoid confusion and delay.[7] Baruch pleaded with the department to draw up full-scale plans for mobilization based on World War I.[8] After years of hesitation, OASW began to plan for economic mobilization as well as procurement. Under Baruch's critical eye, the supply planners between 1929 and 1931 drafted the first official economic blueprint for war—the "Industrial Mobilization Plan" of 1930.[9]

This plan amounted to little more than a proposal for using the methods of World War I to regulate a wartime economy. The key to OASW's blueprint was a War Resources Administration, Comparable to the War Industries Board, the War Resources Administration would rely upon a Commodity Committee-War Service Committee system for economic control. The military services would also organize their procurement networks along commodity lines and integrate their personnel into the War Resources Administration. In a future war, the economy would be mobilized by new federal agencies largely dominated by industrial and military personnel.[10] In 1933, 1936, and 1939, the War Department published revised editions of the plan. With each revision, the proposed mobilization apparatus was simplified and patterned more explicitly after the World War I model.[11]

The fact that the War Department wrote the 1930 plan is of the greatest significance. After ten years of planning, OASW recognized that modern warfare required a totally planned economy; the armed services would have to adapt themselves to the civilian mobilization agencies during hostilities. The Industrial Mobilization Plan did not mean, however, that the army as a whole had accepted the new conditions of warfare. Before that could take place, the supply planners had to convert the chief of staff and the General Staff to their point of view. Throughout the 1920s and into the 1930s, the army's command structure refused to recognize that supply and procurement set limits for tactics and strategy; and the General Staff's war plans provided for raising and fielding an army at rates that exceeded the economy's capacity. The General Staff insisted that supply had to adjust to strategy. OASW and the supply bureaus adamantly opposed such thinking. Both the economy and the military mission, they argued, would be threatened.[12] The admonition went unheeded for years.

The General Staff turned a deaf ear to OASW because, knowing little about procurement, it could not gauge the effects of industrialized warfare on the army or the economy and, therefore, continued to view civilian and military responsibilities as if they were unrelated. In addition, the General Staff and OASW were rivals for power. The General Staff resented the 1920 reorganization which deprived it of control of the bureaus. It was intent upon keeping the supply side of the department subordinate to itself. If the General Staff granted the importance of supply and procurement in military affairs, it would strengthen the hand of its rival. Relations between the two groups in the War Department became so embittered in the 1920s that communication broke down almost completely. In the 1930s, however, the strife began to wane. As relations improved, the General Staff gradually became more receptive to OASW ideas.[13]

A major turning point occurred in 1935-36, when General Malin Craig became chief of staff, and Harry W. Woodring, secretary of war. Woodring, who had served as assistant secretary of war from 1933 to 1936, was convinced of the need for practical war plans. Craig agreed. Under their combined influence, the General Staff's Mobilization Plan of 1933 was scrapped and the Protective Mobilization Plan drawn up and perfected between 1936 and 1939. It was the first war plan based on the nation's industrial potential.[14] A radical change had taken place in the thinking of the army's command structure. It had finally accepted army dependence on the civilian economy in order to fulfill the military mission. Woodring observed: "I believe the reduction of our mobilization program to sensible workable proportions to be one of the highest attainments of the War Department since the World War."[15]

OASW planning naturally led to numerous War Department contacts with the business community. Thousands of industrialists, most of whom had participated in wartime mobilization, guided and assisted the department's efforts in various ways. When the Army Industrial College was organized, it had an advisory board graced with such prominent business figures as Baruch, Elbert H. Gary, and Walter Gifford. The various procurement districts also set up civilian advisory boards composed of army contractors to review the department's supply operations. In 1925 the department organized a Business Council, which included members from the nation's largest corporations, to help introduce modern business techniques into army operations and to familiarize the industralists with army procurement and planning methods.[16]

Most contacts between the War Department and industry involved representatives from trade associations and interested corporation executives. Often these men were or became reserve officers assigned to OASW. By 1931 about 14,000 individuals served in such a capacity. They aided in the drafting of procurement and mobilization plans and sought to further cooperative relations between the military and business.[17]

Mixed motives explain industry's participation in War Department planning.[18] Firms contracting with the army obviously welcomed the opportunity of working closely with OASW in order to secure or advance their special interests. Some business elements assisted the army so that they could identify their products or materials with national defense in order to enhance their chances for tariff protection, government assistance, or other special privileges. Also, their firms received free publicity of a "patriotic" nature. But reasons other than immediate economic concerns must be considered in assessing industry's role in army planning. Industrial preparedness became almost an ideological crusade for some business executives after the war. That was the case with Baruch and his coterie; with Howard E. Coffin, a prominent industrialist and leading participant in wartime mobilization; and with businessmen associated with the American Legion.[19] They participated in army planning as a means of preparing the nation for war. The business community in general was not so disposed. Without being committed to industrial preparedness per se, many businessmen were willing to assist in the planning at the War Department's request because it helped the department to adjust its structure and thinking to modern warfare.

The general trend of the interwar political economy is also significant for measuring the response of business to army planning. World War I greatly strengthened the cooperative ethic within the business community and between it and the government. Before World War II, both business and the government experimented with official and unofficial attempts at economic control through industrial cooperation. The National Recovery Administration was only the most formal example. The army's economic planning accurately reflected this cooperative trend.[20] For that reason, among others, the planning received the endorsement of interested businessmen.

OASW did not confine itself simply to planning for industrial mobilization. It also sought legislative authority for implementing the "Industrial Mobilization Plan" in an emergency.

During the 1920s the department's drive for industrial preparedness was carried on in conjunction with the American Legion. The Legion rank and file seethed with resentment about alleged wartime profiteering and the unequal burden shouldered by the fighting forces. In order to remove the promise of riches as an inducement to war and to distribute the burdens of warfare more equitably, the returning veterans demanded a total draft of manpower and capital in any future emergency. Ironically, the Legion's peace movement, which originated in dissent over the economics of World War I, was ultimately converted into support for the "Industrial Mobilization Plan" based on the wartime model. Legion leadership and its special relationship with the War Department explains why. Substantial business elements and former military officers dominated Legion affairs; throughout the 1920s the secretaries and assistant secretaries of war were usually active Legionnaires. When acting on the proposal for a total draft that was favored by the rank and file, the Legion leaders turned to the War Department for assistance. In 1922, OASW drafted for the Legion a bill that in general terms would have granted the president almost unlimited authority over the nation's human and economic resources in the event of war.[21] The Legion consistently referred to the bill as a "universal draft," as a measure for promoting peace, and as a proposal for "equalizing wartime burdens." That was scarcely the case. The bill was so vague that it could be used for many different purposes. Its grant of authority was so great and its power so general that it could sanction a presidential dictatorship. Once the economic planning of OASW was fully underway, the War Department and the Legion leadership clearly intended the bill to a general grant of authority for implementing the "industrial Mobilization Plan."

Beginning in 1922, the Legion-sponsored bill was repeatedly introduced in Congress. Despite Legion lobbying and War Department support, each Congress sidetracked the proposed legislation. Unable to get its bill through Congress, the Legion asked for a bipartisan commission to study and recommend policies for industrial mobilization. An active campaign by congressmen who were also Legionnaires soon led to action. By a joint resolution in June 1930, Congress created the War Policies Commission (WPC), which consisted of eight congressmen and six cabinet members. Six of the fourteen commissioners were Legionnaires. The commission was to study and make recommendations for equalizing war buurdens and preventing war profiteering, and it was to formulate "policies to be pursued in event of war."[22]

WPC, like the Legion's drive for a "universal draft," quickly became a means for furthering military preparation.[23] Because the War Department dominated the proceedings, WPC emphasized how to mobilize the economy for war and not how to equalize war burdens and eliminate war profits. Secretary of War Patrick J. Hurley, an active Legionnaire, served as WPC's chairman. WPC's staff came almost exclusively from the War Department. The department's presentation of its 1930 "Industrial Mobilization Plan" and Baruch's testimony on the economics of World War I were the highlights of WPC's public hearings. After extended deliberations, WPC, with only one dissenting vote, directly endorsed the department's planning and indirectly endorsed the "Industrial Mobilization Plan."[24] WPC efforts were more impressive as an attempt to popularize and legitimize department planning than as a serious study of wartime economics.

Despite a friendly commission, the department was unable to drum up much overt support for its plans. In addition to the department itself, the principal advocates of the planning before WPC were the American Legion and some wartime mobilization leaders like Baruch, Gifford, and Coffin.[25] The business community in general was either unconcerned about or unwilling to commit itself publicly on issues involving economic mobilization. Of the thousands of businessmen participating in the army planning, only a few came forward to testify.

Although support for department planning was weak, the opposition was vociferous. Witnesses like Norman Thomas, several congressmen, and spokesmen for some peace societies and humanitarian groups were hostile to WPC and the department's plans. Some advocates of peace detected inherent dangers in the department's work. According to their analyses, the promise of wartime riches, while not a major cause of war, was a contributing one that had to be eliminated. The army's plans would not do this. Moreover, the opponents feared that the industrial-military ties resulting from department planning could endanger the nation's future.[26] But the critics—among them a member of WPC, Representative Ross A. Collins of Mississippi—were weak on analysis. Their critique of the department's plans and planning was often nebulous, contradictory, or incomplete. Seymour Waldman, a journalist covering the hearings, articulated more clearly and precisely what appeared to alarm Collins and some witnesses before WPC:

> The hearings revealed a gigantic machine, whose intricate parts touch the entire nation, which is being constructed by the War Department and industrial magnates for use in the event of war. . . . They reveal the dangers inherent in a militarization of industry, an industrialization of the military forces, or a combination of the two. . . .
> I would feel rewarded and gratified if this book should be the precursor of a much needed diagnosis of the whole problem, a study of the interlocking of our war mechanism and our economic system.

. . . Such a work . . . is imperative if we are to be effective in preventing more national and international bloodshed.[27]

Opposition to the department's plans and proposed legislation for implementing them increased after WPC's hearings as the peace and isolationist
movement gained in strength.[28] The most formidable challenge came from
the Senate's so-called Nye Committee. In addition to the munitions makers,
the Nye Committee's purview included economic mobilization for World War
I, interwar military procurement policies, and the "Industrial Mobilization
Plan." In a fragmentary manner, the committee disclosed the dynamics of an
emerging Military-Industrial Complex. The elements were presented in the committee hearings and reports, but they were not fitted together. Senator Gerald
P. Nye and his colleagues still saw only through a glass darkly.*

The Nye Committee clearly perceived that industrialized warfare created
qualitatively new and ominous problems for the nation. To fight a modern
war, even to prepare for one, eroded the barriers between private and public,
civilian and military institutions. The committee observed that during hostilities
"practically every important industry in the country is necessary for the supply
of the armed forces." "Even in time of peace," the committee reported, "the
line of demarkation between the munitions industry and other industries is not
clear and fixed."[29]

From its investigation of interwar defense spending, the committee established that various industries depended upon military contracts for profitable operations and that the military services depended upon them for developing and producing weapons. There were many prime examples. Shipbuilding
indirectly included "the steel companies, the electrical manufacturing groups,
the boiler producers, the instrument people," and "the biggest banking interests in the Nation." Du Pont and other munitions producers were virtual ad-
juncts of the War Department. Industrialists and military leaders regarded their
interests as mutual. Industry favored and worked for increased military appropriations; the armed services granted industry special favors, encouraged monopoly where it served their interests, financed research, and, despite legislation to
the contrary, displayed little concern about profit restraints.[30] Committee members were shocked to find that the War and Navy Departments, and even the
Commerce and State Departments at times, cooperated with munitions firms
in a manner that compromised national policies for disarmament, arms limita-
tion, arms sales, and arms embargoes.[31] The fact that Public Works Administration funds, intended to stimulate industrial recovery, went to the armed

---

*The Nye Committee findings, although not all of its recommendations, received the
unanimous endorsement of all members.

services and that some businessmen favored defense spending as an antidote to the Depression also disturbed Nye and his colleagues.[32]

The Nye Committee found a web of personal as well as contractual ties binding industrial-military elements. Retired army and navy officers often joined firms contracting with the services. Frequently, officials of corporations supplying the armed services became reserve officers. A society like the Army Ordnance Association, organized in 1919, combined in its membership actual or potential military contractors and retired and active army officers. The association lobbied for the army, participated in the industrial mobilization planning, and attempted to influence War Department policies and the selection and promotion of personnel.[33]

The Nye Committee carefully avoided charges of conspiracy. It pointed out that plausible reasons existed for what was done and stated that it was not drawing a one-to-one correlation between expenditures for defense and the causation of war.[34] Nevertheless, argued the committee,

> any close associations between munitions and supply companies . . . and the service departments . . . , of the kind that existed in Germany before the World War, constitutes an unhealthy alliance in that it brings into being a self-interested political power which operates in the name of patriotism and satisfies interests which are, in large part, purely selfish, and that such associations are an inevitable part of militarism, and are to be avoided in peacetime at all costs.[35]

In order to check the growth of an "unhealthy alliance," a majority of the committee favored nationalizing the munitions facilities. Congress never seriously considered the proposal. Upon the advice of the Roosevelt administration, Congress even refused to strengthen regulations governing military procurement as the committee minority recommended.[36]

The army's economic planning for war also disturbed the Nye Committee. The planning, argued the committee, assured that industry and the military would function more effectively as a team than they had in World War I; but, because the "Industrial Mobilization Plan" was patterned after wartime methods, it would not eliminate the "economic evils of war." According to the committee's analysis, World War I mobilization was accompanied by "shameless profiteering" and extravagant waste. The war left a legacy of inflation, debt, and increased concentration of economic power. Similar results would occur in a future war if industry, in conjunction with the armed services, virtually regulated itself.[37]

In order to secure the nation's economic future and to remove the promise of riches as an inducement to war, the Nye Committee maintained that wartime "economic evils" had to be eliminated. That required radical changes in the economic system during hostilities, not the preservation of the status quo as proposed by the "Industrial Mobilization Plan." The profit motive and the prerogatives of private property would have to be modified. To accomplish that purpose, the committee supported legislation drafted under the direction of John T. Flynn. In an emergency, profits would be limited to 3 percent and personal annual income to $10,000. No individual with direct or indirect interests in an industry could serve in a government capacity involving that industry. Moreover, the president would be granted vast authority over the economy to the point of conscripting capital and management if necessary.[38] Although vague at many points, the Flynn legislation amounted to a proposal for state capitalism during wartime with the industrial managers removed from the seats of power.

The War Department opposed the committee's major recommendations. It viewed with alarm any taxation proposals that threatened production. It maintained that conscripting management would not work and insisted that economic mobilization was impossible without the assistance of managers of the industries to be regulated.[39] Baruch responded to the proposed bill with undisguised hostility. Attempting to change the economic system during a war, he argued, was an invitation to disaster.[40]

In its most impressive reports, the Nye Committee curiously agreed with both the War Department and Baruch. The committee's support of the Flynn proposals ignored its own findings. Without constitutional amendments that could be "far worse than the situation of profiteering in a national emergency," the Flynn legislation could not be enforced. The committee recognized that, even if the bill and the necessary amendments were adopted, they would probably be repealed or ignored in an emergency. The only men qualified to administer a wartime economy were industrialists themselves. It was inconceivable that they would attempt to enforce laws they considered detrimental to the economy and to the war effort.[41]

The Flynn bill was introduced into Congress in 1935. For a time, Franklin D. Roosevelt seemed disposed toward the bill. Ultimately, he joined Baruch, the War Department, and, with reservations, the Legion in backing competing legislation that would have granted the president authority for mobilizing the economy, but with few safeguards against abuse. That bill would have sanctioned what the "Industrial Mobilization Plan" proposed. The administration let it be known that it, too, believed that curtailing the profit motive during a war would jeopardize any mobilization program. No legislation was passed.[42]

After the Nye Committee investigation, the nation knew more about the political economy of warfare; but short of avoiding war and excessive spending for defense, there was no viable way to prevent close and compromising relations between business and the armed services. Military spending in the U.S. industrial system inevitably drew industrial and military elements together, and the threat of an "unhealthy alliance" was always present.

War Department planning entered its final and most important phase after the Nye Committee investigation. With the approach of war and the growing U.S. preparedness movement, the department launched a drive for the appointment of a joint industry-military board to review and ultimately to implement the "Industrial Mobilization Plan."

The proposal for a joint board originated with civilians who were concerned about a major flaw in the "Industrial Mobilization Plan." Because of a continuing distrust of civilian institutions, the army determined to dominate the wartime mobilization agencies. To insure that OASW plans were realistic and to keep the nation ready for war, Baruch and others repeatedly recommended that industrialists officially meet each year with the War Department. They would review the department's plans and prepare themselves for the eventuality of official duty.[43]

The War Department resisted suggestions for officially sharing its planning authority with industrialists until Louis Johnson, a past American Legion commander, became assistant secretary of war in June 1937. With international relations deteriorating, Johnson was determined to prepare both the army and the nation for war. He arranged for Baruch, some former WIB members, and younger talent to serve as an advisory board to OASW.[44] For Johnson, that was the first essential step for instituting the "Industrial Mobilization Plan." But the president refused to sanction the scheme.[45] Despite the setback, Johnson was determined to create an advisory board. He was stealthily maneuvering to achieve that end in mid-1939,[46] when Roosevelt, fearing that war was imminent and that the nation might become involved,[47] authorized Johnson to set up a mobilization advisory group called the War Resources Board (WRB). Roosevelt chose Edward R. Stettinius, Jr., of the United States Steel Corporation, as chairman and left the selection of other members to the War Department. With Stettinius serving as an intermediary, Johnson, Acting Secretary of the Navy Charles Edison, Army Chief of Staff George Marshall, and two senior members of OASW selected the others. In addition to Stettinius, WRB included Gifford, president of American Telephone and Telegraph, John Lee Pratt of General Motors Corporation, Robert E. Wood, chairman of Sears, Roebuck, and Company, Karl T. Compton of the Massachusetts Institute of Technology, and Harold G. Moulton, president of the Brookings Institute. The membership was cleared with the president.[48] Why Baruch was excluded is still unclear. He was described as being "sore as hell" about being passed over.[49] WRB did not get his blessing until his close associate, John Hancock, was appointed to it in September. Hancock played a prominent role in WRB proceedings.

Assistant Secretary of War Johnson announced to the nation that WRB would review the "Industrial Mobilization Plan" of 1939, revise it if necessary, and implement it in an emergency.[50] Key to the plan was the War Resources Administration, organized along Commodity Committee-War Service Committee lines with military representatives integrated into it. Unlike earlier plans, the 1939 edition moderated proposed military influence in the civilian agencies.[51]

Working hand in hand with the armed services, WRB, while still reviewing the "Industrial Mobilization Plan," began preparing to institute it. In sharp contrast to its attitude toward WPC, the business community was eager to co-operate with WRB. The National Association of Manufacturers and the U.S. Chamber of Commerce rushed forward to volunteer their services. Through con-ferences with these organizations, former WIB members, the Commerce Depart-ment, and other private and public sources, WRB drew up an industrial who's who to staff the War Resources Administration and also made provisions for the use of War Service Committees.[52] The most daring move was a memorandum drafted for the president's signature that would have granted the WRB and the Army-Navy Munitions Board authority to mobilize the economy and that in-structed all government agencies to cooperate with those two boards.[53]

Roosevelt suddenly cut the ground from under WRB shortly after its cre-ation because the war scare had waned and because of widespread opposi-tion to it within the administration and the nation. Liberal Democrats were aghast at the dominant position held by the major banking and industrial in-terests in WRB. They identified Stettinius, Gifford, and Pratt with J. P. Mor-gan. The anti-Morgan banking elements on Wall Street who were sympathetic to the administration were bitterly disappointed. Labor and agriculture were irate over their exclusion.[54]

The president waited until WRB had completed reviewing the "Indus-trial Mobilization Plan" and had submitted a final report in November 1939 before dismissing it. In its final report, WRB indirectly endorsed the War De-partment plan and fully accepted its basic assumptions. A wartime economy should be regulated by federal agencies largely controlled by industry and the military services. In circumscribed terms, WRB recommended the suspension of the antitrust laws and also suggested that domestic reform would be a casualty of a mobilized economy. It further proposed that the Army-Navy Munitions Board,* through consultation with industry, continue to explore the yet unre-solved issues of industrial mobilization. It concluded by offering its advisory services for the future.[55] Roosevelt thanked WRB members and never called on them again.[56]

WRB's fate did not negate the years of planning. Because of this plan-ning, the War Department adjusted to emergency conditions during World War II with relative ease. In the late 1930s the department began a gradual transition from planning for to participating in a mobilization program. Start-ing in 1937-38, Congress, after years of departmental advocacy, authorized

---

*The Army-Navy Munitions Board (ANMB) was reorganized and strengthened in 1931-1932, and the "IMP" was published by ANMB even though OASW continued to do most of the work.

educational orders* and the stockpiling of essential and strategic raw materials and slowly modified peacetime restraints on military contracting.[57] As the army and military budgets grew, OASW expanded its staff and activities proportionately until the mobilization stage was reached in 1940-41. Writing in mid-1940, Assistant Secretary of War Johnson observed: "Without the benefit of plans perfected by 20 years of study the successful and timely execution of this [expanded munitions] program would have been virtually impossible."[58]

When the War Department began the transition to mobilization in 1937-38, it also launched the drive for implementing the "Industrial Mobilization Plan"; it had been convinced by the years of planning that civilian mobilization agencies were essential for fulfilling the military mission. During 1940-41, the Army-Navy Munitions Board played a more active role in mobilizing the economy than the army plans had envisaged. But that was the case principally because the civilian agencies were weak. After WRB's demise, the Roosevelt administration relied upon the resucitated NDAC and other agencies that were totally inadequate for mobilization. War Department officials were in the vanguard of those working for more effective civilian agencies until the creation in early 1942 of the War Production Board.

Throughout the years 1940-41, the War Department, and the Navy Department as well, sided with industry on most major policies involving economic mobilization. After war was declared, the nation's largest corporations and the armed forces ultimately dominated the War Production Board through an alliance of mutual interests.[59] Though officially rejected in 1939, the principal proposals concurred in by WRB and the military were adopted during World War II. As foreseen by the Nye Committee and others, relations between the business community and the armed services during World War I and the interwar period prepared the way for the full-blown Military-Industrial Complex of World War II and the Cold War years.

---

*Educational orders were intended to help industry and the army through the transitional phase from planning to mobilizing for war. Without the restrictions of competitive bidding, the army could award contracts to selected firms for the limited production of various munitions items. In that way, industry accumulated the tools and worked out the techniques for quantity production and the army tested its munitions designs and procurement plans. Educational orders were first introduced before World War I at the instigation of businessmen and public officials striving to prepare the nation for hostilities. For years after the war, Congress rejected bills authorizing educational orders. Before such legislation was passed in the late 1930s, however, the army interpreted the laws and regulations governing procurement in a way that allowed it to grant some educational orders to selected firms. During the 1930s, the businessmen in the Army Ordnance Association launched a drive for educational orders to help stimulate industrial recovery.

NOTES

1. For example, see C. Wright Mills, *The Power Elite* (New York, 1956), 212; Walter Millis, *Arms and Men: A Study in American Military History* (New York, 1956), 306–07; Fred J. Cook, *The Warfare State* (New York, 1962), 41–65; Jack Raymond, *Power at the Pentagon* (New York, 1964), 167; H. L. Nieburg, *In the Name of Science* (Chicago, 1966), vii–viii, 184–85.

2. Paul A. C. Koistinen, "The 'Industrial-Military Complex' in Historical Perspective: World War I," *Business History Review*, XLI (Winter 1967), 378–403. Further research by the author in the papers of Woodrow Wilson, Newton D. Baker, James W. Wadsworth, Jr., George W. Goethals, and Bernard M. Baruch and in commerce department records has not significantly modifed the conclusions reached in the essay on World War I.

3. *U.S. Statutes at Large*, XLI (1921), Part 1, pp. 762–65.

4. "Reorganization of the Army," Senate, *Hearings before the Subcommittee of the Committee on Military Affairs*, 66 Cong., 2 Sess., 1919, pp. 1760–77; "Army Reorganization," House, *Hearings before the Committee on Military Affairs*, 66 Cong., 1 Sess., 1919–1920, pp. 1801–35; Charles Saltzman, "Reminiscences of the Battle of Washington," Nov. 26, 1935, File No. 020/2/113.1, Planning Branch (PB), Assistant Secretary of War (ASW), Office of the Secretary of War, RG 107 (National Archives); Benedict Crowell and Robert F. Wilson, *The Armies of Industry* (New Haven, 1921), 8–19. See also E. O. Saunders, "National Defense Act—Legislative History of Industrial Mobilization Clauses," Oct. 11, 1923, File No. 628, PB ASW Office of the Secretary of War; A. H. Moran, "Legislative History of the General Staff Corps and the Assistant Secretary of War," Feb. 14, 1928, File No. 46, *ibid.*; Troyer S. Anderson, "Introduction to the History of the Under Secretary of War's Office," 1947, Office of the Chief of Military History, Washington, D.C.; Harry B. Yoshpe, "Economic Mobilization Planning Between Two World Wars," *Military Affairs* XV (Winter 1951), 199–204, XVI (Summer 1952), 71–83.

5. Harold W. Thatcher, *Planning for Industrial Mobilization, 1920–1940* (Washington, D.C., 1943), 16, 24–25, 42–43.

6. J. Mayhew Wainwright to President, Aug. 29, 1940, PPF 1678, Franklin D. Roosevelt Papers (Franklin D. Roosevelt Library, Hyde Park, N.Y.); War Department, *Report of the Secretary of War to the President, 1925* (Washington, 1925), 27–28; War Department, *Report of the Secretary of War to the President, 1926* (Washington, 1926), 30–31; War Department, *Report of the Secretary of War to the President, 1927* (Washington, 1927), 25, 27, 29–35; War Department, *Report of the Secretary of War to the President, 1928* (Washington, 1928), 16–18, 50–58. See also Marvin A. Kreidberg and Merton G. Henry, *History of Military Mobilization in the United States Army, 1775–1945* (Washington, 1955), 502–07; Erna Risch, *The Quartermaster Corps; Organization, Supply, and Services* (2 vols., Washington, 1953), I, 56–57, 208–10, 243–52, 323–29.

7. Bernard M. Baruch, *American Industry in the War: A Report of the War Industries Board* (March 1921) (New York, 1941), 7–8, 36, 102–04; Crowell and Wilson, *Armies of Industry*, 18–19; Grosvenor B. Clarkson, *Industrial America in the World War: The Strategy Behind the Lines, 1917–1918* (New York, 1923), 483–84; "Final Report of the Chairman of the United States War Industries Board to the President of the United States, February, 1919," Senate, Special Committee Investigating the Munitions Industry, *Senate Committee Print No. 3*, 74 Cong., 1 Sess., 1935, pp. 44–52; "Reorganization of the Army," 371–72, 432–41; United States Council of National Defense, *Third Annual Report, Fiscal Year Ended June 30, 1919* (Washington, D.C., 1919), 16–17; United States Council of National Defense, *Fourth Annual Report, Fiscal Year Ended June 30, 1920* (Washington, D.C., 1920), 3–108.

8. Bernard M. Baruch, Speeches Delivered at the Army War College, Jan. 15, Dec. 2, 1925, Dec. 14, 1926, File No. 011.2, Records of the War Production Board, RG 179 (Na-

tional Archives); John W. Weeks to Chairman, House Military Affairs Committee, Feb. 9, 1923, File No. 374, PB ASW Office of the Secretary of War; Baruch to Dwight F. Davis, March 6, 1923, Dec. 11, 1924, June 6, 1925; Baruch to Weeks, Jan. 22, 1923; Baruch to H. E. Ely, Feb. 20, Oct. 29, 1925; Ely to Baruch, Oct. 30, 1925, Bernard M. Baruch Papers (Princeton University Library). Harry B. Yoshpe, "Bernard Baruch: Civilian Godfather of the Military M-Day Plan," *Military Affairs*, XXX (Spring 1965), 1–15.

9. "Plan for Governmental Organization For War," Nov. 12, 1929, File No. 109, PB ASW Office of the Secretary of War (Baruch's comments are written on the Plan); George Van Horn Mosely to Baruch, Jan. 9, Feb. 1, 13, 1930; Baruch to Moseley, Feb. 4, 18, 1930, Baruch Papers.

10. "Industrial Mobilization Plan," 1930 ("IMP"), File No. 110, PB ASW Office of the Secretary of War, In "IMP," 1939, the major mobilization agency was called the War Resources Administration.

11. "IMP," 1933, File No. 112, PB ASW Office of the Secretary of War; "IMP," 1936, File No. 120, *ibid.*; "IMP," 1939, File No. 334/117.3, *ibid.*

12. Kreidberg and Henry, *History of Military Mobilization*, 382–461, 502–03; War Department, *Report of the Secretary . . . 1928*, pp. 56–57; War Department, *Report of the Secretary of War to the President, 1935* (Washington, 1935), 36; Constance McLaughlin Green, Harry C. Thomson, and Peter C. Roots, *The Ordnance Department: Planning Munitions for War* (Washington, 1955), 51–54.

13. Paul A. C. Koistinen, "The Hammer and the Sword: Labor, the Military, and Industrial Mobilization, 1920–1945" (doctoral dissertation, University of California, Berkeley, 1964), 15–16, 24–27; War Department, *Report of the Secretary . . . 1927*, p. 38; War Department, *Report of the Secretary . . . 1928*, p. 58; Kreidberg and Henry, *History of Military Mobilization*, 382–461, 502–03.

14. Kreidberg and Henry, *History of Military Mobilization*, 382–461, 466–92, 502–03; Otto L. Nelson, Jr., *National Security And The General Staff* (Washington, 1946), 303–07; Mark S. Watson, *Chief of Staff: Prewar Plans and Preparations* (Washington, 1950), 78, 81–84.

15. War Department, *Report of the Secretary of War to the President, 1938* (Washington, 1938), 1.

16. War Department, *Report of the Secretary . . . 1925*, p. 27; War Department, *Report of the Secretary . . . 1926*, pp. 30–31; War Department, *Report of the Secretary . . . 1927*, pp. 28, 34, 39; War Department, *Report of the Secretary of War to the President, 1929* (Washington, 1929), 35–65; Senate, *Hearings Before the Special Committee Investigating the Munitions Industry*, 73–74 Congs. (40 parts, Washington, 1934–1943), Part 15, pp. 3623–26, Part 16, pp. 3996–4022; Thatcher, *Planning for Industrial Mobilization*, 26; Green, Thomson, and Roots, *Ordnance Department*, 26–27, 36–37, 54–55; Harry C. Thomson and Lida Mayo, *The Ordnance Department: Procurement and Supply* (Washington, 1960), 13.

17. EFK memo, [circa] Feb. 1922, File No. 46, H. B. Ferguson to Planning Branch, Dec. 12, 1924, File No. 44, PB ASW Office of the Secretary of War; War Department, *Report of the Secretary . . . 1925*, p. 27; War Department, *Report of the Secretary . . . 1927*, pp. 31–33; War Department, *Report of the Secretary . . . 1928*, p. 53; War Department, *Report of the Secretary of War to the Preisdent, 1932* (Washington, 1932), 34–35; U.S. War Policies Commission, "Hearings," *House Doc.*, 72 Cong., 1 Sess., No. 163 (Serial 9538), 188.

18. War Department, *Report of the Secretary . . . 1926*, p. 30; War Department, *Report of the Secretary . . . 1927*, pp. 28, 38; War Department, *Report of the Secretary . . . 1928*, pp. 15, 51, 57; War Department, *Report of the Secretary . . . 1929*, pp. 35–65; War Department, *Report of the Secretary of War to the President, 1931* (Washington, 1931), 26; War Department, *Report of the Secretary . . . 1932*, p. 32; War Department, *Report*

of the Secretary of War to the President, 1934 (Washington, 1934), 31; War Department, *Report of the Secretary . . . 1938*, p. 21; Koistinen, "Hammer and the Sword," 16, 19–21, 29–30, 58–59, 61–62, 71–77; War Policies Commission, "Hearings," 258–65; Thatcher, *Planning for Industrial Mobilization*, 128–29; Green, Thomson, and Roots, *Ordnance Department*, 54–57; Thomson and Mayo, *Ordnance Department*, 22; Dulany Terrett, *The Signal Corps: The Emergency (To December 1941)* (Washington, 1956), 58–69.

19. Concerning Howard E. Coffin, see Koistinen, "'Industrial-Military Complex,'" 381–82, and Coffin's correspondence with the Hoover and Roosevelt administrations, File No. 92819, General Correspondence, Office of the Secretary of Commerce, RG 40 (National Archives). Coffin to Stephen Early, Dec. 21, 1936, OF 172, Roosevelt Papers.

20. The War Department's participation in NRA resulted directly from AWS planning. See Senate, *Hearings Before the Special Committee Investigating the Munitions Industry*, Part 17, pp. 4292–93, 4319–20, 4444–45.

21. D. John Markey to Weeks, Feb. 1, 1922, File No. 62, PB ASW Office of the Secretary of War; correspondence concerning the Legion-war department bill, File No. 560, *ibid.*; "Mobilization of Manpower and Industrial Resources, Legislative History," Feb. 18, 1937, File No. 010/178, *ibid.*; Thatcher, *Planning for Industrial Mobilization*, 100–09; Marcus Duffield, *King Legion* (New York, 1931), 4–12, 109–15, 129–45; Justin Gray with Victor H. Bernstein, *The Inside Story of the Legion* (New York, 1948), 44–70, 87–92. See also Roscoe Baker, *The American Legion and American Foreign Policy* (New York, 1954); Richard Seelye Jones, *A History of the American Legion* (Indianapolis, 1946). The Legion affiliations of the war department officials can be traced through the above volumes.

22. War Policies Commission, "Report to the President," *House Doc.*, 72 Cong., 1 Sess., No. 163 (Serial 9538), vi.

23. In addition to the hearings and reports of the War Policies Commission collection, see War Policies Commission Files No. 1–211, PB ASW Office of the Secretary of War.

24. "Message from the President . . . Transmitting . . . the Final Recommendation of the Commission," *House Doc.*, 72 Cong., 1 Sess., No. 264 (Serial 9549), 2–5. See also War Policies Commission, "Documents by War Policies Commission," *House Doc.*, 72 Cong., 1 Sess., No. 271 (Serial 9549), 1–71.

25. War Policies Commission, "Hearings," 7–72, 85–113, 121–44, 169–90, 218–21, 252–65, 288–323, 481–88, 776–90, 794–836, 854–75.

26. *Ibid.*, 20–24, 66–71, 73–85, 93–94, 119–21, 136–40, 186–89, 258–65, 272–73, 279–80, 323–50, 380–85, 489–502, 535–687, 722–76, 850–54; Seymour Waldman, *Death and Profits: A Study of the War Policies Commission* (New York, 1932), 91, 131–34.

27. Waldman, *Death and Profits*, v–vii. See also *ibid.*, 71, 147–56.

28. File No. 049.12/175, 381/116.4b, PB ASW Office of the Secretary of War; Kreidberg and Henry, *History of Military Mobilization*, 516, 518, 529–31, 538–40; Rose M. Stein, *M-Day: The First Day of War* (New York, 1936).

29. "Report on War Department Bills S.1716–S.1722 Relating to Industrial Mobilization in Wartime," *Senate Report*, 74 Cong., 2 Sess., No. 944, Part 4 (Serial 9884), 7. See also "Report of the Special Committee on Investigation of the Munitions Industry," *Senate Report*, 74 Cong., 2 Sess., No. 944, Part 3 (Serial 9983), 3.

30. "Preliminary Report of the Special Committee on Investigation of the Munitions Industry," *Senate Report*, 74 Cong., 1 Sess., No. 944, Part 1 (Serial 9881) 1–8, 15–343, 384–89; "Report . . . on Investigation of the Munitions Industry," No. 944, Part 3, 159–204; "Report on Government Manufacture of Munitions by the Special Committee on Investigation of the Munitions Industry," *Senate Report*, 74 Cong., 2 Sess., No. 944, Part 7 (Serial 9987), 1–13.

31. "Report . . . on Investigation of the Munitions Industry," No. 944, Part 3, pp. 3–12, 15–17, 159–204; Wayne S. Cole, *Senator Gerald P. Nye and American Foreign Relations* (Minneapolis, 1962), 76, 79–81; John E. Wiltz, *In Search of Peace: The Senate Munitions Inquiry, 1934–36* (Baton Rouge, 1963), 81.

32. Senate, *Hearings Before the Special Committee Investigating the Munitions Industry*, Part 37, pp. 12409-37, 12502-26, 12766; "Report . . . on Investigation of the Munitions Industry," No. 944, Part 3, pp. 204-07; Wiltz, *In Search of Peace*, 116.

33. "Preliminary Report . . . on Investigation of the Munitions Industry," No. 944, Part 1, pp. 220-21; "Report . . . on Investigation of the Munitions Industry," No. 944, Part 3, pp. 10-11, 159-217; Senate, *Hearings Before the Special Committee Investigating the Munitions Industry*, Part 36, pp. 11972-12043; Part 37, pp. 12399-443, 12501-28, 12766. Concern existed about military contractors employing retired officers before World War I. "To Increase the Efficiency of the Military Establishment of the United States," House, *Hearings before the Committee on Military Affairs*, 64 Cong., 1 Sess., 1916, pp. 540-42, 1147-48, 1153-55; "Army Appropriations Bill, [Fiscal] 1917," House, *Hearings before the Committee on Military Affairs*, 64 Cong., 1 Sess., 1916, pp. 848-50.

34. "Preliminary Report . . . on Investigation of the Munitions Industry," No. 944, Part 1, p. 222; "Report . . . on Investigation of the Munitions Industry," No. 944, Part 3, p. 8; Cole, *Senator Gerald P. Nye*, 95-96; Wiltz, *In Search of Peace*, 224-27.

35. "Report . . . on Investigation of the Munitions Industry," No. 944, Part 3, p. 12.

36. *Ibid.*, 15-17; "Preliminary Report . . . on Investigation of the Munitions Industry," No. 944, Part 1, pp. 11-14; "Report on Government Manufacture of Munitions . . . ," No. 944, Part 7, pp. 1-123; Wiltz, *In Search of Peace*, 91-98, 115-16.

37. "Preliminary Report . . . on Investigation of the Munitions Industry," No. 944, Part 1, pp. 345-89; "Report on War Department Bills S.1716-S.1722 . . . ," 74 Cong., 2 Sess., No. 944, Part 4, p. 1-46 (direct quotations, 7, 11), 57-61; "Report on Government Manufacture of Munitions . . . ," No. 944, Part 7, pp. 3-64; "To Prevent Profiteering in War," *Senate Report*, 74 Cong., 1 Sess., No. 577 (Serial 9879), 9-20. See also Senate, *Hearings Before the Special Committee Investigating the Munitions Industry*, Parts 13, 14, 15, 16, 17, 21, 22, 24, 36, 37. The Nye Committee was less critical of World War I military procurement practices than an earlier investigation by the so-called Graham Committee. See "War Expenditures," House, *Hearings before the Select Committee on Expenditure in the War Department*, 66 Cong., 1 Sess., Vol. 3, 1921 (Serial 1), [Reports of Committee]; *ibid.*, Vol. 1, 1921 (Serial 1); *ibid.*, 1920 (Serial 3).

38. "To Prevent Profiteering in War," No. 577, pp. 1-9, 20-35. See also Senate, *Hearings Before the Special Committee Investigating the Munitions Industry*, Part 22, pp. 6179-257, 6425-29, 6643-48, Part 24, pp. 7087-7112.

39. Memo on conference on HR 5529, May 24, 1935, File No. 1401, PB ASW Office of the Secretary of War; Planning Branch Orientation Conference, Oct. 27, 1936, pp. 11-12, File No. 010/178.1A, *ibid.*; "IMP," 1936, pp. 99-113, File No. 120, *ibid.*

40. Senate, *Hearings Before the Special Committee Investigating the Munitions Industry*, Part 22, pp. 6623-43. See also *ibid.*, 6259-423.

41. "Preliminary Report on Wartime Taxation and Price Control," *Senate Report*, 74 Cong., 1 Sess., No. 944, Part 2 (Serial 9882), 1-164 (direct quotation, 3); "Report on War Department Bills S.1716-S.1722 . . . ," No. 944, Part 4, pp. 1-46.

42. Wiltz, *In Search of Peace*, 119-22, 131-46. For some relevant data on the administration and the Nye Committee, see OF 178, 1934-1935, OF 1672, PPF 1820, Roosevelt Papers.

43. "Plan for Governmental Organization for War," Nov. 12, 1929, File No. 109, PB ASW Office of the Secretary of War; "IMP," 1936, pp. 14-21, 34-35, File No. 120, *ibid.*; Assistant Secretary of War and Navy to Joint Board and memo of C. T. Harris and W. S. Farber, July 19, 1934, File No. 112, *ibid.*; W. A. Buck to Harry B. Jordan, April 4, 1936, File No. 1401, *ibid.*; H. K. Rutherford at John Hancock Lecture, "Mobilization of Industry," May 27, 1938, File No. 352/109.1, *ibid.*; War Policy Commission, "Hearings," 38, 55-56, 169-90, 288-309, 481-88, 776-90, 854-56; Senate, *Hearings Before the Special Committee Investigating the Munitions Industry*, Part 22, pp. 6281-82; Thatcher, *Planning for Industrial Mobilization*, 84-91; Kreidberg and Henry, *History of Military Mobilization*, 507-08, 530.

44. Louis Johnson to Baruch, Sept. 19, 1937, File No. 381/116.4b, PB ASW Office of the Secretary of War; War Department, *Report of the Secretary of War to the President, 1937* (Washington, 1937), 21–25; War Department, *Report of the Secretary . . . 1938*, pp. 19–25; War Department, *Report of the Secretary of War to the President, 1939* (Washington, 1939), 15–20.

45. Roosevelt to Johnson in Johnson to Roosevelt, Oct. 23, 1937, OF 813, Roosevelt Papers.

46. Johnson to Roosevelt, Aug. 9, 1939, OF 25, *ibid.*; Charles Hines to John Hancock; July 1, Aug. 11, 1939, Hancock to Hines, July 7, 1939, File No. MB-223-23.1, Records of the Joint Army and Navy Boards and Committees, RG 225 (National Archives); Johnson to Crowell, Aug. 9, 1939, File No. 011/27c, Records of the War Production Board.

47. Charles W. Wiltse to James W. Fesler, July 19, 1946, File No. 011.2, Records of the War Production Board; "Industrial Mobilization Plan," Senate, *Hearings Before the Special Committee Investigating the National Defense Program*, 80 Cong., 1 Sess., 1948, Part 42, pp. 25662–69.

48. War Resources Board (WRB) Minutes, Aug. 17, 1939, pp. 1–2, File No. 011.25, Records of the War Production Board; Wiltse to Fesler, July 19, 1946, File No. 011/2, *ibid.*

49. Memo. Re: "War Industries [sic] Board," undated, PPF 702, Roosevelt Papers.

50. Joint Release, war and navy departments, Aug. 17, 1939, WRB Minutes, File No. 011.25, Records of the War Production Board.

51. "IMP," 1939, File No. 334/117.3, PB ASW Office of the Secretary of War.

52. WRB Minutes, Aug. 17, 1939, p. 2, Aug. 23–25, 1939, pp. 1, 3–4, Aug. 29–31, 1939, pp. 1–3, Sept. 9, 1939, pp. 1–2, Sept. 13–14, 1939, pp. 1–4, File No. 011.25, Records of the War Production Board; Memo of A. B. Anderson, Sept. 1, 1939, *ibid.*; Rutherford to Edward R. Stettinius, Jr., Sept. 4, 1939, *ibid.*; Wiltse to Fesler, July 19, 1939, File No. 011.2, *ibid.* For the fourteen-page list of the names of individuals selected to staff the mobilization agencies, see File No. 011.27c, *ibid.*

53. WRB Minutes, Sept. 6, 1939, p. 1, File No. 011.25, Records of the War Production Board. Memo, acting secretary of war and navy to President, Sept. 6, 1939; "Memorandum for Departments and Executive Agencies, Federal Government," from the President, File No. 334/117.3, PB ASW Office of the Secretary of War. These documents were never sent out.

54. WRB Minutes, Aug. 29–31, 1939, pp. 1–2, Sept. 13–14, 1939, p. 3, File No. 001.25, Records of the War Production Board; Memo. Re: "War Industries [sic] Board," PPF 702, Roosevelt Papers. See also OF 3759, 1939, PPF 5344, PPF 702-H, OF 200XXX, Roosevelt Papers; File No. 011.25, File No. 011.27c, Records of the War Production Board. See also Harold L. Ickes, *The Secret Diary of Harold L. Ickes* (3 vols., New York, 1953–1954), II, 710, 716–20; Albert A. Blum, "Birth and Death of the M-Day Plan," Harold Stein, ed., *American Civil-Military Decisions: A Book of Case Studies* (University, Ala., 1963), 61–96; Eliot Janeway, *The Struggle for Survival: A Chronicle of Economic Mobilization in World War II* (New Haven, 1951), 47–71.

55. "Report of the War Resources Board," Oct. 13, 1939, File No. 334.117.3, PB ASW Office of the Secretary of War.

56. President to Stettinius and others, Nov. 24, 1939, File No. 370.26/110.B, *ibid.*

57. "Investigation of the War Department," Senate, *Hearings Before the Committee on Military Affairs*, 65 Cong., 2 Sess., 1917–1918, pp. 2268–71; War Department, *Report of the Secretary . . . 1927*, pp. 36–38; War Department, *Report of the Secretary . . . 1928*, p. 57; War Department, *Report of the Secretary . . . 1929*, pp. 47–49, 53–65; War Department, *Report of the Secretary . . . 1932*, pp. 32–34; War Department, *Report of the Secretary . . . 1935*, pp. 34–35; War Department, *Report of the Secretary of War . . . 1938*, pp.

21-25; War Department, *Report of the Secretary . . . 1939*, pp. 15-22; War Department, *Report of the Secretary of War to the President, 1940* (Washington, 1940), 1-10; War Department, *Report of the Secretary of War to the President, 1941* (Washington, 1941), 21-46; Senate, *Hearings Before the Special Committee Investigating the Munitions Industry*, Part 37, pp. 12409-37, 12502-26, 12766; "Report . . . on Investigation of the Munitions Industry," No. 944, Part 3, pp. 204-07. See also R. Elberton Smith, *The Army and Economic Mobilization* (Washington, 1959), 61-65; Irvin Brinton Holley, Jr., *Buying Aircraft: Matériel Procurement for the Army Air Forces* (Washington, 1964), 6-193, Edwin H. Rutkowski, *The Politics of Military Aviation Procurement, 1926-1934: A Study in the Political Assertion of Consensual Values* (Columbus, 1966).

58. War Department, *Report of the Secretary . . . 1940*, p. 10.

59. Economic mobilization for World War II is treated extensively in Koistinen, "Hammer and the Sword," 553-831.

4

MOBILIZING THE WORLD WAR II ECONOMY: LABOR AND THE INDUSTRIAL-MILITARY ALLIANCE

Organized labor's participation in the World War II agencies for mobilizing industry and manpower and its relations with the military have been neglected by scholars. Studies of labor during the war largely concentrate on collective bargaining, employment patterns, and income levels.[1] An analysis of the larger topics, however, is critically important for assessing the impact of massive union growth during the 1930s on the nation's power relations, the nature of the New Deal as a reform movement, and the origins and operations of the so-called munitions complex.

Despite the growth of huge unions in the mass production industries during the New Deal years, labor's role in the World War II economy, outside the realm of collective bargaining, did not vary much from that of World War I. In both wars, corporate leaders dominated the mobilized economies. If World War II differed from World War I, in that union spokesmen fought for the right to share authority with management in regulating the economy, it was also similar in that they were consistently rebuffed. Organized labor was also denied equitable economic stabilization policies and other programs intended to protect the nation's work force. While unions grew vigorously during the war years, they frequently had to fight for their organizing prerogatives, and they operated under the constant threat of compulsory manpower controls.

Indeed, the World War II economy hardly justifies the conclusion of Carl N. Degler, and many other scholars, that with the New Deal "Big Labor now

*The following is a reprint of an article which appeared as "Mobilizing the World War II Economy: Labor and the Industrial-Military Alliance," *Pacific Historical Review* 42 (November 1973): 443–78. Permission from the editor to reproduce this essay is gratefully acknowledged.

took its place beside Big Business and Big Government to complete a triumvirate of economic power."[2] Union power had increased during the 1930s, but the whole thrust of the Franklin D. Roosevelt administration's massive intervention in the Depression-ridden economy was designed to preserve, not change, U.S. corporate capitalism.[3] When a planned wartime economy became essential, the administration turned to the business community, which owned the nation's productive plant and had the personnel and knowledge necessary to run it. "Big Government" and "Big Business" had virtually become one. "Big Labor" was a pigmy by comparison.

The emergence of a "Big Military" was the most significant development in the operation of the World War II economy. The army and navy simultaneously became the nation's largest consumers and investors and the most powerful voices within the government, but they did not threaten corporate power. Instead, the armed services became the friendly and immensely useful allies of the industrial community.

Although today an industry-military munitions alliance may appear to be a natural order of events, this was not always the case. During World War I, the army almost disastrously disrupted the economy by refusing to cooperate with the industry-dominated mobilization agencies. Only the threat of losing its procurement responsibilities forced the army to work with the civilian administrations.[4] After the war, 20 years of War Department planning for economic mobilization, constant contact with businessmen, and participation in the National Recovery Administration (NRA) were required before the army fully absorbed the economic significance of modern warfare for itself and the nation.[5] Even then, the industrial and military communities had to go through a difficult adjustment process from 1940 to 1943 before they could function as an effective team.

Modern warfare had a different effect upon the army's attitude towards unions. In World War I, the War and Navy Departments became so absorbed in the massive procurement operations and in their disputes with, and ultimate adjustment to, the civilian production agencies that they had little time to devote to labor issues. Nonetheless, given the context of a relatively weak labor movement that was deeply divided between conservative trade unionists and radical elements and the ambiguity towards unions which characterized the Progressive leadership, the armed services maintained a reasonably neutral attitude towards organized labor and the working population.[6] But in the interwar years, as the services became increasingly involved in planning for industrial mobilization, they began reflecting the anti-union outlook prevalent in large sectors of industry.[7] During World War II, while some subdivisions of the armed services worked in harmony with unions, the services in general joined management in restricting labor's influence to the collective bargaining area and in attempting to place as many restraints on union activity as possible.

I

A rough model of how the enormously complex U.S. economy operated during World War II can be drawn from the distribution of military contracts. Out of wartime expenditures approximating $315.8 billion, the War Department spent about $179.9 billion and the Navy Department $83.9 billion. Through 1944, the armed services contracted with some 18,539 firms. Consistently, however, 100 corporations received at least two-thirds of the contracts; 30 corporations almost one-half. Subcontracting did not significantly change the picture since most of it took place among the larger corporations. Expenditures for research and plants and equipment followed a similar pattern.[8]

Prior to Pearl Harbor, anti-war dissent and interest-group conflict over preparedness prevented the Roosevelt administration from creating a mobilization structure which combined the efforts of the giant corporations and the military services.[9] After the declaration of hostilities in Europe in September 1939, the president, at the instigation of the War Department and as a direct result of its economic mobilization planning, had convened a War Resources Board (WRB) under the leadership of corporate and military representatives in order to begin preparing the economy for the eventuality of war. Vociferous opposition to the board from representatives of labor, agriculture, and some industrial and financial firms as well as anti-war and anti-business spokesmen, however, had forced Roosevelt to retreat. He allowed the WRB to expire in November 1939 and waited until the imminent fall of France before resucitating the World War I National Defense Advisory Commission (NDAC) in May 1940. The Office of Production Management (OPM) replaced the commission in December 1940 and served until January 1942. Both the NDAC and OPM were relatively weak agencies which included spokesmen from a broad spectrum of the industrial-financial community, New Deal academicians and civil servants, and representatives from labor and other interest groups.

The balancing of diverse interests within the mobilization agencies was more apparent than real; industry was dominant and the largest corporations exercised the most influence. Key to the operation of the NDAC, the OPM, as well as the later War Production Board (WPB), was what came to be called Industry Divisions. These divisions formulated and implemented policies for an industry or a group of related industries. They were staffed by industrialists who often came from the same industries they helped to regulate and who usually served without compensation. Industry advisory committees, representing various firms and/or trade associations, assisted the Industry Divisions. The divisions generally functioned under officials like William S. Knudsen, president of the General Motors Corporation, and Edward R. Stettinius, Jr., board chairman of the United States Steel Corporation.

Neither the NDAC nor the OPM prepared the economy adequately for World War II. Most defense production before 1942 was accomplished in addition to normal civilian output and through new or expanded facilities constructed largely at the public's expense. Until there were enough contracts to convert all major firms from private to public use and enough *immediate* demand to justify expanding production capacity for steel, aluminum, and the like, industrialists serving within and advising the mobilization agencies resisted forthright preparation for war. The business community feared disturbing the economic status quo and desired to exploit the growing civilian demand stimulated by spending for defense and war at home and abroad. Roosevelt's public declarations against the nation entering the war served to strengthen industry's aversion to economic mobilization. Additionally, most advocates of maximum conversion and expansion within the NDAC and OPM were New Dealers, like Leon Henderson, civil servants, and labor spokesmen. Industrialists looked upon these "all-outers" as anti-business interlopers who, if allowed to have their way, would threaten business control of the mobilization process.

The inability of the NDAC and the OPM to get the mobilization program off the ground distressed leading civilian and military officials within the War and Navy Departments. Secretary of War Henry L. Stimson and others were also "all-outers," but they viewed the effort of "New Dealers" and labor representatives as a detriment, not an asset, to preparedness because those elements antagonized the business community. According to military spokesmen, industry's cooperation was the sine qua non for any successful mobilization program. A more cooperative attitude on industry's part could be achieved, they argued, if the administration secured from Congress legislation on taxation, profit controls, plant amortization, and the like favorable to business, curbed antitrust activities, and, most importantly, created strong mobilization agencies and placed them securely in the hands of industry or those who had its unquestioned confidence. With anti-war sentiment and conflict over mobilization still running high, however, Roosevelt and his advisers continued to move cautiously on all aspects of preparedness until the nation declared war. Consequently, the War and Navy Departments attempted to expedite war preparation by building up their own procurement systems into a mobilization structure which in part paralleled and competed with the civilian administrations. To help staff this structure, the departments recruited Ferdinand Eberstadt, a prominent New York investment banker, and others from industrial and financial circles. Largely free from NDAC and OPM control, the War and Navy departments distributed contracts, financed the construction of plants and the purchase of equipment, and even granted priority ratings.

After Pearl Harbor, Roosevelt sought to bring more order to the chaotic mobilization program by creating the WPB and granting Donald Nelson, as chairman, almost unlimited authority over all facets of industrial mobilization. By mid-1942, the board was successfully guiding the conversion and expansion of industry, but it encountered severe problems with the War and Navy Departments, and especially the former. The two departments, harboring a prewar distrust of civilian agencies and possessing a competing mobilization system, refused to subordinate their procurement operations to WPB authority. The consequences were dire. Army and navy requirements were increased to levels far beyond the economy's potential, and the two services, between January and June 1942, let over $100 billion of new contracts without a workable priorities system and without proper regard to the availability of facilities, power, transportation, work force, and the like. Economic dislocation to the point of paralysis faced the nation unless the demand functions of the military were coordinated with the supply functions of the WPB.[10]

After a series of bitter encounters between August and December 1942, The WPB and the military services finally arrived at a modus operandi. The army and navy continued to determine their requirements and to conduct their procurement; the board, however, set ceilings for military demands and guided military procurement through the allocation of materials and the scheduling of production. Civilian and military personnel also moved over from the services' procurement systems to occupy positions, and often very prominent ones, in the WPB.[11]

By mid-1943, the WPB began to function smoothly. It had become an enormous production team consisting primarily of spokesmen from the nation's largest corporations and the military. This production team operated principally through the Production Executive Committee (PEC), which had emerged as the major source of authority within the board. Charles E. Wilson, president of the General Electric Corporation, headed the committee and also served as the WPB's executive vice chairman with all Industry Divisions under his control. The War and Navy Departments, along with the U.S. Maritime Commission, which usually sided with the military on mobilization issues, had a majority of representatives on the PEC.[12]

Closely guarding its authority, the PEC largely isolated other groups from WPB decision making. Subdivisions of the board, like the Planning Committee and the Office of Civilian Requirements which were composed mainly of non-business personnel, were relegated to insignificant positions. Offices created to protect small business likewise languished within the WPB.[13]

Organized labor was also consistently denied a meaningful voice in the mobilization agencies. Since late 1939, both the American Federation of Labor (AFL) and the Congress of Industrial Organizations (CIO) had insisted that they be granted equal authority with management in mobilizing the economy. Various unions believed they were achieving that end when, after much agitation on labor's part, the OPM permitted the organization of labor advisory committees. Labor had hoped that its committees would serve jointly with those of industry. Yet, such hopes had been largely dashed. The industry advisory committees, supported by officials from business and later the military, refused to meet with union representatives because, they insisted, unions had no right to intrude upon management functions. Unused and unwanted, labor's committees atrophied within the OPM and WPB structures.[14]

Labor's aspirations regarding industrial mobilization had reflected the liberal to radical orientation engendered in the CIO and, to a lesser degree, the AFL by the massive growth of industrial unions, but more was at stake than ideology and power. Labor leaders believed that they could genuinely aid the nation in its hour of need. Unlike most of industry, unions generally supported converting the economy during 1940–41, even if it meant temporary unemployment for their members, and devised plans for doing so. In instances where unions represented an entire industry and had research staffs, they often proved to be more informed and imaginative about mobilization than management. The United Automobile Workers of America (UAW), for example, rightly insisted that over 50 percent of the auto industry's productive facilities, not 15 percent as management maintained, could be utilized for defense purposes.[15] The UAW, along with other unions and labor spokesmen, also worked for the maximum use of the nation's existing productive facilities before new or expanded plants were built. They were particularly concerned that small business be included in the growing munitions program. Only occasionally was a labor proposal considered, however, let alone adopted. Although union spokesmen always served within the WPB, they rarely had any power.

II

Organized labor also met bitter frustration in the area of manpower management. Unions achieved considerable strength within the War Manpower Commission (WMC) only to have that agency lose much of its authority, first to the WPB and the armed services and later to the Office of War Mobilization, created in 1943 to coordinate the activities of all agencies involved in mobilizing the economy.

Before the creation of the WMC, manpower mobilization had been a source of continuing controversy and bureaucratic infighting within the Roosevelt administration from 1940 through early 1942. The issue in dispute involved the vitally important question of who would be responsible for coordinating labor supply and production programs in a mobilized economy. While assigned manpower responsibilities in the NDAC, OPM, and WPB, labor representatives made little headway in that area because of their isolated position. With unemployment levels still high, the industry divisions assumed that the nation's work force was sufficiently great to adjust to any production effort and, even if that was not the case, they had no intention of allowing union spokesmen to influence their decisionmaking. Industry's atittude led to both the AFL and CIO ultimately advocating that control over manpower be centered in a separate organization in which they had substantial influence. Government agencies like the U.S. Employment Service also supported the idea of an independent labor supply agency, but one that was directed by disinterested civil servants and economists, rather than by either management or labor as interested parties. Faced with conflicting advice and huge manpower reserves, the Roosevelt administration chose to procrastinate and largely ignored labor supply matters until after Pearl Harbor.[16]

Roosevelt finally moved to resolve the labor supply controversy in April 1942 by creating the WMC as an agency which incorporated representatives from all competing groups. Civil servants and academicians headed the commission but they were advised by a Management-Labor Policy Committee (MLPC). Although only an advisory body, the MLPC emerged as a major center of power within the WMC. The unusually able union and industry representives minimized their differences in order to maximize their influence. They had the administration's support because the president was anxious to win the cooperation of the two interest groups most vitally affected by the commission's operations. Organized labor, led by CIO officials, was the more dynamic element; it vigorously fought to protect the interests of the nation's work force. Management members were primarily concerned with guarding industry's prerogatives against further government encroachment.[17]

The WMC's responsibilities encompassed two areas: first, it was to oversee the raising of military forces by supervising the Selective Service System and consulting with the armed services concerning the feasibility of their size; and, second, it was to regulate manpower in labor shortage areas and, most significantly, to determine policies to maximize the use of labor that other agencies and departments would implement.[18] Both assignments made the WMC a competitor with the armed services and the WPB.

At all times, the commission lacked the political and economic muscle for winning any contest with the military brass and the WPB industrialists. The armed services refused with impunity to grant the WMC any influence over determining their size. Through recruitment campaigns and the War Department's control of the Selective Service System, the military also raised its own forces free of the commission's authority.[19] The military weakened the WMC further by insisting upon a free hand in the distribution of contracts and the construction of facilities. For the army, seven technical services and the Army Air Forces procured munitions without centralized control. Army field personnel, along with that of the navy, invariably turned to the large industrial firms regardless of labor supply conditions, with the result that most contracts flowed into labor shortage areas.[20]

The armed services had their way in contracting because the WPB supported their position. The board frustrated the WMC's operations in other ways as well. It refused to curtail nonessential industries in tight labor markets or to concentrate civilian output within a few firms in an industry. More importantly, the WPB would not cooperate with the commission in devising a priority system for the referral of workers. According to board members, those in charge of production and procurement, not the WMC, should assign manpower priorities. The commission balked at such an interpretation. It maintained that government contracts which based compensation on a percentage of production costs or paid the contractor a fixed fee regardless of costs encouraged management to hoard and waste labor. WMC labor-utilization surveys often succeeded in reducing the number of employees in a plant while increasing the production record; but the WPB and the military procurement divisions, arguing that labor utilization was a management prerogative, kept such surveys to a minimum.[21]

Unable to bring the job to the worker, the WMC had to bring the worker to the job. In accomplishing the latter assignment, the commission was largely restricted to voluntary methods at the insistence of the MLPC. By September 1942, the WMC had instituted an employment stabilization plan for labor shortage areas. The commission regulated all hiring, firing, and transferring of employees. In some sections of the nation, the plan, or variations of it, worked well; on the whole it was unsuccessful. WMC subdivisions were inefficient, regulations were easily violated, and, without a priority system, the commission could not effectively guide the referral of employees. In addition, the WMC had no control over the poor working and living conditions and the unsatisfactory community facilities that largely accounted for high turnover rates.[22]

Despite the WMC weakness and the constant turmoil which characterized its relations with the WPB and the military, the nation's manpower pool was so large that labor supply set no major limits for production until mid-1943. When that occurred, a new agency—the Office of War Mobilization (OWM)—became the final arbiter of manpower policy with the result that the WMC was officially reduced to a subordinate and increasingly insignificant status.

Roosevelt created the OWM by executive order in May 1943 and selected James F. Byrnes as its director. He did so to head off growing congressional support for a bill endorsed by, among others, Congressman John H. Tolan and Senator Harry S. Truman. The bill proposed that an office of war mobilization take over military procurement, production, manpower, and economic stabilization functions. Such an office would be staffed with civilians serving as civil servants, not as dollar-a-year men, and advised by representatives from all major interest groups. The bill, which labor and other liberal groups enthusiastically supported was intended to rationalize the mobilization program and break the industry-military hold on the economy.[23]

Byrnes's office was a poor substitute for what Senator Truman and others had in mind. The OWM settled disputes among agencies, but it did not alter the configurations of power within the economy. In making decisions, Byrnes turned principally to the WPB and the War and Navy Departments for advice. This proclivity became clear with Byrnes's resolution of the manpower crisis which erupted in 1943.

The first danger signals involving manpower came from the West Coast, where employers complained that labor shortages were preventing them from meeting their production schedules. Several investigations ensued, the most important of which Bernard M. Baruch and John Hancock conducted for the OWM. In August 1943, the two investigators reported that the manpower crisis stemmed from

> the lack of any system of labor priorities and the hopelessly unbalanced production demands that have been imposed on the Pacific Coast. These demands for the next six months are so far in excess of the available labor supply that a disastrous breakdown of vital production programs all through the region is threatened.[24]

In order to avoid such a calamity, Baruch and Hancock insisted that contract placement, military recruitment, labor utilization and standards, and community facilities must be more effectively handled. To accomplish that end, the two elder statesmen appended a plan for the WMC to implement.[25]

The WMC suffered a major defeat when Byrnes unveiled a manpower program for the West Coast in September. The plan set up a new series of committees for coordinating the procurement, production, and manpower programs—committees that the military services and prominent industrial elements in the WPB dominated. Committee action relieved some immediate problems and prevented labor supply conditions from deteriorating further, but none of the necessary long-range reforms occurred. The WPB and the armed services used the committees to guard the practices which had created the crisis. Nevertheless, Byrnes gradually extended the plan to other regions, and, in June 1944, ordered it into effect throughout the nation.[26]

Organized labor was incensed with Byrnes's action. It had the same representatives serving in both the WMC and the WPB. Those individuals could have coordinated the manpower and production policies had industry not isolated labor within the WPB. Labor considered its position to be even worse after September 1943 because, at the War Department's insistence, Byrnes excluded the MLPC from the new coordinating committees. The WMC was one of the few wartime agencies in which labor had some meaningful representation. But, because of OWM decisions, the commission grew increasingly impotent.[27]

The WMC not only declined in power but its very existence was also threatened by attempts to enact national service legislation. Grenville Clark, the Citizens' Committee for a National War Service Act which he organized and headed,[28] and the War Department (backed by the Navy Department and Maritime Commission) were the driving forces behind the movement. The reasons for supporting such legislation varied. For Clark, Secretary of War Stimson, and Under Secretary of War Robert P. Patterson, the war strengthened their inclination for order, discipline, and regimentation; during the national emergency, they believed, the population should don a hair shirt. An anti-labor bias attracted some adherents to the national service movement. The most important motive for industry and the military was that the conscription of labor would permit them a freer hand in running the waritime economy. The WPB and the armed services had fairly well made the WMC into a service agency for themselves. But since the commission depended upon voluntary controls, it was unreliable as a labor supply administration.

The business community responded to the national service bills in uncertain silence rather than with either vigorous support or opposition. Compulsory work controls could affect how management used its manpower. Yet, the national service movement indirectly benefited industry and the WPB by keeping labor and the WMC on the defensive. Roosevelt was also consistently ambivalent about a "labor draft." Firm manpower controls might be economically sound, but, without union support, they could be politically hazardous. Nonetheless, as the war stretched out, as labor strife and real or imagined mobilization crises grew, and as the harried president became detached from events at home and absorbed in military and diplomatic efforts abroad, he yielded to the armed services' demand for national service. At all times, however, the president hedged his support for compulsory labor controls in a manner designed to placate the opposition.

In July 1942, Clark, War Department personnel, and others drafted a bill which, in substance, was later introduced in Congress by Senator Warren A. Austin and Congressman James W. Wadsworth, Jr. The bill was at once vague and comprehensive. It would have created a universal obligation for all males from 18 to 65 and females 18 to 50. If the need arose, the president, acting through a director of national service, could assign people to jobs in war industries.[29]

The bill's authors maintained that a "national service program does not require that management be subjected to Government regulation."[30] While employers faced few restraints, employees would be without protection. The bill failed to provide for seniority or reemployment rights, did not guard against numerous possible abuses, and would have created an inadequate grievance and appeal procedure. For unions, the proposed legislation was an outright threat. Wadsworth wrote to Clark in March 1942, "Incidentally, it may amuse you to realize that when we have reached that stage [the assignment of labor under national service legislation] there can be no such thing as a closed shop or union dues applicable to men who take orders and go where they are sent."

Roosevelt was tempted to endorse the principle of national service but decided against it in late 1942.[32] Still, early in 1943 the Austin-Wadsworth bill was introduced in Congress and became the subject of extended hearings. Equality of sacrifice and total mobilization of the nation's resources were the principal reasons offered in the bill's defense. Organized labor became the bill's most vociferous opponent. Union spokesmen hit at the bill's grave dangers for the workingman and also argued that manpower problems resulted from a chaotic mobilization program, not a labor shortage.[33]

The Austin-Wadsworth bill never got out of committee. Byrnes's West Coast manpower plan of September 1943 temporarily ended the drive for national service. But the proponents only paused to regroup their forces. As the number of strikes grew in 1943, they successfully increased their pressure on Roosevelt to support compulsory labor controls. On January 11, 1944, the president called upon Congress to enact some form of national service legislation as part of a larger package including bills to achieve a more equitable economic stabilization program.[34] Roosevelt's action led to the re-introduction of the Austin-Wadsworth bill. Its chances for passage were even less than in 1943. Manpower shortages became less critical after the turn of the year as some production programs were cut back. Additionally, most members of Congress opposed further government controls for varying reasons and rejected a "labor draft" as a panacea for resolving the "mobilization muddle."

The last drive for national service began with the "Battle of the Bulge" in December 1944. Prior to that setback, the military had been waging psychological warfare on the homefront in order to kill reconversion planning and to create the right atmosphere for a "labor draft." For months, despite indisputable evidence to the contrary, military spokesmen insisted that strikes, manpower shortages, labor turnover, absenteeism, workers leaving war work, and the like were jeopardizing production and, therefore, the war effort. The homefront, it was charged, had gone sour; the troops overseas were demoralized and the enemy's desire to resist was strengthened.[35] Stimson and his assistant, Goldwaithe Dorr, even attempted unsuccessfully to have Chief of Staff George C. Marshall enlarge the army's proposed size so as to diminish the nation's estimated work force and, thereby, lend further weight to the argument for national service legislation.[36]

The military propaganda campaign increased in intensity with the German offensive and when Byrnes appointed Major General Lucius D. Clay, a key officer in the army's procurement structure, as his chief assistant in December. That month, the OWM issued a work-or-fight order, placed a 12 p.m. curfew on all places of amusement, and took other action to create a crisis atmosphere. The president, acting on the advice of the civilian and military heads of the army and navy, assisted that effort in January 1945 by unequivocally endorsing compulsory labor controls. But the administration would only muster its strength behind a relatively innocuous bill which would have obligated all males between 18 and 45 to remain at or transfer to war employment and which provided varying penalties for violators. That bill passed the House of Representatives on February 1, 1945.[37]

The Senate was less amenable than the House. Organized labor and the MLPC joined forces with public officials to establish that, while spot manpower problems existed, there was no overall labor shortage, that people in general were not rushing to leave essential employment, and that the military was manipulating statistics for its own purposes. Once the allies beat back the

German thrust, the Senate refused to pass any manpower legislation.[38] Stimson observed in his diary:

> It seems funny that in such a situation [end of the Battle of the Bulge] I should be distressed by our successes and our good fortune. But the true fact is that these things are going to make it more difficult than it would have been to get the necessary legislation through our Congress which we had in view at the time when everybody was scared. . . . I never had a more vivid viewpoint of some of the curious characteristics of our noble people in the United States that [sic] have no more notion that they are in a war or the sacrifices which are involved or needed—that is, the great bulk of them do not—just so many children.[39]

III

Organized labor fared better in terms of wartime labor relations, but, even in that area, unions were dissatisfied with the Roosevelt administration's policies and felt themselves to be victimized by the industry-military production team. From May 1940 through early 1942, Sidney Hillman, president of the Amalgamated Clothing Workers of America, headed a Labor Division within the NDAC, OPM, and WPB. Hillman's division was supposed to formulate and enforce a national defense labor policy. In attempting to fulfill its responsibilities, the Labor Division was weakened by internal discord between the AFL, CIO, and other staff members. Uncertain presidential support and the opposition of industry and the military crippled the weakened division. It took Hillman from May through September 1940 to persuade the reluctant NDAC and the armed services to endorse a relatively moderate defense labor policy. According to the policy, unemployment patterns would be a major consideration in the building of defense facilities and the distribution of contracts. In addition, the 40-hour work week and standard overtime compensation should be generally observed, and all defense work carried out in accordance with local, state, and federal labor laws.[40]

Hillman could not enforce the policy. At no time before or during World War II did labor supply significantly affect the location of defense plants or the letting of contracts. In the massive cantonment construction projects, the Quartermaster Corps during 1940–41 insisted that its contractors disregard standard house of work and pay for their employees.[41]

Hillman suffered his worst and most humiliating defeat over interpretations of the National Labor Relations Act. Could federal contracts be awarded to firms violating the Wagner Act? The question became critically important when billions of dollars of contracts went to labor's sworn enemies. With the adoption of the NDAC policy, Hillman got the War and Navy Departments and the attorney general committed to an interpretation denying further contracts to Wagner Act violators. Business representatives in and outside the mobilization agencies and anti-labor forces in Congress screamed their defiance. From September 1940 to June 1941, Hillman fought a spirited battle for labor. At crucial points Roosevelt either opposed him or equivocated. The military services eventually lined up with the industrial community. In the end, Hillman lost the struggle. Throughout the years 1940 to 1945, neither the civilian mobilization agencies nor the armed services would use their enormous power to enforce labor laws.[42]

The Labor Division's weakness eroded its prestige, left the nation without an enforced defense labor policy, and added to the forces creating industrial unrest. Neither the AFL nor the CIO would shelve the strike weapon during a national emergency without having its interests protected. Consequently, as the industrial mobilization program grew, so too did the strike record. By 1941, the incidence of strikes—involving organizational campaigns, jurisdictional disputes, wages, hours, and working conditions, and, in some instances for left-wing unions, political purposes—had reached alarming proportions for numerous government officials. Various new and old federal agencies helped reduce industrial turmoil, but the strike record was still high in December 1941.[43]

When war broke out, Roosevelt summoned the management-labor conference, which produced the no-strike, no-lock out pledge and created the tripartite War Labor Board (WLB) for settling disputes. Unions responded to the board with mixed emotions. By rejecting management's desire to freeze union security for the war's duration in favor of the maintenance-of-membership formula, the WLB granted labor a significant victory. After a brief escape clause, the formula required employees joining a union to remain in it for the duration of the collective bargaining contract. That was a modified form of the union shop which allowed organized labor to continue its organizational drives. Where union membership stood at about 9 million in 1940, it had increased to 14.75 million by 1945. Both the AFL and CIO, as well as other unions, were less satisfied with the WLB's "Little Steel" decision of July 1942, which, along with other government directives, froze wages. The decision created endless strife throughout the war years.

Few areas of union activity escaped government regulation during World War II. As the major consumers of the planned wartime economy, the armed services played an important part in the government's extensive involvement in labor affairs. The relationship between unions and the military was always potentially explosive. Union leaders identified the military with management because of the nature of the army's interwar mobilization planning, the role the services played in the World War II economy, and the inclusion of many industrial and financial executives in the armed services' procurement systems. On their part, the War and Navy Departments tended to view organized labor as an obstruction to full production, and anti-labor attitudes prevailed among the officer corps of both services.

Despite their differences, unions and the armed services worked together in the labor relations area with reasonable harmony. That was the case principally because Secretary of War Stimson and Under Secretary of War Patterson recruited a very talented group of advisers to staff a department Labor Branch (WDLB) which served as a buffer between unions and the army. Since the army was the largest and most powerful procurement agent, the navy and the Maritime Commission usually followed its lead in labor matters.[44]

The military's anti-labor stance and the ameliorating role played by the WDLB were most manifest when the armed services and unions came into direct contact. The operation of government-built plants, ships, and port facilities and the security programs and plant guards for military contractors are outstanding examples.

Prior to and during World War II, the War Department financed the construction of numerous giant plants costing billions of dollars and employing hundreds of thousands of workers. Most of the plants were built under the Ordnance Department's asupices. The department devised a system, designated "Government-Owned, Privately-Operated" (GOPO), whereby firms like Atlas, Hercules Powder, and DuPont would operate the plants as private contractors and be guaranteed all management prerogatives consistent with the government's interests. Specifically, the companies would be solely responsible for hiring personnel. Where organized labor was involved, the Ordnance Department, having apparently made some commitments to Atlas and the other firms, maintained that the plants should be considered as government-owned and operated, with unions practically prohibited for purposes of security and optimum production.[45]

In October 1941, the Ordnance Department attempted to implement its anti-union policy. The WDLB initially blocked Ordnance, but the latter ultimately converted the War and Navy Departments to its point of view. The WLB and the National Labor Relations Board (NLRB) reluctantly agreed to go along with the policy if organized labor approved. During extended negotiations with the armed services, the AFL and CIO, over the vehement opposition of the Navy Department and some members of the War Department, successfully insisted that the Wagner Act, modified only to protect the government's investment, must apply to the GOPO plants. By mid-1942 the new policy was implemented. Throughout the war, the WDLB worked closely with union leaders to maintain amicable labor relations in the GOPO plants.[46]

Labor problems involving the GOPO plants were miniscule compared with what developed in the maritime industry. Army difficulties in this industry stemmed largely from lack of experience and the incompetent and anti-union staff it recruited, mainly from marginal areas of the shipping and waterfront industries. Starting in late 1940, the Army Transportation Corps (ATC), the Army Air

Forces, the Quartermaster Corps, and other bureaus began leasing port facilities and operating fleets of ships for the movement of freight. On the West, East, and Gulf coasts, the army's operation of docks and warehouses produced great confusion. Though the army usually continued to hire union longshoremen, it replaced union freight checkers, shipping clerks, warehousemen, and others with inexperienced personnel hired as civil servants. The practice tended to break down the unity and coordination between docks and warehouses. Port operations in general became hopelessly tangled, facilities were improperly used, and ships sailed only partially or poorly loaded.[47]

The army's management of ships caused as many problems for unions as did its operation of port facilities. When the ATC took over ships, it informed crew members that henceforth they would be civil servants, denied union rights, suffer a cut in pay, and work unlimited hours without overtime pay. The general response was for crews to walk off en masse. In recruiting new crews, the army largely avoided union and government hiring halls with the result that it often ended up with low grade or inexperienced personnel. If union members remained on an army ship and proved to be troublesome, they were usually fired as subversives.[48]

Longshore and maritime unions, AFL and CIO alike, all bitterly protested against the anti-union policies. Beginning in late 1941, the War Department labor office attempted to reform army practices, but it was unable to initiate forthright action until mid-1942. In August 1942, and continuing until February 1943, the department employed a group of labor relations experts, under the direction of Professor Douglass V. Brown of the Massachusetts Institute of Technology, to conduct a thorough investigation of army port and maritime operations.

The Brown Committee investigation revealed that not all problems in the maritime industry originated with the army. The International Longshoremen's Association (ILA), along with many employers on the East Coast, were hopelessly corrupt and unstable. Furthermore, unions from the two major federations added to the industry's instability by competing with one another. Brown and his associates also established that army-labor relations were not uniformly bad. In Baltimore and Hampton Roads, the ATC and ILA worked cooperatively to solve mutual problems. Despite these observations, the Brown Committee established beyond question that the army's practices were intensely anti-union and generally incompetent.[49]

The investigation and the efforts of the WDLB led to reform. The department removed or downgraded inexperienced and anti-union personnel; it eliminated whenever possible the practice of forcing workers into the civil service; and it instituted recognized wages, hours, working conditions, and grievance and discharge procedures. The reforms produced results varying from good to poor.

Plant guards and security programs for military contractors, both of which were under the armed forces' auspices, also caused some serious labor problems.

The military tenaciously fought the unionization of the guards. "Permitting the condition to be brought about," insisted an Army Air Force colonel, "is as preposterous as the thought of surrendering our defense effort to the forces we are trying to destroy."[50] Abuse of the security programs also prevailed. Labor leaders charged that they were not given the chance to transfer suspected individuals to non-sensitive employment and that management and the military discharged undesirable employees as subversives. Also, there were no adequate provisions for review, appeal, reemployment of cleared suspects, or protection of seniority rights. By late 1943, under the constant prodding of unions, the effort of the military labor offices, and rulings of the NLRB, most of labor's complaints had been met. Plant guards could be unionized under conditions consistent with the war effort and procedures protecting the employees' interests were adopted in the security programs.[51]

Military participation in labor affairs did not stop at the point where unions and the armed services came into direct contact. After Pearl Harbor, the Navy Department, the Maritime Commission, and, with some hesitation, the War Department attempted to persuade the president to declare a national labor policy that included freezing union security and wages. In addition, the work week would be increased from 40 to 48 hours and most overtime pay eliminated. Roosevelt turned thumbs down on the policy except for the premium pay proposal. With the president's support, the military services and the Maritime Commission during 1942-43 pressured the Labor Department into restricting standard overtime pay to work over 40 hours per week or for the seventh consecutive day and a few holidays. Operating through an Interdepartmental Committee on Wage Control, the armed services also joined forces with the Office of Price Administration to block various potentially inflationary wage plans and to keep the pressure on the WLB which undoubtedly expedited the adoption of the "Little Steel" formula. Additionally, the military attempted to change most labor laws that might inhibit production, but it met a wall of opposition from unions and other government agencies.[52]

The War and Navy department labor offices also became involved in labor relations through attempts to settle or prevent strikes that would disrupt military production and through the seizure of facilities at the order of the president. At the Washington level, military labor advisers tried to maintain a strict neutrality in dealing with both management and unions. This meant that they often had to restrain field personnel, who tended to be inexperienced, mediocre, or biased towards management, from provoking or aggravating labor unrest.[53]

Despite the skillful performance of the WDLB and, to a lesser degree, its Navy Department counterpart, labor-military relations became increasingly strained from 1943 onward. As strikes grew in number, the armed services, usually over the objection of their labor advisers, launched a publicity campaign against work stoppages, stepped up their efforts for national service, and, within the Roosevelt administration, became the leading advocates of the War Labor

Disputes Act of 1943.[54] That bill was intended to prevent strikes, but, among other provisions, sanctioned them after a 30-day cooling off period and a favorable union vote.

Support for the Disputes Act was based on the assumption that irresponsible labor leaders drove their membership to the picket line—an assumption proven erroneous when the act was implemented. The rank and file usually voted overwhelmingly for strikes.[55] Rather than encouraging strikes, union leaders faced increasing difficulty in controlling their membership. Philip Murray constantly fretted about "an attitude of rebellion on the part of the workers generally."[56] Numerous local union leaders lost their elected positions during 1944–45 because they had demanded moderation on labor's part.[57]

Labor unrest stemmed largely from conservative domestic policies. Union spokesmen believed that the traditional Southern Democrats, whom the president had selected to oversee the economy, were principally responsible for such policies. They were thinking first of Byrnes, who had been appointed director of Economic Stabilization in October 1942 and who later served as head of the OWM, and then of Fred M. Vinson, Byrnes's successor in the stabilization office.

The Byrnes-Vinson leadership prevented a runaway inflation by holding a tighter reign on wages than prices. The Bureau of Labor Statistics (BLS) calculated that the cost of living had risen 23.4 percent between January 1941 and December 1943; labor set the figure at 43.5 percent. Yet the WLB, acting under directives from the stabilization office, generally held wage increases to 15 percent in order to offset a commensurate rise in prices from January 1941 to April 1942. Using the low BLS estimates, the average real spendable income of a manufacturing worker with three dependents went up slightly over 30 percent between 1941 and 1943.[58] But, quite clearly, most of labor's income gains resulted from full employment, overtime work, and the upgrading of workers. Averages, moreover, do not account for the many instances when wages remained substandard and gross inequities existed. Even when wages were good, the American worker did not receive the protection afforded, for example, his British counterpart: a guaranteed 40-hour work week, programs for reemploying displaced workers, separation and relocation pay, preservation of peacetime seniority for those transferring to war work, and an updated social security program.[59]

Other interest groups were protected to a far greater degree than labor. The farmer had the benefits of the parity system. Industry, and especially the large corporations, fared much better. Management salaries were only temporarily controlled and corporate taxes always remained relatively low. Investment in defense and war plants was not only underwritten by the government but the business community also received elaborate facilities and research financed at public expense. Profits on government contracts based on net worth after taxes and renegotiation, according to a conservative estimate, ranged from 15 percent to 48.9 percent.[60]

Although prices remained remarkably stable from December 1943 to V-J

Day, restlessness among the nation's working population grew rather than diminished because of the absence of adequate plans for reconversion. As the least protected economic interest group, labor faced the prospect of peace with foreboding. Predictions of a postwar depression were rife; a few years of war had not erased the painful memories of the Depression decade. To avoid a postwar crash, union spokesmen were among the leading advocates of a carefully planned reconversion program—a program in which they participated and which included the welfare benefits denied the worker during the war. Their proposals were ignored.[61]

Spokesmen from the large corporations and the military services who dominated the WPB were mainly responsible for the nation being unprepared for peace. During 1944, the president and Congress designated the OWM—now the Office of War Mobilization and Reconversion (OWMR)—as the agency to determine demobilization policy. The OWMR's most significant act was to resolve the reconversion controversy which wracked the WPB in favor of the industry-military production team. Nelson, the board's chairman, intended to expand gradually civilian production, beginning in early 1944 as munitions demand tapered off in order to ease the economy into demobilization, protect the interests of small business, and avoid unemployment. Within the WPB, Nelson was consistently supported only by his own staff, the labor and small business offices, and the Office of Civilian Requirements. Industrial and the military representatives vehemently opposed the chairman's position: the latter because they feared that any increase in civilian production could set off a stampede detrimental to munitions output; the former because they wanted to protect postwar market positions by holding civilian production to a minimum until all firms could resume peacetime pursuits simultaneously with the conclusion of hostilities. With the critically important support of Byrnes, the WPB's industry-military production team during 1944 and early 1945 first delayed and then crippled the implementation of Nelson's plan. Thereafter, some planning for reconversion took place, but it was largely inconsequential. When the war ended, the WPB quickly lifted all wartime restrictions.[62]

The postwar depression feared by many did not materialize, but the lack of planning for peace had its consequences. A quick end to the war caught the Truman administration unprepared for maintaining stable economic conditions during demobilization. One result of that failure was the massive explosion in industrial relations—an explosion that had been building up slowly for almost two years.

IV

Organized labor's fate during World War II stemmed from the fact that labor leaders were unable to extend their power beyond the bounds of traditional American "business unionism"; that is, selecting, distributing, and disciplining manpower for management, while bargaining over wages, hours, and working conditions. Throughout the war years, union spokesmen insisted that since the government was planning the economy and serving as the nation's largest consumer and investor, they had the right to share in all economic decisions. At no time, however, did the Roosevelt administration seriously support labor's contention, and without such backing unions never stood a chance of achieving their goal. The commitment of the president and his advisers to preserving a corporate capitalist system precluded the possibility of organized labor serving as other than a subordinate economic interest group.

The way in which the wartime economy functioned was a direct outgrowth of New Deal policies. During the first few years in office, the Roosevelt administration principally concentrated upon economic planning under the National Industrial Recovery Act (NIRA) of 1933. Had the large corporations, which actually, if not nominally, controlled the NRA, been able and willing to use that agency to revive the Depression-ridden economy, the New Deal as a reform movement would probably have ended quickly. The NRA, however, failed to bring about recovery and also exposed the parochial outlook and operation of the corporate giants which had played no small part in bringing about the Crash in 1929. With organized and unorganized labor, smaller business units, and the public at large growing increasingly restive, and with numerous members of the industrial-financial community blaming the Roosevelt administration for the consequences of their own bankrupt leadership, the president and his advisers chose to jettison economic planning.

While new tactics to combat the Depression emerged with the NRA's demise, the president and his advisers in no way tried to modify the nation's corporate structure meaningfully. The administration introduced some business reforms and later launched an anti-trust crusade against collusive pricing, but essentially it allowed the large corporate interests to continue their various oligopolistic practices which were less obvious outside than inside a planning structure. Since the administration remained committed to corporate capitalism, it was forced to protect the system by having the government assume responsibility for the necessary social functions that the economy's private sector could not or would not perform. Otherwise, real or incipient movements of protest threatened to rip the society away from its moorings. Consequently, relief programs were expanded in order to support or employ the millions who could not find jobs, and a rather conservative social security and labor standards program, along with moderate taxation reforms, were introduced in order to mitigate the harshest features of marketplace economics. Additionally, some assistance was offered to smaller business units and those agrarian elements unaffected or adversely affected by the Agricultural Adjustment Act.

More significantly, the National Labor Relations Act became part of the administration's post-NRA program, but, unlike most major New Deal legislation, that act neither originated with nor was shaped by the president and his advisers. It resulted from Congress responding positively to a ground swell of demand for unions among the workers in the mass production industries. After two years of equivocating over the collective bargaining provisions of the NIRA, the president in 1935 finally endorsed the proposed Wagner bill at a time when any lesser move could have been politically hazardous. Even after the Wagner Act was passed, the White House, outside of occasional mediation effort, remained aloof from the tumultuous labor scene. Militant union tactics, combined with the exposure by the so-called LaFollette Committee and the NLRB of management's anti-union practices, forced industry to obey the law. The Roosevelt administration got enormous political mileage out of a unionizing process it had done little to bring about.

The administration's new tactics introduced in 1935 generated a faster rate of recovery, principally because more deficit spending was involved. Rising industrial production, the massive unionizing campaigns, and the relief, welfare, and reform measures all served to convert popular discontent and malaise into great enthusiasm for the president and the Democratic Party. Roosevelt's growing feud with large sectors of the business community proved to be an immense political asset. It acted as a catharsis for the angry, frightened, or distraught population and helped to give the impression of sweeping change to a program that was essentially a modest rescue operation for a foundering corporate economy.

Before the nation was out of the Depression, however, the approach of World War II faced the Roosevelt administration with the need to reintroduce some form of economic planning. A planned economy meant that the New Deal could no longer stand still; it had either to go backward to the NRA or forward to a planning system which actually, not just nominally, included all economic interest groups and particularly representatives from the public and organized labor. Neither alternative was especially appealing to the administration. Resuming NRA-type planning involved turning the economy over to corporations which were myopic concerning the public's larger interests. Additionally, a large population still antagonistic towards business would have to be persuaded or forced to accept such a venture. But the prospect of authentic interest-group planning presented even greater problems. Coercion of almost dictatorial proportions would have been necessary before industry would share its decision-making functions with labor and other groups. Even such drastic measures, however, offered no guarantee that the economy could have been mobilized since those who owned the nation's industrial plant could thwart any planning effort through obstructionist tactics.*

---

*The so-called Nye Committee quite clearly saw that taking power away from industry during a period of war mobilization might result in a cure that was worse than the disease.[63]

Moreover, strong-arming industry in a nation devoted to business values would probably have lacked popular appeal. While there was much discontent with how the American business system worked and a widespread desire for it to function more equitably, there was no consensus over how to reform the system and little sentiment in favor of changing capitalism. The split emotions of American liberalism over marketplace economics, which the New Deal accurately reflected, created enormous obstacles to modifying significantly industry's power.

With the convening of the WRB late in 1939, Roosevelt unmistakably revealed that he was prepared to go backward to the NRA, but anti-business and anti-war dissent temporarily blocked the way. Consequently, the president employed the stratagem of creating mobilization agencies with a facade of broad interest-group representation when actually large corporations were always dominant. Although the NDAC and OPM did little in the way of economic preparedness, they served the important purpose of setting up and manning the mobilization apparatus and mending the administration's fences with the business community. Once wartime necessity and war-induced prosperity had reduced dissent over conservative mobilization schemes to an acceptably low level, corporate America was overtly given control of the WPB.

The WPB's most immediately pressing problem involved integrating the armed services into its structure. That process, although at times difficult, was always possible because no fundamental issues were at stake. Interwar mobilization planning had fully conditioned the army and navy to working in harmony with industrial America. By early 1943, a munitions partnership had been consummated within the WPB which was based upon the mutual needs and benefits of the industrial and military communities. With the armed services' purchasing appartus adapted to the WPB, industry had the assurance that the prewar corporate structure would be used as the approximate pattern for distributing billions of dollars of war contracts. The military was guaranteed a reliable source of supply and, within the economy's potential, was granted almost unlimited authority for determining its own requirements.

The WPB ultimately determined the outline for how the entire World War II economy operated. Inflation, for example, was controlled mainly through squeezing mass spending power and nonmilitary governmental expenditures, while wide latitude was granted for the costs and profits of munitions production. When the board's authority and policies came under fire from various sources, the president created the Office of Economic Stabilization and the OWM, ostensibly to coordinate the activity of the various mobilization agencies, but actually to protect the WPB's decision making.

Organized labor, along with other interest groups, ended up catering to the WPB's needs. Labor had a critically important function to perform in the area of managing a substantial part of the nation's work force for industry. Before war was declared, much of the business community had come to accept unionization not only as inevitable but also as a service useful to itself. Despite all of the chaos that the armed services created in the industrial relations field, the military, as evidenced by the quality and operation of its own labor offices, likewise appreciated the positive attributes of unions. Hence, for industry and the military the existence and growth of unions was no threat so long as labor was denied the power to influence the overall direction of the World War II economy. With labor leaders isolated within the WPB, the WMC subordinated to the board, and the WLB restricted to the rules established by Byrnes and Vinson, businessmen and military officials had good reasons to cooperate with union spokesmen, and did so for the most part, because the WPB's interests were being served.

But organized labor and the working population, still fired by the militance of the 1930s, did not accept their secondary role with equanimity. As the inequities and irresponsibility of the wartime economic machine mounted, so too did the protest and restlessness among labor's ranks. Consequently, more and more manipulation and threats had to be employed to keep the nation's work force in line. While those expedients may have been distasteful to Roosevelt, they were made probable by the adoption of the NRA-planning model. Furthermore, an administration that had proceeded with such agonizing deliberation about labor's right to organize and bargain collectively in the midst of the Depression, obviously grew impatient over labor unrest when unions were permitted to continue organizing in a prosperous wartime economy with full employment.

"Military necessity" became the Roosevelt administration's main justification for most policies during the war, including threats directed at labor. That rationale placed the armed services in a strategic position concerning domestic policies. Both before and after war was declared, Roosevelt and his chief lieutenants consistently allowed a willing military to run interference for conservative mobilization policies. Speaking as guardians of vital national interests, the army and navy became the archadvocates of anti-strike and national service legislation, the principal opponents of interest-group planning, the chief spokesmen for retrogressive economic stabilization and wealth distribution measures, and the most vociferous elements against reconversion planning.

The military's World War II role as defender of the status quo was part of a larger ongoing twentieth-century trend whereby modern warfare had a greater impact than reform upon the nation's political economy. During World War I, the Progressive concern for making concentrated economic power accountable to the public had become submerged in the effort to plan a corporate capitalist economy without changing its basic nature. The ultimate result was a form of industrial self-regulation carried out chiefly by corporate representatives serving as public officials within the War Industries Board (WIB). After the war, the urge for reforming the U.S. economic system remained submerged as the Republican administrations in the 1920s and the Roosevelt administration in the early New Deal years attempted peacetime variations of the wartime planning system, first, to stabilize, and, then, to revive a corporate-dominated economy. The Depression, however, rekindled the nation's reform instincts and, beginning in 1935, drove the Roosevelt administration to the left. Public sentiment for making business answerable to the commonweal remained so strong before and after Pearl Harbor that the combined power and influence of both industry and the military were required to adopt and retain the NRA (essentially the WIB) planning system as the method for mobilizing the World War II economy.

The armed services tenaciously fought for what became the WPB because they had become convinced that mobilization had to be based upon the existing corporate structure. During 20 years of interwar planning, the military services had no other demonstrated mobilization model to guide their effort. After war was declared, the army and navy became even more committed to WPB methods since numerous advocates of interest-group, as opposed to elitist, planning, like Congressman Tolan and Senator Truman, proposed taking away the military's procurement functions. These officials wanted to dissolve completely the wartime munitions partnership by placing under a new source of authority the concentrated buying power of the armed services as well as the concentrated producing power of industry.

The president and his advisers were not about to try restructuring either the corporate community or the armed services, because they believed that the existing power system was essential for achieving the administration's goals abroad. The logical outcome was the Roosevelt administration's defense of the WPB's industry-military alliance—an alliance which dictated policies at home. Modern warfare in the United States, therefore, had produced economic planning schemes that protected the power of both the industrial and military communities.*

With the conclusion of hostilities, the industrial-military alliance appeared to dissolve.[65] While corporate America and the armed services had explored the range of a partnership which was mutually beneficial during the war, business in general was as anxious to reconvert its facilities to peacetime production as it had been resistive to converting its plant to wartime pursuits. This immediate postwar separation did not last. By slow stages, large and sustained military expenditures produced an enduring Military-Industrial Complex with the self-serving consequences suggested by the World War II economy and, more seriously, with the potential for perpetuating the forces of modern warfare which had provided for the initial growth of such a complex.

Gradually, most of organized labor, which had fought the wartime munitions team, became a junior partner in the postwar complex. Unions could not

---

*Most countries starting with World War I did, to varying degrees, take procurement authority away from the military services.[64]

afford endlessly to neglect their immediate self-interest. During the war, they had fought to break out of the crippling role of business unionism without success. As a result, realism dictated that labor accommodate to, instead of resist, an environment which it had neither created nor could do much to change. While unions did not participate, for example, in the decisions which produced the aerospace industry, they developed a vital stake in working for that industry's survival and growth. Other interest groups would respond similarly.

But all of that was in the future. The significant point to be made is that the Roosevelt administration between 1935 and 1939 had been caught up in the strongest drive for reforming the U.S. economic system that the nation probably had ever experienced. During those volatile years, the administration had failed to confront the nation with what would have been necessary to reform corporate capitalism significantly. Instead, it encouraged the population to believe that business could be made responsible to the public without modifying industry's power. The operation of the World War II economy cast great doubt upon that proposition.

Beyond question, the production records of the war years were impressive, but they had been purchased at a very high price. With the conclusion of hostilities, New Deal liberal ideology had been undermined. New Dealers had assumed that an enlarged federal government would operate to protect the public interest. During World War II, however, the government had served certain dominant interests at the expense of those less powerful. Through the functions of the wartime economy, the large corporations concentrated their power even further; the military had been granted and willingly assumed responsibility and authority which drastically distorted the armed services' role in a democratic society; and, although the labor movement had been vastly expanded in size, unions proved to be no match for business, let alone industry working in conjunction with the military.*

Modern warfare lays bare the essential attributes of a society. That being the case, the World War II years, more than the 1930s, should be used to measure the quality of the Roosevelt leadership.

---

*John L. Lewis, largely unmoved by ideology and as shrewd a calculator of power as Roosevelt himself, appeared to have anticipated well in advance of most union leaders that the President would use, more than serve, a massively expanded labor movement. If that was the case, then Lewis may not have blundered, as is generally assumed, in his feud with the President which left the United Mine Workers isolated within the labor movement. Lewis consciously may have chosen to conduct guerilla warfare against the Roosevelt administration in the late 1930s and during World War II instead of accepting a co-opted position within a liberal state.

NOTES

1. For example, see Joel Seidman, *American Labor from Defense to Reconstruction* (Chicago, 1953); Harry A. Millis and Emily C. Brown, *From the Wagner Act to Taft-Hartley* (Chicago, 1950). Aaron Levenstein, *Labor Today and Tomorrow* (New York, 1945), provides a perceptive, although erratic, account of labor during the war. The various monographs, anthologies, and unpublished manuscripts which treat with labor outside the collective bargaining area are included in the footnotes below. For bibliographic studies of the wartime economy in general, see Barton J. Bernstein, "Economic Policies," *The Truman Period as a Research Field*, ed. Richard S. Kirkendall (Columbia, 1967), 87–147; Jim F. Heath, "Domestic America during World War II: Research Opportunities for Historians," *Journal of American History*, LVII (1971), 384–414; Richard Polenberg, *War and Society: The United States, 1941-1945* (Philadelphia, 1972), 261–279.

2. *Out of Our Past* (New York, 1970), 406. See also Milton Derber, "Growth and Expansion," *Labor and the New Deal*, eds. Derber and Edwin Young (Madison, 1961), 38–42; Walter Galenson, *The CIO Challenge to the AFL* (Cambridge, 1960), xvii, 583–644. For the best and most balanced analysis of labor during the New Deal, see Irving Bernstein, *Turbulent Years* (Boston, 1970).

3. Ellis W. Hawley, *The New Deal and the Problem of Monopoly* (Princeton, 1966), remains the most impressive analysis of New Deal economic policies. See also William E. Leuchtenburg, "The New Deal and the Analogue of War," 79–143, and Arthur M. Johnson, "Continuity and Change in Government-Business Relations," 206–209, in *Change and Continuity in Twentieth Century America*, eds. John Braeman, Robert H. Bremner, and Everett Walters (New York, 1966). New Left views on the New Deal are discussed by Ronald Radosh, "The Myth of the New Deal," *A New History of Leviathan*, eds. Radosh and Murray N. Rothbard (New York, 1972), 146–187.

4. Paul A. C. Koistinen, "The 'Industrial-Military Complex' in Historical Perspective: World War I," *Business History Review*, XLI (1967), 378–403.

5. Paul A. C. Koistinen, "The 'Industrial-Military Complex' in Historical Perspective: The InterWar Years," *Journal of American History*, LVI (1970), 819–839.

6. There are no satisfactory studies of the entire labor movement during World War I. For an introduction to the subject, see Gordon S. Watkins, *Labor Problems and Labor Administration in the United States During World War I* (Urbana, 1920); George Soule, *Prosperity Decade* (New York, 1968), 64–76; James Weinstein, *The Corporate Ideal in the Liberal State: 1900-1918* (Boston, 1968), 226–254; Daniel R. Beaver, *Newton D. Baker and the American War Effort, 1917-1919* (Lincoln, 1966), 66–71.

7. Paul A. C. Koistinen, "The Hammer and the Sword: Labor, the Military, and Industrial Mobilization, 1920-1945" (Ph.D. dissertation, University of California, Berkeley, 1964), 8–77. See also Albert A. Blum and J. Douglas Smyth, "Who Should Serve: Pre-World War II Planning for Selective Service," *Journal of Economic History*, XXX (1970), 379–404.

8. Smaller War Plants Corporation, "Economic Concentration and World War II," 79 Cong., 2 sess., *S. Doc. 206* (1946), 21–54; E. Elberton Smith, *The Army and Economic Mobilization* (Washington, D.C., 1959), 6, 215.

9. Koistinen, "Hammer and Sword," 554–637. Further research by the author in numerous additional document collections and other primary sources has not significantly modified the conclusions reached in the dissertation.

10. *Ibid.*, 637–703.

11. *Ibid.*

12. *Ibid.*

13. *Ibid.*

14. AFL, *Annual Proceedings, 1939*, pp. 509-517; AFL, Executive Council Minutes, Jan. 29-Feb. 9, 1940, pp. 57-58, 147; CIO, *Annual Proceedings, 1939*, pp. 5-6, 235-236; "Joint A.F. of L-CIO Statement on War Production Crisis," Aug. 25, 1942, file "War Production Crisis-AFL-CIO Statement," Correspondence, World War II Policy (Series B), William Green Papers, Wisconsin State Historical Society, Madison; G. Warren Morgan to Philip J. Clowes, Oct. 29, 1942, and other documents, file 240.1, Records of the War Production Board, RG 179, National Archives; Philip Murray to Roosevelt, Dec. 20, 1940, file 631.0423, *ibid.*; William J. Schuck, "Industry and Labor Advisory Committees of the War Production Board (1942-1945)" (1947), *ibid.*; J. Carlyle Sitterson, "Industry and Labor Advisory Committees" (1944), *ibid.*; Richard J. Purcell, "Labor policies of the War Production Board (April 1942 to November 1945)," 5 vols. (1946), *ibid.*; Merton W. Ertell, "The CIO Industry Council Plan–Its Background and Implications" (Ph.D. dissertation, University of Chicago, 1955); Edythe W. First, *Industry and Labor Advisory Committees in the National Defense Advisory Commission and the Office of Production Management, May 1940 to January 1942* (Washington, D.C., 1946), 55-64, 169-229.

15. Robert R. Russell, "Expansion of Industrial Facilities Under Army Air Force Auspices, 1940-1945" (1947), p. 86, Wright-Patterson Airfield, Ohio.

16. Koistinen, "Hammer and Sword," 341-377.

17. Ellen S. Parks, "Management-Labor Policy Committee: A Case Study of Organized Group Participation in Administration," Records of the Bureau of the Budget, RG 51, National Archives.

18. Ellen S. Parks, "Creation of the War Manpower Commission: Administration of the War Labor Market through the Device of Coordination" (1944), Records of the Bureau of the Budget.

19. Koistinen, "Hammer and Sword," 346-351, 367-372, 415-429. Albert A. Blum, *Drafted or Deferred* (Ann Arbor, 1967), 1-209, analyzes the draft system within the context of the over-all wartime manpower programs.

20. Robert P. Patterson to Paul V. McNutt, Dec. 28, 1942, and other documents, file "War Manpower Commission," Julius Amberg Papers, Records of the Office of the Secretary of War (OSW), RG 107, National Archives; James P. Mitchell to Brehon B. Somervell, May 27, 1943, file "Placement of Contracts with Regard to Labor Supply," John H. Ohly Papers (in Ohly's possession); Constance Kiehl, "U.S. War Manpower Commission," Chap. 2, pp. 13-14, Chap. 4, pp. 53-54, Records of the Bureau of the Budget; Labor Department, "Short History of the War Manpower Commission" (1948), 115-116, Records of the War Manpower Commission, RG 211, National Archives; Edmond Kanwit, "War Department Facility Allocation, Contract Placement, and Cutback Distribution from the Standpoint of Labor Supply and Labor Relations, June 1940 to May 1945," Office of the Chief of Military History (OCMH), Washington, D.C.; Herman M. Somers and John H. Ohly, "The War Department Organization for the Handling of Labor Problems" (1945), Part II, 4-18, *ibid.*

21. Memo from Samuel Lubell, Sept. 4, 1943, file "National Service," Washington File, 1942-45, Bernard M. Baruch Papers, Princeton University Library; Minutes, Advisory Board, Office of War Mobilization and Reconversion (OWMR), Feb. 19-20, 1945, Records of the OWMR, RG 250, National Archives; Earl Latham, "First Narrative on the 'Coordination of War Manpower Commission's Relations with the War Production Board,'" 2-23, Records of the Bureau of the Budget; R. Burr Smith, "Labor and Manpower Administration in War Production" (1943), 34-37, Records of the WPB; WMC, "History of the Bureau of Manpower Utilization in the War Manpower Commission," Records of the WMC.

22. Parks, "Management-Labor Policy Committee"; Koistinen, "Hammer and Sword," 380-387. See also MLPC Minutes (verbatim and summaries); WMC, Minutes and numerous documents in the files on National War Service Legislation, Records of the WMC.

23. *S. Doc. 607*, 78 Cong., 1 sess. (Feb. 1, 1943); Herman M. Somers, *Presidential Agency: OWMR: The Office of War Mobilization and Reconversion* (Cambridge, 1950), 35-38.

24. Baruch and Hancock to Byrnes, Aug. 19, 1943, file "Manpower—West Coast Reports," Washington File, 1942–45, Baruch Papers.

25. *Cong. Rec.*, 78 Cong., 1 sess., 7589–7596. See also Baruch to President, Sept. 8, 1943, and other documents, OF 1413F, Franklin D. Roosevelt Papers, Franklin D. Roosevelt Library, Hyde Park, N.Y.; John Hertz to Patterson, Sept. 30, 1943, and other documents, file "Final Report," John Hertz Papers, Records of the OSW.

26. "West Coast Manpower Program," Sept. 4, 1943, file "Master Plan—West Coast Aircraft Shortage Plan," Goldwaithe H. Dorr Papers, Records of the OSW; Dorr to John J. McCloy, Aug. 28, 1943, file "Papers Used at Conf., 10 A.M. Sunday Morning," *ibid.*

27. Koistinen, "Hammer and Sword," 387–414.

28. Grenville Clark and Arthur L. Williston, *The Effort for a National Service Law in World War II: 1942-1945—Report to the National Council of the Citizens Committee for a National War Service Act* (Massachusetts, 1947).

29. Clark to James V. Forrestal, May 10, 1944, and other documents, file "National Service-Official File," Records of the OSW; memo, "The Austin-Wadsworth Bill" and other documents, file "Austin-Wadsworth Bill," Dorr Papers; "Preliminary Report . . . National War Service Act," circa July 1942, file "National Service," *ibid.*

30. William Haber, *et al.* to McNutt, Aug. 4, 1942, file "National Service-Misc.," *ibid.*; Dorr to Stimson, Dec. 10, 1942, file "Manpower," Records of the OSW.

31. Wadsworth to Clark, March 26, 1942, *ibid.*

32. Clark to Benjamin Long, July 6, 1942, file "National Service-Correspondence—1942,." Dorr Papers; R. Irwin, "Report on War Manpower Programs," Nov. 2, 1942, file "Management-Labor Policy Committee—Book II," *ibid.*; Dorr to Stimson, Nov. 4, 1942, file "Selective Service System-National Service Act," *ibid.*; McNutt to President, circa Nov. 1942 and other documents, file "Mobilization Resources, Director of," *ibid.*; Bureau of the Budget, *The United States at War* (Washington, D.C., 1946), 188–189.

33. Senate Committee on Military Affairs, "Hearings on Manpower (National War Service Bill)," 78 Cong., 1 sess. (1943); House Committee on Military Affairs, "Hearings on Full Utilization of Manpower," 78 Cong., 1 sess. (1943).

34. Henry L. Stimson Diary, June 29, 30, July 1, Sept. 15, 16, Dec. 8, 23, 25, 28, 30, 1943, Yale University Library; Stimson to President, July 1, 1943, file "National Service—Correspondence—Jan. '43–Jan. '44," Dorr Papers; Stimson, *et al.* to President, Dec. 28, 1943, file "White House Correspondence," Records of the OSW; Clark to Stimson, Dec. 8, 1943, file "National Service–Official File," *ibid.*; Clark to Samuel I. Rosenman, Sept. 17, 1943, file 60–13, Box 1, Samuel I. Rosenman Papers, Roosevelt Library; Samuel I. Rosenman, *Working with Roosevelt* (New York, 1952), 417–425; *New York Times*, Jan. 12, 1944. See also "Meeting on National Service Legislation," April 20, 1944, file 42-3-42, Records of the Office of the Secretary of the Navy, RG 80, National Archives.

35. Koistinen, "Hammer and Sword," 478–480, 503–521.

36. Stimson Diary, May 11 (with attached memo, May 10), 1944, Jan. 4, 9, 1945; Dorr to Stimson, April 11, 1944, file "Manpower," Records of the OSW; Dorr to Stimson, Jan. 1, 1945, and other documents, file "Size of Army," Dorr Papers; Amberg to Patterson, May 2, 1944, file "War Production Board," Amberg Papers.

37. Koistinen, "Hammer and Sword," 521–530.

38. *Ibid.*, 530–541.

39. Stimson Diary, Jan. 15, 1945.

40. Richard J. Purcell, *Labor Policies of the National Defense Advisory Commission and the Office of Production Management, May 1940 to April 1942* (Washington, D.C., 1946), 1–41, 170; Matthew Josephson, *Sidney Hillman: Statesman of American Labor* (New York, 1952), 504–528; Koistinen, "Hammer and Sword," 88–93, 128–129, 144–147.

41. Koistinen, "Hammer and Sword," 129–132.

42. Fredrick M. Eaton To William S. Knudsen, Dec. 20, 1940, and other documents, files "Labor—1941-42 (1) and (2)," Amberg Papers; M. H. Pettit to Burton O. Lewis, Dec. 17, 1940, file "Policies, Labor," *ibid.*; Patterson to Hillman, Sept. 27, 1940, and other documents, file "Labor-Award of Contracts—Policy and General," Ohly Papers; "Conversations with Julius Amberg," April 19, 1945, file "Misc.," *ibid.*; President to Patterson, Nov. 14, 1940, file "Labor—Labor Factors in Award of Contracts—Particular Contracts," *ibid.*; Ohly interview with Blackwell Smith, Dec. 23, 1940, and other documents, file "Labor," Howard C. Petersen Papers, Records of the OSW; Ohly to Edward F. McGrady, Feb. 22, 1941, file 230.1404, Under Secretary of War (USW) Papers, *ibid.*; Procurement Circular No. 43 and other documents, file 160, *ibid.*; *Verbatim Record of Proceedings of the House Committee Investigating Labor Boards and Wagner Act,* Vol. IV, No. 9, Oct. 8, 1940—copy in Ohly Papers; Byron Fairchild and Jonathan Grossman, *The Army and Industrial Manpower* (Washington, D.C., 1959), 35-42.

43. Seidman, *American Labor*, 41-73.

44. Somers and Ohly, "War Department," Pt. 1, p. 4; author's interview with Ohly, Aug. 1, 1962; Troyer S. Anderson, "Introduction to the History of the Office of the Under Secretary of War's Office" (1947), OCMH, Chap. 4, pp. 28-31, Chap. 5, pp. 34-38. See also Army Air Force, "A History of AAF Activities During World War II in the Field of Industrial Manpower," Wright-Patterson Airfield, Ohio.

45. C. M. Wesson to Patterson, Oct. 25, 1941, file 230.1405, USW Papers; J. L. Saltonstall, Jr., to Ohly, Jan. 30, 1942, and other documents, file "Labor—GOPO's—Background and Development of Labor Policy," Ohly Papers.

46. McGrady to Patterson, Oct. 27, 1941, and other documents, *ibid.*; Ohly for files, July 14, 1942, and other documents, file "Labor—GOPO's—Interpretation and Application of Labor Policy," *ibid.*; Wesson to Patterson, Feb. 21, 1942, and other documents, file "Leg.—Dead Bills (HofR)," *ibid.*; Wesson to Patterson, Nov. 22, 1941, and other documents, file "Labor," Petersen Papers; Patterson to Wesson, Feb. 28, 1942, and other documents, file 049.12/175, Planning Branch, Assistant Secretary of War, Records of the OSW; Lee Pressman to McGrady, May 29, 1942, and other documents, file "Plant Protection and Subversive Activity," Edward F. McGrady Papers, *ibid.*

47. Joseph W. Battley, Jr., to McGrady, Aug. 11, 1941, and other documents, file "Longshore up to March, 1943," Labor Relations Branch (LBR), Records of the Army Service Forces, RG 160, National Archives; Ohly for files, Feb. 18, 1942, and other documents, file "Longshore work on the Eastern and Gulf Coasts," Ohly Papers; Bishop for files, July 16, 1942, and other documents, file "Labor—Unions—Longshoremen, ALF-CIO," *ibid.*

48. Ohly for files, Aug. 27, 1942, and other documents, file "Labor-Maritime Labor Problems (including ATS)," *ibid.*; Douglass V. Brown to Bishop, Oct. 29, 1942, and other documents, file "Longshore up to March, 1943," LBR, Records of the Army Service Forces.

49. Brown Reports, parts I and II, file "Pacific and East Coast Longshore Reports (Brown)," *ibid.*; author's interview with Brown, June 1962. See also the numerous reports and correspondence among Brown, his staff, and the army, Douglass V. Brown Papers (in Brown's possession).

50. Memo, W. F. Volandt, Dec. 8, 1941, unlabeled folder, Ohly Papers.

51. Koistinen, "Hammer and Sword," 108-110, 214-215.

52. *Ibid.*, 164-196.

53. *Ibid.*, 99-124, 249-251, 285-332.

54. Stimson Diary, June 16, 17, 1943; Stimson and Frank Knox to Harold D. Smith, June 17, 1943, file 004.07, USW Papers; John H. Ohly, "History of Plant Seizures During World War II," 3 vols., OCMH, I, 137-143.

55. Seidman, *American Labor*, 189-190.

56. CIO, Executive Board Minutes, July 13–14, 1945, pp. 48–57. See also Institute of Labor Studies, *Labor Views on Current Issues* (New York, 1943–1945).

57. John T. Dunlop, "The Decontrol of Wages and Prices," *Labor in Postwar America*, eds. Colston E. Warne, *et al.* (New York, 1949), 4–5.

58. Lenore A. Epstein and Eleanor M. Snyder, "Urban Price Trends," *ibid.*, 143; "Changes In The Cost of Living During 1943," *Yearbook of American Labor*, eds. Colston E. Warne, *et al.* (New York, 1945), 51–68.

59. Purcell, "Labor Policies of the WPB" (no pagination). Labor representatives also consistently worked for more effective price controls. See Executive Offices–Labor Office, Labor Policy Committee Records, Correspondence, Minutes of Meetings, Office of Price Administration, RG 188, National Archives.

60. Koistinen, "Hammer and Sword," 283–284, 577–584, 664–672.

61. *Ibid.*, 747–773; Philip Murray to Donald Nelson and Byrnes, March 7, 1944, Box 3, Philip Murray Papers, Catholic University Library.

62. The Records of the WPB are the best primary source on reconversion; secondary sources are legion. Some of the better ones include Barton J. Bernstein, "The Debate on Industrial Reconversion," *American Journal of Economics and Sociology*, XXVI (1967), 159–172; J. Carlyle Sitterson, *Development of the Reconversion Policies of the War Production Board, April 1943 to January 1945* (Washington, D.C., 1945); Jack Peltason, *The Reconversion Controversy* (Washington, D.C., 1950); Civilian Production Administration, *Industrial Mobilization for War: History of the War Production Board and Predecessor Agencies, 1940–1945* (Washington, D.C., 1947); Donald M. Nelson, *Arsenal of Democracy* (New York, 1946); Bruce Catton, *The War Lords of Washington* (New York, 1948); Drummond Jones, *The Role of the Office of Civilian Requirements in the Office of Production Management and the War Production Board, January 1941 to November 1945* (Washington, D.C., 1946); John D. Millett, *The Organization and Role of the Army Service Forces* (Washington, D.C., 1954); Robert H. Connery, *The Navy and Industrial Mobilization in World War II* (Princeton, 1951). See also, Koistinen, "Hammer and Sword," 703–793.

63. See Koistinen, "The 'Industrial-Military Complex' . . . InterWar Years," 831–835.

64. For further discussion about the significance of maintaining procurement rights with the military as part of the strategy for preserving a corporate capitalist economy during a time of war, see Koistinen, "The 'Industrial-Military Complex' . . . World War I," 395–398.

65. For a perceptive analysis of conspiracy, warfare, and other themes, see Keith L. Nelson, "The 'Warfare State': History of a Concept," *Pacific Historical Review*, XL (1971), 127–143.

5

THE MILITARY-INDUSTRIAL
COMPLEX

In his paper, "The Waning of the Warfare State," Professor James L. Clayton's analysis presents some difficult obstacles to serious discussion for several reasons. First, his purview is enormously broad and comprehensive. Second, key terms and concepts remain undefined, vaguely defined, or shift in definition. Third, the focus of the essay is uncertain, and, finally, critically important and controversial issues are touched upon in passing and not dealt with directly. Nonetheless, I shall attempt to respond to most of Clayton's major points in four principal ways.

My first line of criticism involves methodology. Here, it should be pointed out that quantification provides no magic resolution to the debate concerning defense and war spending. Clayton's "hard and irrefutable evidence" that the "warfare state"—or "national security state," as I would prefer—is "already in a state of decay" is far from absolute. In an appendix unavailable to the audience, Clayton observes that there is no norm for measuring defense spending, that dif-

---

This chapter is a comment on a paper presented by Professor James L. Clayton at the Annual Meeting of the Organization of American Historians, April 1974, in Denver, Colorado, entitled "The Waning of the Warfare State." Clayton proposed that when any nation spends over 10 perccent of its GNP or 30 percent of its net public outlays on either war-related or welfare-related programs, a "Warfare" or "Welfare State," respectively, has been created. Using that paradigm, he went on to point out that the United States had a Warfare State in 1918-20, 1942-46, 1951-63, and 1968. The American Welfare State, according to Clayton, had its origins with the New Deal, became the hallmark of the Great Society, and has grown exponentially since the Nixon administration. Clayton has published a significantly modified and elaborately illustrated version of this paper as "The Fiscal Limits of the Warfare-Welfare State: Defense and Welfare Spending in the United States Since 1900," *The Western Political Quarterly* 24 (1976): 364-83.

ferent approaches produce different results, and, I might add, different conclusions. Indeed, nowhere in his paper does Clayton define precisely what he means by either warfare or welfare spending, although certainly such a definition is crucial to his analysis. In the same appendix, however, the author warns that studies by the Joint Economic Committee of the Congress and the Brookings Institution must be treated with caution because they favor defense cuts, yet the substance of Clayton's analysis is based upon a Department of Defense publication, *The Economics of Defense Spending: A Look At The Realities* (1972).[1] Additionally, in a source cited by Clayton—Rosen's *Testing the Theory of the Military-Industrial Complex*[2]—various social scientists employing quantitative methods reach conflicting conclusions. The editor, however, maintains that C. Wright Mills' formulation of the Military-Industrial Complex, in *The Power Elite*,[3] still stands up remarkably well after 18 years of often critical and searching analysis. Hence, in calling upon liberal and radical critics of the warfare state to give up their politically and ideologically biased impressionism in favor of "objective measurement," Clayton distorts what other scholars have done, what he is doing, and what is possible through quantification.

Several points concerning Clayton's approach can and should be made. First, in gauging welfare versus warfare, the analysis should be kept to federal budgets, since local and state spending have virtually nothing to do with national security per se. Second, sources of revenue as well as spending on the federal level must be considered in any analysis. When revenue as well as budgets are reviewed, the assertion that welfare budgets have risen dramatically and defense spending has dropped drastically appears in a different light. My calculations concerning revenue versus expenditures are drawn from a Brookings Institution volume.[4] On the civilian side of federal expenditures, by far the greatest increase has occurred in the area of cash transfers (that is, social security and related programs, civil service and railroad retirement, veterans' benefits, aid to the aged, blind, disabled and families with dependent children, and other assistance, but not, I stress, spending for Medicare and Medicaid, food stamps, housing, grants for education, health, manpower efforts, or revenue sharing). In 1950, these cash outlays totaled $6.7 billion, or 15.2 percent of the federal budget; in 1974, estimated expenditures are for $81.3 billion or 30.3 percent of the budget. However, the overwhelming percentage of increase in cash transfers between 1950 and 1974 has been covered by growing social insurance taxes. Social insurance taxes accounted for 59.7 percent of all federal cash transfers in 1950, 98.9 percent in 1970, and an estimated 96.2 percent in 1974. And, whereas in 1950 only 18.8 percent of cash transfers were tied to recipient contribution, in 1974, 70.5 percent of cash transfers were related to recipient contributions. The famous, or infamous, federal contribution of Aid to Families with Dependent Children totaled about one-third of 1 percent of cash transfers in 1950, and has risen to only 5 percent in 1974.

Most of the increase in so-called federal welfare spending, therefore, has been financed by one of the nation's most regressive taxes (disguised as social insurance in order to make it palatable to the public) at a time when the percentage of federal revenue from corporation and excise taxes has been dropping sharply and income taxes have been steadily reduced. Since this is the case, welfare versus warfare in federal budgets looks different if we eliminate as spending all cash transfers covered by social insurance contributions. When this is done, defense and defense-related spending (which includes outlays for space and foreign affairs but not the Atomic Energy Commission, veterans benefits, or interest on defense and war debts, and hence is a conservative calculation) constituted 46 percent of the federal budget in 1950 and will constitute an estimated 46.6 percent in 1974. To me, these figures indicate that funeral orations for the defense community are somewhat premature.

My second line of criticism involves, as they say in the behaviorist business, power models. Implicit in Clayton's discussion is the pluralist, as opposed to the elitist, power model. As a matter of fact, Clayton goes much further than many enthusiastic pluralists when he contends that "early in the Cold War years" the large defense establishment stemmed from public demand. Nonetheless, it is fashionable today among advocates of a pluralist model to admit that a defense community involving some of the nation's major corporations, the federal executive, and the armed services does exist, but to assert, as Clayton implies, that such a power grouping is only one of many pressure groups vying for benefits and favor. Hence, a Military-Industrial Complex is balanced off against a medical complex, an educational complex, a welfare complex, and the like.[5] I find this type of reasoning exceedingly flimsy. Medical and educational establishments, like labor unions, do have power, but they do not include U.S. corporate giants, do not involve the concentrated power and clout of the armed services, are not covered by the mantle of national security, and are not tied in with the nation's foreign policy and foreign involvement which spreads across the globe. On this last point, Clayton notes that only about 10 percent of corporate capital is invested abroad. As of 1969 that was true, but what he fails to note is that this figure has doubled since 1950. According to available data, nearly 30 percent of the aggregate foreign investment is held by only 16 of the nation's top industrial corporations, and 13 of these 16 corporations receive more than 40 percent of the nation's total foreign income. Finally, on the average, 25-30 percent of total sales, assets, and earnings of the nation's leading 25 corporations are transacted abroad. Clayton also fails to point out that this development also involves armaments. Significant and frightening linkages exist between U.S. multinational corporations and top defense contractors and these firms' dominant or substantial investment in foreign defense companies. To the degree that a Military-Industrial Complex exists at home, it appears to be expanding from a national to an international base.[6] And while this multinational phenomenon includes mostly developed countries, it also indirectly involves developing countries as suppliers of raw materials to the industrial nations.

Let us return to the national scene. Comparing educational, medical, and welfare groupings with the defense establishment is invidious in ways other than that suggested above. Resources and power invested in education and medicine promise, if they do not fulfill, a better life for more people. Resources and power devoted to defense and war may provide for national security, but they also threaten to destroy civilization. Regardless of current events, a blatantly escalated and blatantly lethal arms race with the Soviet Union remains possible, and the existing defense system remains extraordinarily hazardous. (Clayton notes, however, that the post-World War II reconstruction of Western Europe and Japan are an example of the positive spin-off of a warfare state. I can only respond by saying that such a result involves quite a price to pay for progress, financially and ethically.) Moreover, while the man-in-the-street has a way, crude though it may be, of measuring the need for education, medicine, and welfare, and how well existing programs in those areas work, he has no way of knowing how much defense is essential and how well the nation's defense system functions. (Although the national security state as we know it, paradoxically, cannot withstand a prolonged war like that of Vietnam, principally because the nature and values of that system are laid bare to scrutiny and criticism.)

Current budgets illustrate the mystique and sacrosanct quality of defense spending. The defense community has weathered the withering criticism generated by the Vietnamese War combined with budgetary crises and the spirit of detente with amazing resilience. U.S. military managers have stretched out procurement schedules and cut back manpower without modifying in any meaningful way the nature of the defense system. Existing budgets stand somewhere around 6.8 percent of the GNP and most likely will remain there or grow throughout the decade. The Department of Defense notwithstanding, cost overruns, generous profits, waste reaching perhaps as high as 25 percent of budgets, and often poor or useless products will also probably continue.

Additionally, Clayton's notion that defense spending is unrelated to inflation is unsupportable. The current inflationary spiral which began around 1967-68 is clearly related to defense spending and the "guns and butter" political decisions stemming from the Vietnamese War which were intended to check the erosion of public support for a war effort that was becoming highly unpopular and suspect. Once inflation was set off, defense spending, much more than welfare expenditures, has fed inflationary fires principally because in terms of forward and backward linkages military output is much less tied into the nation's production and distribution system than are goods purchased by consumers. Furthermore, the effects of national security are not easily confined simply to munitions production. The skyrocketing price of petroleum products stems at least in part from private-public policies worked out under the aegis of national security. Likewise, wheat, diplomacy, and war have been closely intertwined in the last few years. Fuel and food lead the list in runaway prices today.

Clayton is no doubt right that American opinion concerning the military and potential enemies has changed dramatically. But those changes have not been reflected significantly in defense appropriations. Unlike defense programs, however, social welfare projects are constantly scrutinized, criticized, and, quite often, disestablished. When the current administration faced a budget crunch for fiscal year 1974, it chose to cut social spending instead of increasing taxes or reducing military expenditures to any great extent—a process of warfare on welfare, as it were.[7]

My third line of criticism involves warfare, welfare, and social systems. Few would question Clayton's contention that capitalism has no monopoly on warfare, although who originates cold or hot wars is far from conclusive. The Soviet Union has as potent a Military-Industrial Complex as that of the United States.[8] Hence, such power gropings do not stem from social systems alone. Nevertheless, when we look at the U.S. military establishment over time, what becomes clear is that it has gradually evolved during at least the last three-quarters of a century. Modern warfare has dictated an intricate institutional adjustment process involving corporations, the military services, and a growing regulatory state, to say nothing of lesser institutions. Even when military budgets were comparatively small, during the interwar years, that adjustment process went on apace. It only reached its most accelerated phase during and after World War II. Viewed in this historical context, Clayton's notion that a warfare or national security state appears and disappears according to some arbitrary budget figure becomes most questionable. It is like asserting that a mature industrial system ceases to exist if the annual growth in the GNP falls below 3 percent, 6 percent, 10 percent, or any other random figure. Massive institutional arrangements simply do not come and go like the tides.

Clayton's analysis, however, ignores more than the institutional adjustments of modern warfare; it also ignores reality. According to his analysis, the intense agony this nation went through over the Vietnamese War between 1968 and 1972 had nothing to do with warfare because defense spending did not reach 10 percent of the GNP or some other quantitative measure of reality. American fighting men, the people of Indochina, the Kent and Jackson State students, and countless other Americans will no doubt be relieved to hear that their death, their wounds, and their heartbreak were all a figment of the imagination of the Eisenhowers, the Mills, and the impressionistic liberal and radical scholars.

Turning briefly from social systems and warfare to social systems and welfare, several observations are in order. Clayton's assertion that "virtually all historians and economists accept the *Welfare* State" as an accurate description of the New Deal is far from correct. More and more historians are beginning to view the New Deal as a modest rescue operation for a foundering corporate economy.[9] Since the 1930s, the United States' so-called welfare system, while exhibiting some humane aspects, could be described more accurately as a government-administered program for underwriting the future of a mature corporate capitalist system. Through a generally regressive taxation system and a very regressive social security system, the state insures the minimum consumption level the economy requires. By and large, the masses end up paying themselves for the welfare benefits received. Because this is the case, in this country and other modified capitalist countries with even more elaborate social welfare systems than our own, little progress has been made in altering significantly the distribution of wealth. Some movement usually takes place in the income positions of the very poorest and the very richest elements of the society, but the degree of change is remarkably slight. A skewed distribution of income appears to be endemic to capitalism.[10]

In the light of the discussion above, the welfare-warfare paradigm set up by Clayton must be judged misleading and even irrelevant. So-called welfare comes out of the pocketbook of the masses, but with some return to most. Defense expenditure, at whatever level, also comes out of the pocketbook of the masses, but, to the degree that it is excessive, the interests of the mass are not served and the continued existence of the mass may be threatened. Where welfare and warfare spending may relate, however, is in the purpose of supporting the economic system. That welfare expenditures help support the economy goes without saying. Whether the economy could prosper, let alone survive, without defense spending is still a very open and hotly debated issue.

My remarks on welfare, warfare, and social systems now come to the very heart of my criticism of Clayton's essay. He has carried out his examination in a vacuum. Both welfare and warfare must be examined not only through budgets but also through the total operations of an enormously complex society within an enormously complex world. When an examination of warfare and welfare is reduced to shibboleths, simplistic thinking, or facile observations, the whole nation can suffer. The election campaign of 1972 was carried out largely around slogans and distortions involving defense and welfare, and some of the techniques of warfare, with results that have practically paralyzed the nation today. The warfare state is more than figures; it is also a way of life and a reflection of values. Perhaps one of the cruelest injuries perpetrated upon this nation by the national security mentality is the destruction of language. When blatant aggression becomes labeled "reinforced protective reaction raids,"[11] then the vital requirement of communication has been dealt a severe blow. The same holds true for welfare. When those in genuine need are stigmatized as failures when measured against the demands of the rugged individual image, then the sense of community which is imperative for the real welfare of us all has also been greviously damaged.

My last line of criticism is reserved for Clayton's last sentence: "This exploding Welfare State phenomenon, rather than the waning Warfare State, ought now to take center stage among historians interested in the contemporary era." Even if all of Clayton's assumptions were valid, I maintain that the historian's task would not be that of dropping warfare for welfare. What exists today has its roots in a past we still know much too little about. To adapt the phraseology of our commander-in-chief, let the behaviorists wallow in the instant analysis of today's headlines. The historian has more important work to do: to give depth and breadth to today's headlines, depth through an examination of the past, and breadth through a comparison of this nation's culture with that of other nations and peoples. Such a task, in my estimation, is absolutely essential, fully worthwhile, and entirely noble.

NOTES

1. U.S., Assistant Secretary of Defense (Comptroller), *The Economics of Defense Spending: A Look At The Realities*, by Robert C. Moot (Washington, D.C.: Department of Defense (Comptroller), 1972).

2. Steven Rosen, ed., *Testing the Theory of the Military-Industrial Complex* (Lexington, Mass.: D. C. Heath, 1973).

3. Mills, *The Power Elite* (New York: Oxford University Press, 1956).

4. Edward R. Fried, et al., *Setting National Priorities: The 1974 Budget* (Washington, D.C.: Brookings Institution, 1973), pp. 5, 7, 69.

5. See, for example, Charles Wolf, Jr., "Military-Industrial Simplicities, Complexities and Realities," in *The Military-Industrial Complex: A Reassessment*, ed. Sam C. Sarkesian (Beverly Hills, Calif.: Sage, 1972), pp. 25–52.

6. Thomas E. Weisskopf, "United States Foreign Private Investment: An Empirical Survey," in *The Capitalist System: A Radical Analysis of American Society*, ed. Richard C. Edwards, Michael Reich, and Thomas E. Weisskopf (Englewood Cliffs, N.J.: Prentice-Hall, 1972), pp. 426–35; and Jonathan F. Galloway, "Multinational Corporations and Military-Industrial Linkages," in *Testing the Theory of the Military-Industrial Complex*, ed. Steven Rosen (Lexington, Mass.: D. C. Heath, 1973), pp. 267–90.

7. Fried, et al., *The 1974 Budget*, pp. 1–22, 290–408.

8. Vernon V. Aspaturian, "The Soviet Military-Industrial Complex—Does It Exist?" *Journal of International Affairs* 26 (1972): 1–28. See also "Editor's Forward," p. xiv; Roman Kolkowicz, "Strategic Elites and Politics of Superpower," pp. 40–59; Walter Darnell Jacobs, "Soviet Strategic Effectiveness," pp. 60–72; and William T. Lee, "The 'Politico-Military-Industrial Complex' of the U.S.S.R.," pp. 73–86, all in *Journal of International Affairs* 26 (1972).

9. Otis L. Graham, Jr., "The Age of the Great Depression, 1929–1940," in *The Reinterpretation of American History and Culture*, ed. William H. Cartwright and Richard L. Watson, Jr. (Washington, D.C.: National Council for the Social Studies, 1973), pp. 491–508. See also Ronald Radosh, "The Myth of the New Deal," in *A New History of Leviathan: Essays on the Rise of the American Corporate State*, ed. Ronald Radosh and Murray N. Rothbard (New York: E. P. Dutton, 1972), pp. 146–87.

10. Edwards, "Who Fares Well in the Welfare State? " in *The Capitalist System*, ed. Edwards, Reich, and Weisskopf, pp. 244–51; Fried, et al., *The 1974 Budget*, pp. 40–43.

11. Stuart H. Loory, *Defeated: Inside America's Military Machine* (New York: Random House, 1973), pp. 338–41.

6

THE POLITICAL ECONOMY OF WARFARE IN THE UNITED STATES

I

The political economy of warfare in the United States is simply too broad and complex to analyze in depth in a relatively brief essay. Some sense can be made of the subject, however, by treating in some detail one of the nation's wartime situations while making relevant comparisons or contrasts with other periods of hostility.

World War I was selected as the period for more extended treatment because, by comparison with other wartime situations, it lends itself more readily to clear explication. The Revolutionary War requires dealing with an extremely complicated and confusing emergence, and often intertwining, of institutions in the political, economic, and military spheres. The Civil War, while less intricate than the revolutionary period, still involves focusing upon 23 states in the Union as well as the federal government—to say nothing of the Confederacy—and, hence, also becomes quite tangled. Since society and its institutions were more complex during World War II than during World War I, the period of the earlier war has the advantage in terms of clarity of analysis. Finally, to have concentrated the focus upon the Cold War years would have contradicted this writer's own conviction that the post-World War II period can only be understood when viewed in historical perspective.

The following is based on a seminar report delivered at the Charles Warren Center for Studies in American History, Harvard University, January 15, 1975.

II

Before getting into the analysis of warfare, let us examine the scholar and the study of war in the United States. The enormous trauma of World War I generated intense effort on the part of scholars and other analysts to develop a better understanding of warfare as a means of resolving international conflict. Perhaps the best known products of this inquiry are the over 100 volumes written under the aegis of the Carnegie Endowment for International Peace and the University of Chicago study, which resulted in the publication of Quincy Wright's *A Study of War*.[1] Much less familiar to scholars is a plethora of studies about war and defense policies written during the interwar years that focused almost exclusively upon the U.S. experience. Most of these works, along with the prolific output of the Nye Committee, have been largely ignored since shortly after they were published.[2] This phenomenon can be attributed to the influence of World War II and the Cold War. These interwar publications have been dismissed by most traditionalists as another manifestation of the United States' lost weekend of interwar isolation and, therefore, considered unworthy of serious consideration. For scholars and the American public, the ignoring of this body of work has been a misfortune. Various of these studies raised many of the vital issues involving war, defense, and national interests that plague our society today.

I am not referring to polemical literature like Helmuth C. Engelbrecht and Frank C. Hanighen's *Merchants of Death: A Study of the International Armament Industry*.[3] Instead, I have in mind, to cite a few, Mauritz H. Hallgren, *The Tragic Fallacy: A Study of America's War Policies*[4] and three works by Charles A. Beard: *The Navy: Defense or Portent?, The Idea of National Interest: An Analytical Study in American Foreign Policy,* and *The Open Door at Home: A Trial Philosophy of National Interest.*[5] As a result of studies like these, and under the stimulus of the outbreak of World War II, the American Historical Association in 1940 devoted its Annual Meeting primarily to the topic of war, with some of the better papers published in a volume edited by Jesse D. Clarkson and Thomas C. Cochran.[6]

From this scholarly ferment concerning warfare during the interwar years came the first full-scale study of war and military institutions considered within the context of the entire American experience: Harold and Margaret Sprout's *The Rise of American Naval Power, 1776-1918* and a companion volume, *Toward a New Order of Seapower: American Naval Policy and the World Scene, 1918-1922.*[7] The Sprouts' study served as an inspiration for Walter Millis's *Arms and Men: A Study in American Military History*, a work which has held up remarkably well over the years as a comprehensive analysis of warfare and American society.[8] Following Millis's book by one year was Samuel P. Huntington's *The Soldier and the State: The Theory and Politics of Civil-Military Relations.*[9] Then in 1960 came Morris Janowitz's *The Professional Soldier: A Social and Political Portrait.*[10] The last three volumes are by a journalist-scholar, a political scientist, and a sociologist, respectively. In terms of sweep of coverage and level of insight, no historian has yet matched the quality of these individual books. Nonetheless, a new generation of post-World War II historians, including Weigley, Coffman, Shy, Karsten, Kohn, and others, are constantly breaking new ground in the study of the military, war, and the American experience, with Weigley's work being the most comprehensive to date. Perhaps what began during the interwar years, in the last measure, was not lost effort.

III

Turning from the literature of warfare to the subject of warfare itself, I will now take up the four criteria, set forth in Chapter One, as the determining forces for how the nation mobilized its economy. For each category, I will first deal with World War I and then establish how other wartime situations differed from that war. Then, after digressing briefly from my analysis of the political economy of warfare to comment on Civil War bibliography, I will return to the principal theme and present a quite extensive analysis of mobilizing the economy for World War I. The report will conclude with a few observations about the operations of the so-called Military-Industrial Complex in the post-World War II years.

First, the maturity of the economy: By 1917, the United States had a mature industrial economy characterized by a high degree of concentration and consolidation of economic power. While hundreds of thousands of corporations existed in the nation, several hundred corporations, and particularly those in the vital sector of heavy industry, clearly dominated the nation's economic system. In 1909, the 200 largest non-financial corporations accounted for 41 percent of the gross assets of all non-financial corporations. By 1929, when statistical information about the nation's economic structure is much better, 100 corporations, according to cautious estimates, legally controlled 44 percent of the net capital assets of all manufacturing firms. Such highly concentrated economic power vitally affected industrial mobilization for both world wars. That same consolidating process also affected the nature of the United States' post-World War II "national security state." By 1962, 100 corporations had expanded their control of all capital assets of manufacturing firms to 58 percent.[11] Moreover, the growth of U.S. multinational corporations after 1945, and especially since 1965-67, has created an international, rather than just a national, dimension to the U.S. "defense" posture.[12]

By comparison with 1917, the nation in 1776 had a pre-industrial economy with a vast majority of the nation's population involved in agrarian pursuits. The 13 colonies/states did not even constitute an integrated economy. About six economically functional geographic regions tended to have more contact with the outside world than they did with one another because of extremely poor modes of overland transportation and differing relations with the mother country prior to 1776. Consequently, one of the central tasks facing revolutionary America in terms of economic mobilization was the necessity of attempting to get the varying independent economies to work together for a common cause. To a limited degree, interregional cooperation was accomplished by merchants who served as private businessmen or as public officials and, quite often, as both simultaneously—a condition that led to gross irregularities. Nonetheless, enormously difficult transportation problems combined with the vagaries of currency created immense obstacles in the way of economic coordination, let alone integration.

By 1860, the North had a rigorously competitive and diversified economy; and with the exceptionally rapid growth of the railroad system east of the Mississippi in the decade before the Civil War, that economy was already quite well integrated. Industrialization was also already well advanced in the New England and Middle Atlantic states.

The maturity of the economy and the magnitude and relative success of economic mobilization during various periods of hostility are indicated by some statistical computations. Available figures on the cost of war, war revenue (primarily taxation), rate of inflation, war expenditures as a percentage of total wartime GNP, and revenue as a percentage of spending are presented in Table 1.[13] Statistics are either unavailable or too unreliable to include the Revolutionary War in that table. However, E. James Ferguson has estimated total war costs in specie at between $158-$168 million, and total war revenue at $65,056,917. With revenue accounting for about 40 percent of costs, the remainder of the expenditures were covered by depreciating currency, repudiated currency, lost, destroyed, or unredeemed currency and certificates of debt, the impressment of goods, and unpaid assessments made against the states after the war. Currency of all kinds to 1781 depreciated at rates that ultimately made it practically useless.[14] Jumping from the first years of the republic to the present, rough estimates place military spending between 1946 and 1974 at about $1.5 trillion.[15] Such sustained and lavish expenditures during "peacetime" are new in the American experience and simply do not lend themselves to the categorization offered in Table 1. In one way or another, naturally, all of these expenditures have or will come out of revenue, and especially taxation, and unquestionably have been a major source of inflation in key periods since World War II.

Now to take up the second criterion: the size, strength, and scope of the federal government. By 1917, the national government had clearly eclipsed the states in terms of power, and it was beginning to expand its role as economic regulator and also to a degree as social welfare agent. But among the branches of the federal government, while the executive was beginning to emerge as supreme, the legislature was still formidable and responsible within its proper sphere. Since World War I, and especially since the 1930s, the executive branch

TABLE 1

Comparative Wartime Statistics
(billions of dollars)

Period	Cost of War	Total Wartime GNP	War Cost as % of GNP	War Revenue	War Revenue as % of War Cost	Wholesale Price Increase (index of 100)	GNP, Selected Years
Civil War, 1861-66	3.54	34.97[a] 34.01[c]	10.1 10.4	0.9885	27.9	100-190 (215, 1865)	6[b] (1865)
World War I, 1917-20	38.00	260.00	14.6	13.7000	36.0	100-181	49.9 (1917)
World War II, 1942-46	301.50	995.90	30.3	121.1000	40.1	100-138	161.6 (1942)

Note: Without getting into all of the complexity and controversy involving economic growth during the Civil War era, I am, at best, offering some very crude estimates in order to facilitate comparison of the Civil War with other wartime periods.

[a]This is a calculation based on Robinson source (see note b) and on Simon Kuznets' estimated average annual growth of 1.99 percent for the GNP during the decade 1859-69: "Notes on the Pattern of U.S. Economic Growth," in *The Reinterpretation of American Economic History*, ed. Robert W. Fogel and Stanley L. Engerman (New York: Harper & Row, 1971), pp. 17-24.

[b]Marshall A. Robinson, "Federal Debt Management: Civil War, World War I, and World War II," *American Economic Review, Papers and Proceedings of the Sixty-seventh Annual Meeting of the American Economic Association* 45, pt. 2 (May 1955): 389.

[c]This is a calculation based on Robinson source (see note b) and an estimated growth of the Union economy at 4 percent annually, a figure slightly less than Kuznets (see note a) establishes for the entire nation during the decades 1849-59 and 1869-79.

Source: All statistics, unless otherwise indicated are from Charles Gilbert, *American Financing of World War I* (Westport, Conn.: Greenwood, 1970), pp. 224-32.

has expanded its power enormously at the expense of the legislative branch. This development would have far-reaching consequences for economic mobilization during World War II and for "defense" policies in the post-World War II years.

During the Revolutionary War, while the Continental Congress assumed leadership in the conduct of the war, the states always played a significant and, at times, dominant role. Both at the state and congressional levels the antipathy to executive power remained strong. Nevertheless, to meet the exigencies of war mobilization, the Continental Congress increasingly delegated power to essentially executive agencies of its own making—most significantly, the creation of the office of the secretary of finance in 1781. Filling that office, Robert Morris adopted economic policies favorable to and favored by the mercantile community, supposedly in order to rescue the failing war effort. Ironically, most of Morris's conservative economic reforms were instituted after Yorktown, when hostilities had practically ceased.

With the outbreak of the Civil War, the states carried a major part of the burden of economic mobilization throughout 1861 because of the debilitated state of the national government. Thereafter, power passed to Washington. Although wartime finances made the Treasury Department of key importance, the War and Navy Departments, especially the former under Edwin M. Stanton, emerged as the principal mobilization agencies. In this role those departments were remarkably efficient, and their activities were largely free of the waste and corruption that characterized the Revolutionary War. Contrary to the suggestion of several historians, a World War II-type war production board, besides being politically and administratively unfeasible, was unnecessary during the Civil War.[16] With a competitive economy, the existing military departments, unlike those in the twentieth century, could procure and contract for the required goods and services without either elaborate economic controls or the assistance and expertise of the business community. Only in the case of the railroads, which had been organized as modern corporations, was it imperative for the War Department to integrate businessmen into its structure. Railway executives within the department were necessary in order to use and control for war purposes a transportation system that had already become huge in size and sophisticated in structure. Significantly, the Lincoln administration's experience with the railroads, not the larger mobilization program, anticipated very accurately what industrial mobilization for modern warfare would require in the future.

The absence of elaborate economic controls during the Civil War contrasts with twentieth-century warfare; the absence of such controls also contrasts with that of the Revolutionary War and the Confederacy. Both revolutionary and Confederate leaders attempted centralized control of their economies. Weak political and economic institutions, by sharp contrast with the two world wars, consistently undermined these endeavors. The South's mobilization program, no doubt, suffered additionally from the limited quality and quantity of its merchant class, a condition which did not exist in either the North or during the Revolutionary War period.

Despite the growth of national power at the expense of the states during the Civil War in the North, state governments still continued to play an active and vital role in most aspects of economic mobilization until the conclusion of hostilities. Throughout the war years, the power of the states was significantly less than during the Revolutionary War but considerably more than in the twentieth century. (The Civil War provides a superb opportunity, unexploited to date, for studying directly the operations of both economic and political power at the state level and, indirectly, at the federal level as well. Most governors organized executive and advisory staffs to help them carry out their responsibilities during the war. Those staffs often read like a *Who's Who* for the state and the nation.)

Also of significance during the Civil War was the role played by Congress, which then, by contrast with the period after 1940, played an active role in the conduct of defense and war matters. It was alert to its responsibilities, it demanded to be kept informed concerning the war effort, and it exercised its powers in a judicious but firm fashion. The Committee on the Conduct of the War was not the bête noire often portrayed by historians. Its relations with the Lincoln administration were not uniformly bad, its activities were constitutional, and it served as an effective agency for helping to maintain congressional prerogatives during wartime. Most importantly, the committee refused to suspend its judgment in deference to asserted military expertise, and it rejected any assertion of executive privilege in the area of national security.

For all intents and purposes, the conclusion of the Civil War marked the end of formal state influence in formulating national military policy. The Enrollment Act of 1863 in theory freed Washington from reliance upon the states for raising an army. Although a volatile political climate in the North prevented Lincoln's vigorous use of the draft, the federal government in the twentieth century could conscript even "peacetime" armies without difficulty until recently. Furthermore, after the Civil War, the states maintained their militias, now renamed the National Guard, only at the price of granting effective control over them to the federal government. With Congress in the twentieth century gradually surrendering the initiative in military affairs to the executive, the founding fathers' inspiration for maintaining civilian control over the military by dividing authority over it between branches and levels of government has been drastically altered.

This discussion leads to my third category: the character and structure of the military services and their relationship to civil society and authority. This category is the most difficult to deal with briefly because of the complexities involved. Some grasp of civil-military relations in general is essential before the impact of those relations on economic mobilization can be appreciated. The present discussion will be restricted to some comments about overall civil-military relations for the various periods involved. In my more detailed discussion of World War I, I will attempt to demonstrate, for this one warfare situation, how the larger issue of the interaction between the civilian and military worlds affected the political economy of warfare.

Throughout World War I, civilian dominance over the military remained secure. Woodrow Wilson, while not personally taking an active role in matters of strategy, did maintain in his office the decision-making authority over the military. Although Newton D. Baker as secretary of war was not a strong leader, he was an exceptionally capable conciliator who consistently acted to mollify the various squabbling factions in his department. Josephus Daniels, by contrast, was both unorthodox and tough as secretary of the navy. Additionally, Congress, through its statutory authority over the military's structure and budgets, kept a vigilant eye on the armed services. Finally, officers of both services were still firmly wedded to the traditional notion of civilian supremacy. In circumstances where civilian control over the armed services was not as tight as it should have been, intra-service tension facilitated civilian control. Wilson and Baker, for example, granted General John J. Pershing exceptional latitude in both military and diplomatic matters as head of the American Expeditionary Force (AEF). Suspicion and real or imagined rivalry between Pershing and Chief of Staff Peyton O. March, however, necessitated the constant intervention of both Baker and Wilson in order to maintain reasonable harmony between two exceptionally strong leaders and their staffs. Also, when Pershing, acting on past precedents and assuming powers he had not been granted, attempted to set terms for the armistice, Wilson and Baker moved swiftly and emphatically to establish their precedence. The AEF commander quickly backed off.

During the American Revolution, with most of the population wedded to the tradition of the civilian-soldier, the United States, ironically, came closer to the usurpation of power by the military than at any other time in its history. During periods of economic and military distress, conservatives both within and outside the military more than once sought to persuade George Washington to assume extraordinary, if not dictatorial, power as commander of the nation's armies. The aborted Newburgh conspiracy dramatically demonstrated the desperate irresponsibility of various conservative elements. Beyond question, substantial and sustained abuse of military power at any time during the Revolutionary War would have destroyed absolutely the precarious bonds holding the states and the people together. Exploiting to the maximum the numerous differences among the revolutionaries, it should be noted, was a continuing element of British military and political policy from 1775 to 1783. Most important, however, is that if the military constituted even a potential threat to civilian authority, then that threat stemmed not so much from the strength of the armed forces as from the weakness of all institutions during that time of crisis, when serious divisions existed over the nature and role of the nation's institutions then and in the future.

President Lincoln, during the conduct of the Civil War, gradually and masterfully worked out as effective a civilian-military command structure as the nation has ever witnessed, either before or since. Once the president found his commander in General Ulysses S. Grant, he quickly and clearly delineated the proper spheres of power and function between the secretary of war and the commanding general, all the while maintaining in his own office the final authority. Moreover, Lincoln stands almost alone among modern leaders in devising the appropriate military strategy for achieving the desired national policy goals without allowing the remorseless nature of warfare to get out of control. As I have suggested above, however, Congress, and the states as well, set definite limits upon Lincoln's role as commander-in-chief. In view of those realities, Lincoln's achievement appears all the greater.

During World War II, unlike previous wars, Congress largely surrendered its responsibilities in the military area to the executive. Moreover, and more importantly, Franklin D. Roosevelt, in conjunction with the Joint Chiefs of Staff, and at the expense of other highly placed civilian officials, largely determined not only major strategic policies but significant diplomatic matters as well. Although scholars differ over the degree to which the State Department was eclipsed as a source of power in formulating World War II foreign policy, certainly the armed services acquired more influence in that area than ever before in the nation's history.[17] Additionally, operating with wide latitude from 1941 to 1945, the military as early as 1941 began preparing for its postwar role in terms of plans, structure, and weapons. The freewheeling nature of the armed forces in the years after World War II, by contrast with the past, has actually been a continuation of World War II activity, not a departure from it.

The conduct of World War II, it should be pointed out, grew out of prewar conditions. Roosevelt's wartime leadership was an extension of the enormous power granted to the executive by the other branches of government during the 1930s to meet domestic, not foreign, crises. Additionally, the military's expanded role within the executive branch was also made possible by interwar developments. It was only during World War I that the army actually learned what a general staff was and how it should be used. In the 1920s and 1930s, the army and the navy capitalized on the wartime experience to plan for future hostilities. Hence the military, unlike during World War I, was fully prepared to exploit all opportunities for enhancing its influence and power during World War II.

The Vietnamese debacle and its manifold consequences both at home and abroad have impressed upon Congress the disastrous outcome of its witting or unwitting surrender of power to the executive in the area of defense and war. But even if Congress manages to balance the scales of power in the future, a return to pre-World War II, not to mention pre-World War I, conditions is impossible. U.S. commitments abroad, even if reduced, mean a substantial military establishment with a voice in the formulation of foreign policy. This fact, combined with the weapons revolution begun in the late nineteenth century and accelerated exponentially during World War II and after, has removed the possibility of establishing any clear and precise lines of demarcation between civilian and military affairs and has complicated enormously the problem of even defining, let alone implementing, civilian control over the military.

Our fourth and last category is the state of military technology. By the early twentieth century, scientific and technological progress had already advanced to the point where weapons of war could have been much more destructive and heinous than they actually were. Surprisingly, the inventive genius as applied to the "tools of war" was still quite restrained. Advances in transportation and communication, including the railroad and telegraph systems and steam-propelled vessels, were as important to combat as any weapon system per se, perhaps even more important. Nonetheless, the so-called naval revolution, with fleets of steam, steel, propeller, armor, and modern ordnance, was of great significance. For the land forces, continued progress in breech-loading and repeating weapons, the use of cartridges and shells, and the invention of smokeless powder in the 1880s, introduced fully the age of withering firepower, featuring the modern rifle, the machine gun, and various forms of artillery. Battlefield casualties also went up at an alarming rate as the accuracy of all weapons was improved by the introduction of new aiming devices. During World War I, airplanes, wheeled and tracked vehicles, modern submarines, poison gas, and the like were just making their debut on the fields of slaughter.

By comparison, weaponry during the Revolutionary War was quite unsophisticated. The basic weapon was the early seventeenth-century smoothbore, muzzle-loading, flintlock musket with bayonet. Artillery, also smoothbore and muzzle-loading, supplemented the small arm. These same weapons also served the navy. Moreover, while naval warships had their special design, it was not difficult to convert commercial vessels for limited forms of combat, such as commerce-raiding.

By 1861, weaponry had progressed much more in terms of improvements upon what had existed in the late eighteenth century, rather than along new lines of development. As I have already noted, inventions in the fields of transportation and communication were more significant than anything involving the actual expertise of killing. The smoothbore musket had been officially replaced by the rifled musket, which was now fired by the percussion cap instead of the flintlock. Rifled artillery was also standard weaponry. Although towards the end of the Civil War breech-loading and repeating rifles were introduced, much more refinement was essential before these instruments of death could become standard weapons for the line. For the navy, iron vessels, the armored monitors, and breech-loading artillery suggested the coming revolution in naval warfare. By the measure of weapons used and introduced and the use of new forms of land and sea transportation and communication, the Civil War is transitional when compared with warfare of both the Revolutionary Era and the twentieth century.

The Civil War is likewise transitional in terms of the nation's economic and political systems and the structure and operation of the military services and their interaction with civilian society.

World War II, of course, witnessed the full impact of the industrial and scientific revolutions as applied to weapons of land, air, and sea. Post-World War II trends have unloosed most of the restraints on weapons development, with the result that the very survival of civilization as we know it has become precarious.

The central and obvious point to be made about military technology is that is has advanced along with scientific and industrial development; such development, in some instances, has been accelerated by weaponry. In and of themselves, however, weapons have not dictated economic mobilization methods. During the Revolutionary War, when weapons were quite primitive, total control of the economy was tried, albeit unsuccessfully, in an attempt to bring unity to a disjointed economic system. With the Civil War, when military technology was more sophisticated, economic controls for the Union were limited because the economic and political systems were developed but not yet fully bureaucratized. During the twentieth century, practically the same elaborate mobilization structures were used, even though weaponry had advanced enormously between the wars. The sophistication of the economic and political systems had as much or more to do with the means for industrial mobilization as weapon systems per se. This is not to say that the "tools of war" were unimportant in terms of twentieth-century political economy. On the contrary, beginning in the late nineteenth century with the building of a modern navy, production teams consisting of military, political, and economic personnel had come into existence for war preparation. These teams would steadily grow in size, number, complexity, and power until a full-blown Military-Industrial Complex appeared during World War II, to continue in modified form in the postwar years.

IV

Of all the mobilization periods I have discussed, none is so barren in terms of secondary literature relevant to economic mobilization as the Civil War. Thomas C. Cochran's essay of 1961 challenging the Beard-Hacker thesis about the Civil War viewed as the "Second American Revolution"[18] should have precipitated a vigorous reexamination of the U.S. political economy in general and, more specifically, how economic policy during and after the war affected the composition of the economy's manufacturing and agricultural sectors, the distribution of income between sections and classes, technological innovation, economic growth or the lack thereof, and so forth. Instead, Cochran's article tended to mislead readers concerning what the Beards, if not

Hacker, actually said, and it also appears to have encouraged many readers to assume that, first, gauging economic growth is relatively simple and, second, once that growth was gauged, the results could readily be used to answer basic questions involving the structure and operation of total social systems.

Cochran's essay was inspired by Robert E. Gallman's commodity output figures (first published in 1960 and subsequently supplemented), which refined and expanded existing historical statistics.[19] Since the appearance of Cochran's essay, the debate over the Beard-Hacker thesis has not been advanced much. Even the most sophisticated scholars are reduced to cautious speculation about the economic consequences of the Civil War, not simply because the data are unavailable but also because a great deal have not been collected and analyzed.

Because econometric methods are still relatively new and controversial, the absence of studies employing the more elaborate quantitative techniques is understandable. But the lack of written history involving crucial issues traditionally within the historian's range is surprising. No general economic history of the Civil War exists. Some valuable studies of individual firms or industries that include the Civil War years are available, but no business history for the years 1860 to 1865 has ever been written. While numerous works treating in whole or in part with relations between the government and business, between branches of the national government, between the states and the federal government, and among the various states themselves do exist, most are marginal or outdated. On war mobilization in general, Fred A. Shannon's *The Organization and Administration of the Union Army, 1861–1865* is still the standard source.[20] William B. Hesseltine's *Lincoln and the War Governors* remains the best available examination of the war and U.S. federalism.[21] Both of these works are sound history, but both also cry out for revision, reworking, and updating.

Going from the general to the specific in Civil War historiography, two subjects deserve special mention: the Committee on the Conduct of the War and the activities of the states. The purview of the committee included many matters of significance during the years of hostility, and for this reason alone it should have attracted the keen attention of the historian. But it has not. Our perception of the committee is presumably based on T. Harry Williams' 1937 dissertation, several articles he published a few years later, and the abbreviated rendition of his findings and interpretation included in *Lincoln and the Radicals,*[22] as well as the earlier but more general work of other historians.[23] Williams' work is the only full-scale study, and his analysis has been questioned by other historians. Interpretations that differ from Williams' are presented in articles published by William W. Pierson, Jr. in 1918, and Hans L. Trefousse in 1965, but both of these essays are necessarily brief and, apparently, have not had much impact.[24] Until an updated and comprehensive study of the Committee on the Conduct of the War is written, historians, other scholars, and the reading public are at a disadvantage. The Committee on the Conduct of the War has become the standard measure of what a congressional committee should *not* be in assessing the performance of investigating committees during World War I, the interwar years, and World War II. That measure is questionable and will remain so until more in-depth scholarship involving the committee becomes available. For decades, the Nye Committee suffered from a negative image perpetrated by historians and others who knew little about the committee's activities and had not bothered to read its work. To the degree that the intent and achievements of the Nye Committee were unappreciated, the historian's grasp of economic mobilization for the world wars and developments during the interwar years was less than it should have been. The same evaluation may hold true for the Committee on the Conduct of the War and the Civil War, although probably not to the extent of that of the Nye Committee.

If the Committee on the Conduct of the War has been slighted by historians, then the Union states have suffered from gross neglect. A fine and comprehensive history exists for only one state, John Niven's *Connecticut for the Union: The Role of the State in the Civil War*.[25] Through a combination of works, a reasonably good coverage of Ohio, Indiana, Illinois, and Wisconsin, and the interaction of those states with the federal government, is available.[26] But, for the economically and politically key states of New York, Pennsylvania, and Massachusetts, the available studies are most inadequate.

The lack of recent and revised work on the Committee on the Conduct of the War and of first-rate scholarship on many of the states seriously detracts from our understanding of economic mobilization during the Civil War. Concerning that crucial subject and other topics of importance as well, significant scholarship exists in Ph.D. dissertations, M.A. theses, and articles in obscure journals. A historian would be doing the profession a worthy service simply by writing an essay calling the profession's attention to this material.

For the multi-volume accounts of the Civil War, Allan Nevins's *The War for the Union*, in four volumes, at least for my purposes, advances little beyond his predecessors.[27] The series which Nevins began editing, entitled *The Impact of the Civil War*, and which Harold M. Hyman has subsequently taken over, has had mixed results to date. Paul W. Gates' *Agriculture and the Civil War* is weak,[28] but this is not so for Hyman's *A More Perfect Union: The Impact of the Civil War and Reconstruction on the Constitution*.[29] While Hyman's volume is rather amorphous and meandering, and the organization and development of ideas as well as the writing leave something to be desired, he has written one of the most significant works on the Civil War period. By breaking free of the restraints of traditional constitutional history, Hyman has employed legal and constitutional issues to examine the Civil War and its place in

U.S. history in a fresh, perceptive, and exciting manner. If the other proposed volumes in *The Impact of the Civil War* series come even close to approximating Hyman's achievement, written history about the Civil War and the historical profession will indeed be enriched.

V

After this brief survey of U.S. wars and bibliographic interruption, I am now prepared to turn to the mobilization of the World War I economy. While various agencies were created during the war to deal with food and fuel, finances, and transportation, the War Industries Board (WIB), designed to harness the nation's economic power, was by far the most important.[30] The process of creating that agency involved enormous confusion, conflict, and resistance. In the end, the planning apparatus consisted of negotiated compromises, patchwork arrangements, piecemeal controls, unclear lines of authority, and obliterated lines of demarcation between civilian and military, private and public institutions. Nonetheless, the job was done and in relatively short order under the most trying circumstances.

The WIB, as it finally operated, was created by slow stages and through trial and error between mid-1915 and March 1918. Essentially, the board functioned as follows. The chairman, Barnard M. Baruch, and his staff, starting in March 1918 (operating on instructions and information from higher levels of government), collated the major requirements for the economy in terms of civilian, military, and foreign demand and determined the allocation of resources to facilitate the production of these requirements. Once these decisions were made, subdivisions of the board, called Commodity Committees or Commodity Sections, which consisted of representatives from one industry or a group of related industries, then implemented the decisions. Some 57 Commodity Committees existed in the board's system. In fulfilling their responsibilities, the Commodity Committees were advised by what were euphemistically called War Service Committees—in effect, trade associations which, in order to avoid the appearance of conflicts of interest, were technically not part of the board's formal structure and which financed their own operations.

Several key points about this Commodity Committee-War Service Committee system need to be made. In the first place, the committees not only served to implement the larger decisions rendered by the WIB involving production for civilian, military, and foreign use, but they also played a crucial role in making those decisions since they were practically the sole source of information about the economy's production capacity.

Secondly, while the board, the Wilson administration, and members of Congress tried to give the impression that conflicts of interest were minimized in the board's operation, such conflicts were standard operating procedure. For example, the Commodity Section on Rubber was headed by the president of the Fish Rubber Company. Most of the committee's members and staff came either from Fisk or other companies in the rubber industry. If a contract involving Fisk came before the committee, members of the company on the committee would absent themselves from the room while that contract was being considered so as to avoid the appearance of impropriety. Appearance and reality were far apart. Most businessmen in the WIB served for a nominal salary, or no salary, while maintaining their corporate affiliations. Moreover, in order to insure that the WIB made no decisions that did not have industry's approval, a Commodity Committee usually avoided making any major decision until it had the acquiescence of the War Service Committee or trade association advising it. While a Price Fixing Committee was established independent of the board to minimize abuse in contracting, it turned out to be less than a disinterested body. Those who sat on the committee were generally sympathetic to industry's point of view and were also committed to the proposition that maximizing production, not insuring equitable prices, was their primary function. Even if the members of the committee had been dedicated to the notion that excess profits should be minimized, there was not much they could do, since they operated in a situation in which industry, not the government, possessed most of the information necessary to determine what prices were essential to guarantee maximum production without price gouging. That profiteering was rampant during the war is beyond question and even admitted by industry members when they were under oath in postwar congressional investigations. What heights the profiteering reached will never be known fully. After World War I, 22 accountants spent five years auditing the records of the United States Steel Corporation and its subsidiaries to determine income, excess profits, and war profits just for the years 1917–18.

The third point to be made in terms of the WIB's operations is that it was dominated by the same huge corporations that maintained substantial control over the peacetime economy. Within the board, small and middle-sized firms were represented and had a voice in decision making, but in the major power plays these businesses could do little to protect their interests if they pitted themselves against the corporate giants.

In effect, the WIB was a significantly modified form of industrial self-regulation writ large. Industrialists and financiers served simultaneously as private and public representatives as they formulated and implemented the mobilization policies. Although they had a great deal of room for maneuvering, business leaders still operated within vaguely set and defined boundaries established by the Wilson administration, Congress, and the public. Those who glibly assert that the United States from 1917 to 1918 had a form of wartime socialism either consciously obfuscate or fail totally to grasp the nature and complexity of the nation's wartime political economy.

In the long and arduous process of devising the structure and operation of the WIB, the military, and particularly the War Department, proved to be the major obstacle to success. The difficulty stemmed from two sources. First, the War and Navy Departments and the Wilson administration operated on the assumption that, as during the Civil War, the military departments could act as the principal mobilization agencies. Second, the War Department was unable to conduct its own supply and procurement activities effectively.

Beginning in 1915, the Wilson administration created, under vague authority from Congress, the various civilian advisory mobilization agencies, the most important of which was the WIB. These agencies were intended only to assist the military services in carrying out their mobilization functions. In retrospect, the War and Navy Departments were incapable of serving as mobilization bodies because conditions had dramatically changed from the Civil War period. A mature industrial system required elaborate economic controls, which only civilian agencies like the WIB could formulate and institute, in order to mobilize its strength for war.

If the War Department, like the Navy Department, had had an efficient supply structure on the eve of World War I, then it would have become readily apparent that the military departments could not mobilize the economy. This reality was obscured by the blatant inadequacies of the army's supply system. During the post-Civil War nineteenth century, the armed services had gone through a professionalizing process, but, because of its isolation from, hostility to, and myopia about civilian America, the army, by contrast with the navy, had failed to appreciate the critically important idea that industrial might was essential to fulfilling its combat role. Had the army accepted this fact, it would have been prepared to work with an agency like the WIB before the onset of hostilities. Because the army had not done so, upon the outbreak of war the War Department suddenly became the nation's largest consumer when it was unprepared for such a crucial role. The department proceeded to dump billions of dollars of contracts upon a highly complex industrial system through its antiquated supply and procurement system without regard for the availability of facilities, manpower, transportation, power, and the like. While members of the WIB and the business community in general looked on with trepidation, they could do little more than protest, since Wilson depended primarily upon Secretary of War Baker for advice on economic mobilization. Baker was convinced that the war should be fought with the minimum amount of change in the nation's institutional structure. He also reflected the army's fear of losing its supply operations to civilians. Hence, the secretary of war tenaciously resisted either granting the advisory civilian mobilization agencies any real authority or reforming the War Department's disruptive supply and purchasing system.

In effect, several mobilization systems were proceeding simultaneously on different levels and with varying degrees of authority. Demand, as represented by the War Department and other purchasing agents, had the authority but not the ability to manage economic mobilization. Supply, as represented by the WIB, had the capability of acting as a comprehensive mobilization body, but it had only advisory powers. With demand always exceeding supply and neither adequately coordinated with the other, the only outcome could be growing chaos. And confusion mounted. By winter 1917, War Department procurement and WIB impotence had severely dislocated the economy.

Since the Wilson administration was unable to resolve the conflict between the WIB and the War Department because of internal squabbles and power struggles, Congress stepped in to remedy the situation. Key members of Congress, strongly influenced by members of the WIB, the Chamber of Commerce, and other business elements, threatened to remove supply functions completely from the army unless reform was instituted forthwith. Operating under that threat, the Wilson administration for the first time granted the WIB a substantial measure of authority. The War Department also began quickly to reorganize its supply and procurement systems to match those of the WIB's Commodity Committee system and to integrate its representatives, along with those of the other purchasing agents, into the board's structure. Once inside the WIB, military representatives quickly learned that civilians constituted no threat to their prerogatives. On the contrary, WIB personnel granted military members a fair share of authority within the board and demonstrated to the War and Navy Departments that they were fully committed to assisting the military in meeting its combat mission. Once the WIB's conflict with the military was resolved, the board was then able effectively to coordinate supply and demand during the emergency and operated with reasonable efficiency until the conclusion of hostilities.

Several observations about the WIB are in order.

First, the WIB's structure and staffing demonstrated that Progressive reforms in the area of political economy had not gone very far. Throughout the war, the government had to turn to businessmen for mobilizing the economy because it lacked the information, the organization, and the personnel to do the job itself. This is not to say, however, that the federal government was without power or simply served to grant legitimacy to private power in the form of the industrial community. The business community was far from being a homogeneous unit, and business leaders needed the authority of the government during the emergency to resolve conflict within their system, to hold recalcitrant members in line, and to gain acceptability from the public for their massive endeavor. Moreover, no matter to what degree the business community controlled the WIB, until the military services cooperated with the board, the board was largely impotent. The twentieth-century state as we know it today was still in its incipient stage on the eve of World War I. Since then the industrial community and the American public have come to know in dramatic ways that the national government has exercised and can exercise formidable power.

Second, industrial-military relations during World War I revealed some interesting and very significant trends both for the war itself and for the future. While angry and frustrated members of the business community were most anxious to remove procurement operations from the armed services, the more shrewd and perceptive business leaders realized that such a development would be most untoward. If military contracts had been placed directly in the hands of the WIB, then public outrage over industrialists negotiating among themselves billions of dollars of public contracts would unquestionably have forced major reforms and, more likely, the dissolution of the board. But, as long as the armed services maintained the legal right of contracting and adjusted themselves to the board's operations, distinctions between government and business operations were preserved and, in the process, the WIB's existence guaranteed.

Also of significance in terms of business-military relations during World War I was the attitude of industry toward the armed services' requirements. Throughout the war, business leaders never attempted to establish a system for reviewing military demand either in terms of the armed services' objectives or the potential of the economy. Why this was the case is not entirely clear. Three reasons suggest themselves. First, civilians were unwilling to place themselves in a position where they could be blamed for military failure because of inadequate weapons or material. Second, business leaders wanted to avoid any conflict with the armed services once the WIB began to function effectively after March 1918, because industry needed the military's cooperation in order to maintain the relatively free hand it had in conducting the board's affairs. Finally—and the least generous, but perhaps the most realistic, interpretation—management, contrary to numerous analysts, was extremely shortsighted. It either would not or could not focus on larger issues if such concerns threatened to interfere with the short-run maximization of profits and power. Whatever the case, a crisis over unexamined military requirements was averted during World War I only because of its quick end in 1918.

During World War II, however, the subject of military demand became a matter of paramount importance for the operations of the War Production Board (WPB), the WIB's counterpart. Throughout 1942, the military insisted upon the right to set its requirements at whatever level it determined to be necessary, without regard for the limits of the economy. Industrial leaders within the WPB, who were in the process of working out an alliance of mutual interest with the army and navy in conducting the board's affairs, once again made no move to counter the armed services' parochial outlook. With the entire economy in jeopardy, the WPB's Planning Committee stepped in to provoke what has since come to be called the "Feasibility Dispute." The Planning Committee consisted primarily of two scholars, Robert R. Nathan and Thomas

C. Blaisdell, Jr., and a construction engineer, Fred Searls, Jr. Simon Kuznets, the eminent statistician, and his staff assisted the committee. After months of argument and bureaucratic infighting, the Planning Committee in late 1942 finally impressed upon business and military leaders the indisputable truth that overloading the nation's economic system threatened to bring about economic disaster. While the Planning Committee succeeded in placing some limits on military demand, it did not achieve its more ambitious and important goal: the creation of a supreme war production council. This council would have been a war ministry superior to all other departments and agencies. With broad representation, it would establish, monitor, and enforce military, production, social, and political strategies. Had the Planning Committee's larger recommendations been implemented, U.S. war and postwar policies at home and abroad might well have been substantially different. However, modified power relations within the nation during the 1930s, if not even before, would have been essential preconditions for the success of the Planning Committee's proposals. Because of its efforts on behalf of rationalized military supply programs and fundamentally altered institutions for conducting the war, the Planning Committee shortly found itself relegated to a position of insignificance within the WPB's structure.

Third and finally, throughout and after World War I, numerous critics were distressed by the government's surrendering such vast power in its name to private interests with little or no check upon the operations of such groups. They also became alarmed about modern warfare forging an alliance between economic and military elements. This was especially true of Midwestern and Southern neo-Jeffersonians. However, both during and after the war, critics of the WIB found themselves caught on the horns of a cruel dilemma. Any realistic alternative to the WIB as a mode of economic mobilization involved either state capitalism or socialism. While these solutions were acceptable to some radicals, for the neo-Jeffersonians the state as a source of power was as much to be feared as the growing power of the corporation. Consequently, many of the latter group, after unsuccessfully exploring various substitutes for the WIB as a mobilization model, ultimately ended up opposing war and excessive preparation for hostilities during times of peace as the only sure means of avoiding the feared consequences of war, including what would later be termed a Military-Industrial Complex.

VI

The critics of the present-day political economy of warfare face conditions that make the problems and perceived threats of World War I appear much less threatening. Too often, however, many of those who look upon today's "national security state" with despair often confuse cause with effect; they attribute to the so-called Military-Industrial Complex a major responsibility for the Cold War and the United States' crusade against Communism and revolution in the developing world. That the mammoth military establishment, which incorporates or at least touches upon almost all institutions in U.S. society today, is a formidable force for perpetuating an expansionist and aggressive foreign policy and a lethal arms race is beyond question. But to assert that this multi-institutional complex of death originated the policies of imperialism and arms expansion is most questionable.

In the first place, the United States has been an expansionist nation since the late nineteenth and early twentieth centuries when, with the exception of World War I, its armed forces and military suppliers were relatively small in size and number. "Open Door" imperialism was predicated more upon the strength of the nation's economy and ideology than upon its military establishment. Second, for a complex set of reasons, even for several years after World War II, the nation's military system was substantial, although not gargantuan. Only with the real or assumed international perils that led to the adoption of NSC-68 in 1949-50 did the U.S. leadership fully embrace the proposition that massive military might was essential for maintaining the world community the United States sought. Third, the chief architects of the United States' post-1950 foreign policy and the military establishment to implement it have been principally neither the armed services nor the defense contractors and their numerous allies. Instead, the United States' Cold War imperial design has been shaped by a group of elite civilians who came to power during World War II, who remained in positions of power and influence for years thereafter, and who selected and trained proteges to carry on their tradition. Prominent among such men are Robert A. Lovett, Dean Acheson, James V. Forrestal, Harvey H. Bundy, Averell Harriman, William Clayton, John J. McCloy, and William Draper. During World War II and after, writes Richard J. Barnet,

> the temporary civilian managers who come to Washington to run America's wars and preparations for war [holding down "the very top jobs" as counselors to the president, secretaries of defense and state, secretaries of the three services, the chairman of the old Atomic Energy Commission, and the director of the CIA, or advising those who hold those posts] were so alike one another in occupation, religion, style, and social status that, apart from a few Washington lawyers, Texans, and mavericks, it was possible to locate the offices of all of them within fifteen city blocks in New York, Boston, and Detroit. Most of their biographies in Who's Who read like minor variations on a single theme—wealthy parents, Ivy-League education, leading law firm or bank (or entrepreneur in a war industry), introduction to government in World War II.[31]

While these "national security managers" have been motivated by a desire to preserve and expand U.S. economic interests abroad, their policies have hardly been cast in such a narrow mold. Basic to their thinking has been the notion that this nation has not only the ability but also the duty to impose a *Pax Americana* upon the world as the only hope for a civilized international community. Serving in the government while total victory was achieved during World War II and when the United States played a key role in the rebuilding and reconstructing of Europe and Japan, these men became accustomed to a level of success which they believed a nation as powerful and as principled as the United States should be able to achieve. Believing that their policies had been successful in containing the spread of Soviet Communism, they approached the task of controlling or squelching revolution in the developing countries with confidence, if not arrogance.

Advocates of power in the resolution of international conflict, fascinated, even obsessed, with the use, intricacies, and manipulation of power, these national security managers, operating from the highest levels of government, created the perfect environment for a Military-Industrial Complex to grow, prosper, and even take on power that has at times gone beyond the reach of the national security managers themselves.

Any attempt to control fundamentally the extraordinary power wielded by the MIC must start not with reforms in procurement or even cuts in the military budgets (although such developments can only be welcome and are long overdue). First the idea that the nation can and should play world policeman must be abandoned, and military solutions to what are essentially social, political, ideological, and economic issues must be foregone. This is not to propose a new form of isolationism or "fortress America," as Cold War hawks are so eager to charge. Instead, it means a foreign policy of sane and reasonable priorities for the world's major power, reasonable priorities that stand somewhere between attempting to ignore the world and attempting to mold the world in the American image. Whether such dramatic changes in our foreign policy are possible, given the structure of the U.S. political economy and its inextricable global ties, without a fundamental reordering of our entire social system is highly problematical.

NOTES

1. Wright, *A Study of War*, 2 vols. (Chicago: University of Chicago Press, 1942). The one-volume second edition of Wright's work, issued in 1965 by the same publisher, comments on war since 1942. Appendix 2 of this work lists and discusses briefly the various national and international war and peace study programs of the interwar years. See the 1965 edition, pp. 414–22.

2. For an excellent bibliography which makes reference to some of this literature, see Ronald Schaffer, comp., *The United States in World War I: A Selected Bibliography* (Santa Barbara, Calif.: Clio Press, 1978).

3. (New York, Dodd, Mead, 1934).

4. (New York: Alfred A. Knopf, 1937).

5. (New York: Harper and Brothers, 1932); (New York: Macmillan, 1934); and (New York: Macmillan, 1935), respectively.

6. *War as a Social Institution: The Historian's Perspective* (New York: Columbia University Press, 1941).

7. (Princeton, N.J.: Princeton University Press, 1939) and (Princeton, N.J.: Princeton University Press, 1946), respectively.

8. (New York: Putnan, 1956).

9. (Cambridge, Mass.: The Belknap Press, 1957).

10. (Glencoe, Ill.: Free Press).

11. Adolf A. Berle and Gardiner C. Means, *The Modern Corporation and Private Property*, 2nd rev. ed. (New York: Harcourt, Brace and World, 1968), pp. xxix-xxx, 36.

12. Ronald Müller, "Nation-State Instability and the Global Corporation: The Quest of Control and Accountability," *Peace and Change: A Journal of Peace Research* 3 (Spring 1976): 14-23; Jonathan F. Galloway, "Multinational Corporations and Military-Industrial Linkages," in *Testing the Theory of the Military-Industrial Complex*, ed. Steven Rosen (Lexington, Mass.: D. C. Heath, 1973), pp. 267-90.

13. There are quite a few sources for comparing the economics of U.S. wars. Some of the titles include Chester W. Wright, ed., *Economic Problems of War and Its Aftermath* (Chicago: University of Chicago Press, 1942); Curtis P. Nettels, "Economic Consequences of War: Costs of Production," *The Journal of Economic History*, supplement 3 (December 1943): 1-8; Chester W. Wright, "The More Enduring Economic Consequences of America's Wars," ibid.: 9-26; Simon Kuznets, *National Product in Wartime* (New York: National Bureau of Economic Research, 1945); Milton Friedman, "Price, Income, and Monetary Changes in Three Wartime Periods," *American Economic Review, Papers and Proceedings of the Sixty-Fourth Annual Meeting of the American Economic Association* 42, pt. 2 (May 1952): 612-25; and John G. B. Hutchins, "The Effect of the Civil War and the Two World Wars on American Transportation," ibid.: 626-38. The *Papers and Proceedings of the American Economic Association* in the post-World War II period include numerous essays on the economic consequences of war and comparative studies of wartime situations.

14. Ferguson, *The Power of the Purse: A History of American Public Finance, 1776-1790* (Chapel Hill: The University of North Carolina Press, 1961), pp. 43-44, 57-69, 130, 333-34. See also Anne Bezanson, et al., *Prices and Inflation During the American Revolution, 1770-1790* (Philadelphia: University of Pennsylvania Press, 1951).

15. Seymour Melman, *The Permanent War Economy: American Capitalism in Decline* (New York: Simon and Schuster, 1974), p. 19. See also Ruth Leger Sivard, *World Military and Social Expenditures* (Leesburg, Va.: WMSE, 1978).

16. Allan Nevins, *The War for the Union*, vol. 1: *The Improvised War, 1861-1862*, pp. 202-3, 264-65; vol. 4: *The Organized War to Victory, 1864-1865*, pp. 62 63 (New York: Charles Scribner's Sons, 1959-71); and Russell F. Weigley, *Quartermaster General of the Union Army: A Biography of M. C. Meigs* (New York: Columbia University Press, 1959), pp. 217-18.

17. For differing views on the State Department during World War II, see Gabriel Kolko, *The Politics of War: The World and United States Foreign Policy, 1943-1945* (New York: Random House, 1968), pp. 242-45; and Samuel P. Huntington, *The Soldier and State: The Theory and Politics of Civil-Military Relations* (Cambridge, Mass.: Belknap Press, 1957), pp. 320-22.

18. Thomas C. Cochran, "Did the Civil War Retard Industrialization?" *Mississippi Valley Historical Review* 48 (September 1961): 197-210; Charles A. Beard and Mary R. Beard, *The Rise of American Civilization*, vol. 2 (New York: Macmillan, 1927), chap. 18; Louis M. Hacker, *The Triumph of American Capitalism: The Development of Forces in American History to the End of the Nineteenth Century* (New York: Simon and Schuster,

1940), chap. 24. For some of the other more important literature on the subject, see Ralph Andreano, ed., *The Economic Impact of the American Civil War* (Cambridge, Mass.: Schenkman, 1962); Pershing Vartanian, "The Cochran Thesis: A Critique in Statistical Analysis," *The Journal of American History* 51 (June 1964): 77–89; David T. Gilchrist and W. David Lewis, eds., *Economic Change in the Civil War Era* (Greenville, Del.: Eleutherian Mills-Hagley Foundation, 1965); Harry N. Scheiber, "Economic Change in the Civil War Era: An Analysis of Recent Studies," *Civil War History* 11 (December 1965): 396–411; Stanley L. Engerman, "The Economic Impact of the Civil War," in *The Reinterpretation of American Economic History*, ed. Robert W. Fogel and Stanley L. Engerman (New York: Harper & Row, 1971), pp. 369–79; Jeffrey G. Williamson, "Watersheds and Turning Points: Conjectures on the Long-Term Impact of Civil War Financing," *The Journal of Economic History* 34 (September 1974): 636–61; and Claudia D. Goldin and Frank D. Lewis, "The Economic Cost of the American Civil War: Estimates and Implications," *The Journal of Economic History* 35 (June 1975): 299–326.

19. Gallman, "Commodity Output, 1839–1899," in *Trends in the American Economy in the Nineteenth Century*, by the Conference on Research in Income and Wealth, National Bureau of Economic Research (Princeton, N.J.: Princeton University Press, 1960), pp. 13–71; Gallman, "Gross National Product in the United States, 1834–1909," in *Output, Employment, and Productivity in the United States After 1800*, by the Conference on Research in Income and Wealth, National Bureau of Economic Research (New York: National Bureau of Economic Research, 1966), pp. 3–90.

20. Two vols. (Cleveland: Arthur H. Clark, 1928).

21. (New York: Alfred A. Knopf, 1948).

22. (Madison: University of Wisconsin Press, 1941).

23. Williams, "The Committee on the Conduct of the War: A Study of Civil War Politics," (Ph.D. diss., University of Wisconsin, 1937); Williams, "The Committee on the Conduct of the War," *Journal of the American Military History Institute* 3 (1939): 139–56; Williams, "Benjamin F. Wade and the Atrocity Propaganda of the Civil War," *Ohio Archaeological and Historical Quarterly* 48 (1939): 33–43; Williams, "The Attack upon West Point during the Civil War," *Mississippi Valley Historical Review* 25 (1939): 491–504; and Williams, "Andrew Johnson as a Member of the Committee on the Conduct of the War," *The East Tennessee Historical Society's Publications*, no. 12 (1940): 70–83. For a later analysis that is very similar to Williams, see Virgil Calvin Stroud, "Congressional Investigations of the Conduct of War" (Ph.D. diss., New York University, 1954). The analysis of other historians is referred to in footnote 24.

24. Pierson, "The Committee on the Conduct of the Civil War," *American Historical Review* 23 (April 1918): 550–76; and Trefousse, "The Joint Committee on the Conduct of the War: A Reassessment," *Civil War History* 10 (March 1964): 5–19. Trefousse cites the work of other historians in reference to the committee.

The brilliant essay by Eric L. McKitrick, "Party Politics and the Union and Confederate War Efforts," in *The American Party Systems: Stages of Political Development*, ed. William Nisbet Chambers and Walter Dean Burnham (New York: Oxford University Press, 1967), pp. 117–51, sets forth the most insightful framework for analyzing Civil War politics and the role played by the Committee on the Conduct of the War. James A. Rawley, *The Politics of Union: Northern Politics during the Civil War* (Hinsdale, Ill.: Dryden Press, 1974), largely draws upon McKitrick's ideas in presenting his anlaysis. Much earlier, Pierson suggested some of the main points McKitrick makes. Of course, David Donald's "The Radicals and Lincoln," in his *Lincoln Reconsidered: Essays on the Civil War Era*, 2nd rev. ed. (New York: Vintage, 1956), pp. 103–27, is most relevant to this subject. Donald, "Devils Facing Zionwards," and Williams, "Lincoln and the Radicals: An Essay in Civil War History and Historiography," reexamine their differing interpretations in *Grant,*

Lee, Lincoln and the Radicals, ed. Grady McWhiney (Evanston, Ill.: Northwestern University Press, 1964), pp. 72–117.

25. (New Haven: Yale University Press, 1965).

26. For Ohio, see Ernest L. Bogart, *Financial History of Ohio* (Urbana: University of Illinois Press, 1912); Louis C. Hunter, *Studies in the Economic History of the Ohio Valley*, Smith College Studies in History, no. 19, (Northhampton, Mass.: Smith College, 1933–34); Robert L. Jones, *Ohio Agriculture during the Civil War* (Columbus: Ohio State University Press, 1962); Isaac Lippincott, *A History of Manufactures in the Ohio Valley to the Year 1860* (New York: Knickerbocker Press, 1914); Samuel P. Orth, *The Centralization of Administration in Ohio* (1903; reptd. New York: AMS, 1968); George H. Porter, *Ohio Politics During the Civil War Period* (1911; reptd. New York: AMS, 1968), Emilius O. Randall and Daniel J. Ryan, *History of Ohio*, vols. 4 and 5 (New York: Century History, 1912); Whitelaw Reid, *Ohio in the War*, 2 vols. (Cincinnati: Moore, Wilstach and Baldwin, 1868); Eugene H. Roseboom and Francis P. Weisenburger, *A History of Ohio* (New York: Prentice-Hall, 1934); Eugene H. Roseboom, *The Civil War Era* (Columbus: Ohio State Archaeological and Historical Society, 1944); and Harry N. Scheiber, *Ohio Canal Era* (Athens: Ohio University Press, 1969).

For Illinois, see Cora A. Benneson, "The Work of Edward Everett of Quincy in the Quarter-Master's Department in Illinois During the First Year of the Civil War," *Transactions of the Illinois State Historical Society for the Year 1909* (Springfield: Illinois State Historical Library, 1910): 147–53; Charles A. Church, *History of the Republican Party in Illinois, 1854–1912* (Rockford, Ill.: Wilson Brothers Press, 1912); Arthur C. Cole, *The Era of the Civil War* (Springfield: Illinois Centennial Commission, 1919); Thomas M. Eddy, *The Patriotism of Illinois* (Chicago: Clarke, 1865–66); Edward Everett, "Operations of the Quartermaster's Department of the State of Illinois, 1861–62," *Transactions of the Illinois State Historical Society for the Year 1905* (Springfield: Illinois State Historical Library, 1906): 230–36; Victor Hicken, *Illinois in the Civil War* (Urbana: University of Illinois Press, 1966); Robert P. Howard, *Illinois* (Grand Rapids, Mich.: W. B. Eerdmans, 1972); Theodore C. Pease, *The Story of Illinois*, rev. 3rd ed., by Marguerita J. Pease (Chicago: University of Chicago Press, 1965); and Richard Yates and Catharine Yates Pickering, *Richard Yates, Civil War Governor*, ed. John H. Krenkel (Danville, Ill.: Interstate, 1966).

For Indiana, see Donald F. Carmony, ed., *Indiana* (Bloomington: Indiana University Press, 1966); William A. Rawles, *Centralizing Tendencies in the Administration of Indiana* (1903; reptd. New York: AMS, 1968); Kenneth M. Stampp, *Indiana Politics during the Civil War* (Indianapolis: Indiana Historical Bureau, 1949); George W. Starr, *Industrial Development of Indiana* (Bloomington: School of Business Administration, Indiana University, 1937); William H. H. Terrell, *Indiana in the War of the Rebellion* (reprint of vol. 1 of 1869 edition; Indianapolis: Indiana Historical Bureau, 1960); and Emma L. Thornbrough, *Indiana in the Civil War Era* (Indianapolis: Indiana Historical Bureau, 1965).

For Wisconsin, see Larry Gara, *A Short History of Wisconsin* (Madison: State Historical Society of Wisconsin, 1962); Frederick Merk *Economic History of Wisconsin during the Civil War*, 2nd ed. (Madison: State Historical Society of Wisconsin, 1971); Robert C. Nesbit, *Wisconsin* (Madison: University of Wisconsin Press, 1973); William F. Raney, *Wisconsin* (New York: Prentice-Hall, 1940); Alice E. Smith, *From Exploration to Statehood* (Madison: State Historical Society of Wisconsin, 1973); and Margaret Walsh, *The Manufacturing Frontier* (Madison: State Historical Society of Wisconsin, 1972).

Space limitations preclude the citation of many fine state histories. However, because of their quality and importance, several works require citation: Oscar and Mary Handlin, *Commonwealth . . . Massachusetts, 1774–1861* (New York: New York University Press, 1947); Louis Hartz, *Economic Policy and Democratic Thought: Pennsylvania, 1776–1860* (Cambridge; Harvard University Press, 1948); and Duane Lockard, *The New Jersey Governor: A Study in Political Power* (Princeton, N.J.: Van Nostrand, 1964).

27. (New York: Charles Scribner's Sons, 1959–71).

28. (New York: Alfred A. Knopf, 1965).

29. (New York: Alfred A. Knopf, 1973).

30. Important scholarly work on World War I economic mobilization has been published since my 1967 article. The most significant include Robert D. Cuff, *The War Industries Board: Business-Government Relations during World War I* (Baltimore: The Johns Hopkins University Press, 1973); Melvin I. Urofsky, *Big Steel and the Wilson Administration: A Study in Business-Government Relations* (Columbus: Ohio State University Press, 1969); and Charles Gilbert, *American Financing of World War I* (Westport, Conn.: Greenwood Press, 1970). James Weinstein, *The Corporate Ideal in the Liberal State, 1900–1918* (Boston: Beacon Press, 1968), and Richard L. Watson, Jr., *The Development of National Power: The United States, 1900–1919* (Boston: Houghton Mifflin, 1976), analyze economic mobilization for World War I within the larger context of the Progressive movement, but from differing perspectives. Far and away the best broadly conceived military history of the war is Edward M. Coffman, *The War to End All Wars: The American Military Experience in World War I* (New York: Oxford University Press, 1968).

31. *Roots of War: The Men and Institutions Behind U.S. Foreign Policy* (New York: Atheneum, 1972), pp. 48–49.

A SELECTIVE BIBLIOGRAPHY

The following bibliography indicates the range of sources I have drawn upon for my analysis for the years from the colonial period to the early twentieth century. No work referred to in either the footnotes or the text in any part of this volume is recited in the bibliography. The bibliography is divided into two portions: the colonial years to 1860, and the Civil War to the earlier years of the twentieth century. Most studies that span all or a substantial portion of U.S. history are included in the first section and not recited in the second. A few of the more comprehensive works are placed in the second section because of their special relevance to the Civil War. I am not citing sources for the Confederacy because I have barely mentioned the subject in my essays. However, a fine and current bibliographic essay is included in Emory M. Thomas's *The Confederate Nation, 1861-1865* (New York: Harper & Row, 1979). The following bibliography is basically that which existed in 1975, with the addition of some important studies published after that date.

COLONIAL PERIOD TO CIVIL WAR

Books

Abbot, William W., III. *The Colonial Origins of the United States: 1607-1763*. New York: John Wiley and Sons, 1975.

Adams, Henry. *History of the United States During the Administrations of Jefferson and Madison*. 9 vols., 1921 edition. New York: Charles Scribner's Sons, 1921.

Albion, Robert, and Pope, Jennie, *Sea Lanes in Wartime: The American Experience, 1775-1945*. 2d ed. enlarged. Hamden, Conn.: Archon Books, 1968.

Alden, John R. *A History of the American Revolution*. New York: Alfred A. Knopf, 1969.

Ammon, Harry. *James Monroe: The Quest for National Identity*. New York: McGraw-Hill, 1971.

Aronson, Sidney H. *Status and Kinship in the Higher Civil Service: Standards of Selection in the Administrations of John Adams, Thomas Jefferson, and Andrew Jackson*. Cambridge: Harvard University Press, 1964.

Atherton, Lewis E. *The Frontier Merchant in Mid-America*. 2d rev. ed. Columbia: University of Missouri Press, 1971.

Bailyn, Bernard. *The Ideological Origins of the American Revolution*. Cambridge, Mass.: Belknap Press, 1967.

Baker, Norman. *Government and Contractors: The British Treasury and War Supplies, 1775-1783*. London: Athlone Press, 1971.

Balinky, Alexander. *Albert Gallatin: Fiscal Theories and Politics*. New Brunswick, N.J.: Rutgers University Press, 1958.

Banner, James M., Jr. *To the Hartford Convention: The Federalists and the Origins of Party Politics in Massachusetts, 1789-1815*. New York: Alfred A. Knopf, 1970.

Bauer, K. Jack. *The Mexican War, 1846-48*. New York: Macmillan, 1974.

Baxter, W. T. *The House of Hancock: Business in Boston, 1724-1775*. Cambridge; Harvard University Press, 1945.

Bell, Rudolph M. *Party and Faction in American Politics: The House of Representatives, 1789-1801*. Westport, Conn.: Greenwood Press, 1973.

Bernardo, C. Joseph, and Bacon, Eugene H. *American Military Policy: Its Development Since 1775*. Harrisburg, Penn.: Military Service, 1955.

Boorstin, Daniel J. *The Americans: The Colonial Experience*. New York: Random House, 1958.

——. *The Americans: The National Experience*. New York: Random House, 1965.

Borden, Morton. *Parties and Politics in the Early Republic, 1789-1815*. New York: Thomas Y. Crowell, 1967.

Bowler, Arthur. *Logistics and the Failure of the British Army in America, 1775-1783*. Princeton, N.J.: Princeton University Press, 1975.

Brown, Roger. *The Republic in Peril: 1812*. New York: Columbia University Press, 1964.

Brown, Stuart G. *The First Republicans: Political Philosophy and Public Policy in the Party of Jefferson and Madison*. Syracuse: Syracuse University Press, 1954.

Brownlee, W. Elliot. *Dynamics of Ascent: A History of the American Economy*. New York: Alfred A. Knopf, 1974.

Bruchey, Stuart. *The Roots of American Economic Growth, 1607-1861: An Essay in Social Causation*. New York: Harper & Row, 1965.

——. ed. *The Colonial Merchant*. New York: Harcourt, Brace and World, 1966.

——. *Cotton and the Growth of the American Economy, 1790-1860*. New York: Harcourt, Brace and World, 1967.

Buel, Richard, Jr. *Securing the Revolution: Ideology in American Politics, 1789-1815*. Ithaca: Cornell University Press, 1972.

Burns, James J. *The Colonial Agents of New England*. 1935; reptd. Philadelphia: Porcupine Press, 1975.

Bush, Martin H. *Revolutionary Enigma: A Re-appraisal of Gencral Philip Schuyler of New York*. Port Washington, N.Y.: I. J. Friedman, 1969.

Caldwell, Lynton K. *The Administrative Theories of Hamilton and Jefferson*. 1944; reptd. New York: Russell and Russell, 1964.

Carter, William H. *The American Army*. Indianapolis: Bobbs-Merrill, 1915.

Cassell, Frank A. *Merchant Congressman in the Young Republic: Samuel Smith of Maryland, 1752-1839*. Madison: University of Wisconsin Press, 1971.

Chadwick, French E. *The American Navy*. Garden City: Doubleday, Page, 1915.

Chandler, Alfred D., Jr., ed. *The Railroads: The Nation's First Big Business*. New York: Harcourt, Brace and World, 1965.

Clark, George R., et al. *A Short History of the United States Navy*. Rev. and continued by Carrol S. Alden. Philadelphia: J. B. Lippincott, 1939.

Clark, Victor S. *History of Manufactures in the United States*. 3 vols. 1929; reptd. New York: Peter Smith, 1949.

Cochran, Thomas C. *Business in American Life: A History*. New York: McGraw-Hill, 1972.

——. *New York in the Confederation: An Economic Study*. Philadelphia: University of Pennsylvania Press, 1932.

——. *200 Years of American Business*. New York: Basic Books, 1977.

Cohen, Henry. *Business and Politics in America from the Age of Jackson to the Civil War: The Career Biography of W. W. Corcoran*. Westport, Conn.: Greenwood, 1971.

Coles, Harry L. *The War of 1812*. Chicago: University of Chicago Press, 1965.

Crenson, Matthew A. *The Federal Machine: Beginnings of Bureaucracy in Jacksonian America*. Baltimore: The Johns Hopkins University Press, 1975.

Cromwell, Giles. *The Virginia Manufactory of Arms*. Charlottesville: University Press of Virginia, 1975.

Crowley, J. E. *This Sheba Self: The Conceptualization of Economic Life in Eighteenth Century America*. Baltimore: The Johns Hopkins University Press, 1974.

Cunliffe, Marcus. *The Nation Takes Shape, 1789-1837*. Chicago: University of Chicago Press, 1959.

——. *Soldiers and Civilians: The Martial Spirit in America, 1775-1865*. Boston: Little, Brown, 1968.

Cunningham, Noble. *The Jeffersonian Republicians: The Formation of Party Organization, 1789-1801*. Chapel Hill: University of North Carolina Press, 1957.

——. *The Jeffersonian Republicans in Power: Party Operations, 1801-09*. Chapel Hill: University of North Carolina Press, 1963.

Dangerfield, George. *The Awakening of American Nationalism, 1815-1828*. New York: Harper & Row, 1965.

Dauer, Manning J. *The Adams Federalists*. Baltimore: The Johns Hopkins Press, 1953.

Davis, John P. *Corporations: A Study of The Origin and Development of Great Business Combinations and of Their Relation to the Authority of the State*. Introduction by Abraham Chayes. 1961 edition. New York: Capricorn, 1961.

Davis, Joseph S. *Essays in the Earlier History of American Corporations*. 2 vols. 1917; reptd. New York: Russell and Russell, 1965.

Davis, Lance E.; Hughes, Jonathan R. T.; and McDougall, Duncan M. *American Economic History: The Development of a National Economy*. 3d ed. Homewood, Ill.: Richard D. Irvin, 1969.

Davis, Lance E., and North, Douglass C. *Institutional Change and American Economic Growth*. Cambridge; Cambridge University Press, 1971.

Day, Clive. *A History of Commerce*. 1907; reptd. New York: Longmans, Green, 1914.

Dorfman, Joseph. *The Economic Mind in American Civilization, 1606-1933*. 5 vols. New York: Viking Press, 1946-59.

Douglass, Elisha P. *The Coming of Age of American Business: Three Centuries of Enterprise, 1600-1900*. Chapel Hill: University of North Carolina Press, 1971.

Doyle, James T. *The Organizational and Operational Administration of the Ohio Militia in the War of 1812*. Papers on the War of 1812 in the Northwest, no. 4. Columbus, O.: Anthony Wayne Parkway Board, 1958.

Dupree, A. Hunter. *Science in the Federal Government: A History of Policies and Activities to 1940*. Cambridge; Harvard University Press, 1957.

Dupuy, R. Ernest, and Dupuy, Trevor N. *Military Heritage of America*. New York: McGraw-Hill, 1956.

East, Robert A. *Business Enterprise in the American Revolutionary Era*. New York: Columbia University Press, 1938.

Eckert, Edward K. *The Navy Department in the War of 1812*. Gainesville: University of Florida Press, 1973.

Elazar, Daniel J. *The American Partnership: Intergovernmental Co-operation in Nineteenth-Century United States*. Chicago: University of Chicago Press, 1962.

Ernst, Joseph A. *Money and Politics in America, 1755-1775: A Study in the Currency Act of 1794 and the Political Economy of Revolution*. Chapel Hill: University of North Carolina Press, 1973.

Fairlie, John A. *The National Administration of the United States of America*. New York: Macmillan, 1905.

Ferguson, E. James. *The American Revolution: A General History, 1763-1790*. Homewood, Ill.: Dorsey Press, 1974.

Fischer, David H. *The Revolution of American Conservatism: The Federalist Party in the Era of Jeffersonian Democracy*. New York: Harper & Row, 1965.

Fishlow, Albert. *American Railroads and the Transformation of the Ante-Bellum Economy*. Cambridge: Harvard University Press, 1965.

Fogel, Robert W. *Railroads and American Economic Growth: Essays in Econometric History*. Baltimore: The Johns Hopkins Press, 1964.

Foulke, Roy A. *The Sinews of American Commerce*. New York: Dun and Bradstreet, 1941.

Friedman, Lawrence. *Contract Law in America: A Social and Economic Case Study*. Madison: University of Wisconsin Press, 1965.

Giesecke, Albert A. *American Commercial Legislation Before 1789*. 1910; reptd. New York: B. Franklin, 1970.

Gilchrist, David T., ed. *The Growth of Seaport Cities, 1790-1825*. Charlottesville: University Press of Virginia, 1967.

Goetzman, William H. *Army Explorations in the American West, 1803-1863*. New Haven: Yale University Press, 1959.

Goodrich, Carter. *Government Promotion of American Canals and Railroads, 1800-1890*. New York: Columbia University Press, 1960.

——, ed. *Canals and American Economic Development*. New York: Columbia University Press, 1961.

——, comp. *The Government and the Economy, 1783-1861*. Indianapolis: Bobbs-Merrill, 1967.

Green, Constance M. *Eli Whitney and the Birth of American Technology*. Boston: Little, Brown, 1956.

Green, Fitzhugh. *Our Naval Heritage*. New York: Century, 1925.

Greene, Evarts B. *The Revolutionary Generation, 1763-1790*. New York: Macmillan, 1943.

Greene, Francis V. *The Revolutionary War and the Military Policy of the United States*. New York: Charles Scribner's Sons, 1911.

Greene, Jack P., ed. *The Reinterpretation of the American Revolution, 1763-1789*. New York: Harper & Row, 1968.

Hammond, Bray. *Banks and Politics in America: From the Revolution to the Civil War*. Princeton, N.J.: Princeton University Press, 1957.

Hatch, Louis Clinton. *The Administration of the American Revolutionary Army*. 1904 reptd. New York: B. Franklin, 1971.

Hedges, James B. *The Browns of Providence Plantation*. 2 vols. Providence: Brown University Press, 1968.

Higginbotham, Don. *The War of American Independence: Military Attitudes, Policies, and Practice, 1763-1789*. New York: Macmillan, 1971.

Hill, Forrest G. *Roads, Rails, and Waterways: The Army Engineers and Early Transportation*. Norman: University of Oklahoma Press, 1957.

Hindle, Brooke. *The Pursuit of Science in Revolutionary America, 1735-1789*. Chapel Hill: University of North Carolina Press, 1956.

Hoffman, Ronald. *A Spirit of Dissension: Economics, Politics, and the Revolution in Maryland*. Baltimore: The Johns Hopkins University Press, 1973.

Hofstadter, Richard. *The Idea of a Party System: The Rise of Legitimate Opposition in the United States, 1780-1840*. Berkeley: University of California Press, 1969.

Holt, Michael F. *Forging a Majority: The Formation of the Republican Party in Pittsburgh, 1848-1860*. New Haven: Yale University Press, 1969.

Howe, John R. *From the Revolution through the Age of Jackson: Innocence and Empire in the Young Republic*. Englewood Cliffs, N.J.: Prentice-Hall, 1973.

Hurst, James W. *Law and the Conditions of Freedom in the Nineteenth Century United States*. Madison: University of Wisconsin Press, 1956.

——. *Law and Economic Growth: The Legal History of the Lumber Industry in Wisconsin, 1836-1915*. Cambridge: Harvard University Press, 1964.

Huston, James A. *The Sinews of War: Army Logistics, 1775-1953*. Washington, D.C.: Office of the Chief of Military History, U.S. Army, 1966.

Ingersoll, L. D. *A History of the War Department of the United States*. Washington, D.C.: Francis B. Mohun, 1879.

Jackson, W. Turrentine. *Wagon Roads West: A Study of Road Surveys and Construction in the Trans-Mississippi West, 1846-1869*. Berkeley: University of California Press, 1952.

Jacobs, James R. *The Beginning of the U.S. Army, 1783-1812*. Princeton, N.J.: Princeton University Press, 1947.

Jensen, Merrill. *The American Revolution Within America*. New York: New York University Press, 1974.

——. *The Articles of Confederation: An Interpretation of the Social-Constitutional History of the American Revolution*. Madison: University of Wisconsin Press, 1940.

——. *The Founding of a Nation: A History of the American Revolution, 1763-1776*. New York: Oxford University Press, 1968.

——. *The Making of the Constitution*. Princeton, N.J.: Van Nostrand, 1964.

——. *The New Nation: A History of the United States During the Confederation, 1781-1789*. New York: Alfred A. Knopf, 1950.

Johnson, Edgar A. J. *The Foundations of American Economic Freedom: Government and Enterprise in the Age of Washington*. Minneapolis: University of Minnesota Press, 1973.

Johnson, Emory R. et al. *History of Domestic and Foreign Commerce of the United States*. Washington, D.C.: Carnegie Institution of Washington, 1915.

Johnson, Victor L. *The Administration of the American Commissariat During the Revolutionary War*. Philadelphia: University of Pennsylvania, 1941.

Jones, Fred M. *Middleman in the Domestic Trade of the United States, 1800-1860*. Urbana: University of Illinois, 1937.

Kammen, Michael G. *Empire and Interest: The American Colonies and the Politics of Mercantilism*. Philadelphia: Lippincott, 1970.

Kerber, Linda K. *Federalist in Dissent: Imagery and Ideology in Jeffersonian America*. Ithaca: Cornell University Press, 1970.

Kimmel, Lewis H. *Federal Budget and Fiscal Policy, 1789-1958*. Washington, D.C.: Brookings Institution, 1959.

Kirkland, Edward C. *Men, Cities, and Transportation: A Study in New England History, 1820-1900*. 2 vols. Cambridge: Harvard University Press, 1948.

Klingaman, David C., and Vedder, Richard K., eds. *Essays in Nineteenth Century Economic History: The Old Northwest*. Athens: Ohio University Press, 1975.

Knollenberg, Bernhard. *Washington and the Revolution: A Reappraisal*. New York: Macmillan, 1940.

Knox, Dudley W. *A History of the United States Navy*. New York: G. P. Putnam's Sons, 1936.

Kohn, Richard H. *Eagle and the Sword: The Federalists and the Creation of the Military Establishment, 1783-1802*. New York: Free Press, 1975.

Kraft, Herman F., and Norris, Walter B. *Sea Power in American History: The Influence of the Navy and Merchant Marine upon American Development*. New York: Century, 1920.

Krooss, Herman E., and Blyn, Martin R. *A History of Financial Intermediaries*. New York: Random House, 1971.

——, and Gilbert, Charles. *American Business History*. Englewood Cliffs, N.J.: Prentice-Hall, 1972.

Krout, John A., and Fox, Dixon R. *The Completion of Independence, 1790-1830*. New York: Macmillan, 1944.

Kurtz, Stephen G. *The Presidency of John Adams: The Collapse of Federalism, 1795-1800*. Philadelphia: University of Pennsylvania Press, 1957.

——, and Hutson, James H., eds. *Essays on the American Revolution*. Chapel Hill: University of North Carolina Press, 1973.

Labaree, Benjamin W. *Patriots and Partisans: The Merchants of Newburyport, 1764-1815*. Cambridge; Harvard University Press, 1962.

Leach, Douglas E. *Arms for Empires: A Military History of the British Colonies in North America, 1607-1763*. New York: Macmillan, 1973.

Lemmon, Sarah M. *Frustrated Patriots: North Carolina and the War of 1812*. Chapel Hill: University of North Carolina Press, 1973.

LeRoy, Perry E. *The Weakness of Discipline and Its Consequent Results in the Northwest During the War of 1812*. Papers on the War of 1812 in the Northwest, no. 3. Columbus, O.: Anthony Wayne Parkway Board, 1958.

Lesser, Charles H., ed. *The Sinews of Independence: Monthly Strength Reports of the Continental Army*. Chicago: University of Chicago Press, 1976.

Levy, Leonard W., and Siracusa, Carl, eds. *Essays on the American Republic, 1789-1815*. Hinsdale, Ill.: Dryden Press, 1974.

Livermore, Shaw. *The Twilight of Federalism: The Disintegration of the Federalist Party, 1815-1830*. Princeton, N.J.: Princeton University Press, 1962.

Lloyd, Alan. *The Scorching of Washington: The War of 1812*. Washington, D.C.: Robert B. Luce, 1975.

Love, Robert A. *Federal Financing: A Study of the Methods Employed by the Treasury in Its Borrowing Operations*. New York: Columbia University Press, 1931.

McDonald, Forrest. *The Presidency of George Washington*. Lawrence: University Press of Kansas, 1974.

——. *The Presidency of Thomas Jefferson*. Lawrence: University Press of Kansas, 1976.

——. *We The People: The Economic Origins of the Constitution.* Chicago: University of Chicago Press, 1958.

McFaul, John M. *The Politics of Jacksonian Finance.* Ithaca: Cornell University Press, 1972.

Main, Jackson T. *The Anti-Federalists: Critics of the Constitution, 1781-1788.* Chapel Hill: University of North Carolina Press, 1961.

——. *Political Parties Before the Constitution.* Chapel Hill: University of North Carolina Press, 1973.

——. *Rebel versus Tory: The Crisis of the Revolution, 1773-1776.* Chicago: Rand McNally, 1963.

——. *The Social Structure of Revolutionary America.* Princeton, N.J.: Princeton University Press, 1965.

——. *The Sovereign States, 1775-1783.* New York: New Viewpoints, 1973.

——. *The Upper House in Revolutionary America, 1763-1788.* Madison: University of Wisconsin Press, 1967.

Martin, James K. *Men in Rebellion: Higher Governmental Leaders and the Coming of American Revolution.* New Brunswick, N.J.: Rutgers University Press, 1973.

Miller, John C. *The Emergence of the Nation, 1783-1815.* Glenview, Ill.: Scott, Foresman, 1972.

——. *The Federalist Era, 1789-1801.* New York: Harper & Row, 1960.

——. *Toward a More Perfect Union: The American Republic, 1783-1815.* Glenview, Ill.: Scott, Foresman, 1970.

——. *Triumph of Freedom, 1775-1783.* Boston: Little, Brown, 1948.

Miller, Richard G. *Philadelphia—The Federalist City: A Study of Urban Politics, 1789-1801.* Port Washington, N.Y.: Kennikat Press, 1976.

Miller, William, ed. *Men in Business: Essays in the History of Entrepreneurship.* Cambridge; Harvard University Press, 1952.

Mintz, Max M. *Gouverneur Morris and the American Revolution.* Norman: University of Oklahoma Press, 1970.

Mirsky, Jeanette, and Nevins, Allan. *The World of Eli Whitney.* New York: Macmillan, 1952.

Morgan, Edmund S. *The Birth of the Republic, 1763-89.* Chicago: University of Chicago Press, 1956.

——, and Morgan, Helen M. *The Stamp Act Crisis: Prologue to Revolution.* Chapel Hill: University of North Carolina Press, 1953.

Morison, Samuel E. *The Maritime History of Massachusetts, 1783-1860.* Boston: Houghton Mifflin, 1941.

Morris, Richard B. *Government and Labor in Early America.* 1946; reptd. New York: Octagon Books, 1965.

Nash, Gary B. *Class and Society in Early America.* Englewood Cliffs, N.J.: Prentice-Hall, 1970.

Navin, Thomas R. *The Whitin Machine Works Since 1831: A Textile Machinery Company in an Industrial Village.* Cambridge: Harvard University Press, 1950.

Nettels, Curtis P. *The Emergence of a National Economy, 1775-1815.* New York: Holt, Rinehart and Winston, 1962.

——. *George Washington and American Independence.* Boston: Little, Brown, 1951.

——. *The Roots of American Civilization: A History of American Colonial Life.* 2d ed. New York: Appleton-Century-Crofts, 1963.

Neuenschwander, John A. *The Middle Colonies and the Coming of the American Revolution.* Port Washington, N.Y.: Kennikat Press, 1973.

North, Douglass C. *The Economic Growth of the United States, 1790-1860.* Englewood Cliffs, N.J.: Prentice-Hall, 1961.

——. *Growth and Welfare in the American Past: A New Economic History.* 2d ed. rev. Englewood Cliffs, N.J.: Prentice-Hall, 1974.

——, and Thomas, Robert P., eds. *The Growth of the American Economy to 1860.* Columbia: University of South Carolina Press, 1968.

Oberholtzer, Ellis P. *Robert Morris: Patriot and Financier.* New York: Macmillan, 1903.

Paullin, Charles O. *Paullin's History of Naval Administration, 1775-1911.* Annapolis: U.S. Naval Institute, 1968.

Peckham, Howard H. *The War for Independence: A Military History.* Chicago: University of Chicago Press, 1958.

Pletcher, David M. *The Diplomacy of Annexation: Texas, Oregon, and the Mexican War.* Columbia: University of Missouri Press, 1973.

Ponko, Vincent, Jr. *Ships, Seas, and Scientists: U.S. Naval Explorations and Discovery in the Nineteenth Century.* Annapolis: Naval Institute Press, 1974.

Porter, Glenn, and Livesay, Harold C. *Merchants and Manufacturers: Studies in the Changing Structure of Nineteenth-Century Marketing.* Baltimore: The Johns Hopkins Press, 1971.

Potter, Elmer B., ed. *The United States and World Sea Power.* Englewood Cliffs, N.J.: Prentice-Hall, 1955.

Poulson, Barry W. *Value Added in Manufacturing, Mining, and Agriculture in the American Economy from 1809 to 1839*. New York: Arno Press, 1975.

Pratt, Fletcher. *The Compact History of the United States Navy*. Revised by Hartley E. Howe, New York: Hawthorn, 1962.

——. *The Navy: A History; The Story of a Service in Action*. Garden City: Doubleday, Doran, 1938.

Price, Don K. *Government and Science: The Dynamic Relation in American Democracy*. New York: New York University Press, 1954.

Remini, Robert V. *Andrew Jackson and the Course of American Empire, 1767-1821*. New York: Harper & Row, 1977.

Risch, Erna. *Quartermaster Support of the Army: A History of the Corps, 1775-1939*. Washington, D.C.: Quartermaster Historian's Office, Office of the Quartermaster General, 1962.

Robson, Eric. *The American Revolution in Its Political and Military Aspects, 1763-1783*. Hamden, Conn.: Archon Books, 1965.

Rockoff, Hugh. *The Free Banking Era: A Re-Examination*. New York: Arno Press, 1975.

Rose, Lisle A. *Prologue to Democracy: The Federalists in the South, 1789-1800*. Lexington: University of Kentucky Press, 1968.

Rosenberg, Nathan. *Technology and American Economic Growth*. New York: Harper & Row, 1972.

Rossie, Jonathan G. *The Politics of Command in the American Revolution*. Syracuse: Syracuse University Press, 1975.

Rossman, Kenneth R. *Thomas Mifflin and the Politics of the American Revolution*. Chapel Hill: University of North Carolina Press, 1952.

Rutland, Robert A. *Madison's Alternatives: The Jefferson Republicans and the Coming of War, 1805-1812*. Philadelphia: J.B. Lippincott, 1975.

Sanders, Jennings. *Evolution of Executive Departments of the Continental Congress, 1774-1789*. 1935; reptd. Gloucester: Peter Smith, 1971.

Sapio, Victor A. *Pennsylvania and the War of 1812*. Lexington: University Press of Kentucky, 1970.

Scheiber, Harry N.; Vatter, Harold G.; and Faulkner, Harold U. *American Economic History*. New York: Harper & Row, 1976.

Schlesinger, Arthur M. *The Colonial Merchants and the American Revolution, 1763-1776*. Reptd. New York: F. Ungar Publishing Company, 1957.

Schroeder, John H. *Mr. Polk's War: American Opposition and Dissent, 1846-1848*. Madison: University of Wisconsin Press, 1973.

Seaburg, Carl, and Paterson, Stanley. *Merchant Prince of Boston: Colonel T. H. Perkins, 1764-1854*. Cambridge: Harvard University Press, 1971.

Sellers, Charles G. *James K. Polk: Jacksonian, 1795-1843*. 2 vols. Princeton, N.J.: Princeton University Press, 1957.

Setser, Vernon G. *The Commercial Reciprocity Policy of the United States, 1774-1829*. 1937 reptd. New York: Da Capo Press, 1969.

Short, Lloyd M. *The Development of National Administrative Organization in The United States*. Baltimore: The Johns Hopkins Press, 1923.

Shy, John. *A People Numerous and Armed: Reflections on the Military Struggle for American Independence*. New York: Oxford University Press, 1976.

——. *Toward Lexington: The Role of the British Army in the Coming of the American Revolution*. Princeton, N.J.: Princeton University Press, 1965.

Simpson, William H. *Some Aspects of America's Textile Industry with Special Reference to Cotton*. Columbia: University of South Carolina Press, 1966.

Sisson, Daniel. *The American Revolution of 1800*. New York: Alfred A. Knopf, 1974.

Smelser, Marshall. *The Congress Founds the Navy, 1787-1798*. Notre Dame: University of Notre Dame Press, 1959.

——. *The Democratic Republic, 1801-1815*. New York: Harper & Row, 1968.

——. *The Winning of Independence*. Chicago: Quadrangle, 1972.

Smith, Page. *John Adams*. 2 vols. Garden City: Doubleday, 1962.

Smith, Theodore C. *The Wars Between England and America*. 2d ed. rev. Port Washington, N.Y.: Kennikat Press, 1969.

Spaulding, Oliver L. *The United States Army in War and Peace*. New York: G. P. Putnam's Sons, 1937.

Studenski, Paul, and Krooss, Herman E. *Financial History of the United States: Fiscal, Monetary, Banking, and Tariff, including Financial Administration and State and Local Finance*. New York: McGraw-Hill, 1952.

Sumner, William G. *The Financier and Finances of the American Revolution*. 2 vols. New York: Dodd, Mead, 1892.

Tausigg, F. W. *The Tariff History of the United States*, 8th ed. rev. New York: Capricorn Books, 1964.

Taylor, George R. *The Transportation Revolution, 1815-1860*. New York: Holt, Rinehart and Winston, 1951.

Temin, Peter. *Iron and Steel in Nineteenth Century America: An Economic Inquiry*. Cambridge, Mass.: MIT Press, 1964.

Thayer, Theodore G. *Nathanael Greene: Strategist of the American Revolution*. New York: Twayne, 1960.

Trescott, Paul B. *Financing American Enterprise: The Story of Commercial Banking*. New York: Harper & Row, 1963.

Ver Steeg, Clarence L. *Robert Morris: Revolutionary Financier*. Philadelphia: University of Pennsylvania Press, 1954.

Wade, Richard C. *The Urban Frontier: Pioneer Life in Early Pittsburgh, Cincinnati, Lexington, Louisville, and St. Louis*. Chicago: University of Chicago Press, 1964.

Wallace, Willard W. *Appeal to Arms: A Military History of the American Revolution*. New York: Harper and Brothers, 1951.

Walters, Raymond. *Albert Gallatin: Jeffersonian Financier and Diplomat*. New York: Macmillan, 1957.

Walther, Daniel. *Gouverneur Morris: Witness of Two Revolutions*. New York: Funk and Wagnalls, 1934.

Ward, Harry M. *The Department of War, 1781-1795*. Pittsburgh: University of Pittsburgh Press, 1962.

Weigley, Russell F. *History of the United States Army*. New York: Macmillan, 1967.

———. *Towards an American Army: Military Thought from Washington to Marshall*. New York: Columbia University Press, 1962.

Westcott, Allan, ed. *American Seapower Since 1775*. Rev. ed. Philadelphia: J. B. Lippincott, 1952.

White, Howard. *Executive Influence in Determining Military Policy in the United States*. Urbana: University of Illinois Press, 1925.

White, Leonard D. *The Federalist: A Study In Administrative History—1789-1801*. New York: Macmillan, 1948.

———. *The Jacksonians: A Study in Administrative History—1829-1861*. New York: Macmillan, 1954.

———. *The Jeffersonians: A Study in Administrative History—1801-1829*. New York: Macmillan, 1951.

Williams, William A. *The Contours of American History*. Cleveland: World, 1961.

Wiltse, Charles M. *The New Nation—1800-1845*. New York: Hill and Wang, 1961.

Wood, Gordon S. *The Creation of the American Republic, 1776-1787*. Chapel Hill: University of North Carolina Press, 1969.

Wright, Chester W. *Economic History of the United States*. 2d ed. rev. New York: McGraw-Hill, 1949.

Wright, Esmond. *Fabric of Freedom: 1763-1800*. Rev. ed. New York: Hill and Wang, 1978.

Young, Alfred F., ed. *The American Revolution: Explorations in the History of American Radicalism*. DeKalb: Northern Illinois University Press, 1976.

Young, Eleanor. *Forgotten Patriot: Robert Morris*. New York: Macmillan, 1950.

Young, James S. *The Washington Community, 1800-1828*. New York: Columbia University Press, 1966.

Articles and Dissertations

Baker, Norman. "The Treasury and Open Contracting, 1776-1782." *The Historical Journal* 15 (September 1972): 433-54.

Balinky, Alexander S. "Gallatin's Theory of War Finance." *The William and Mary Quarterly* 16 (January 1959): 73-82.

Bruchey, Stuart. "Success and Failure Factors: American Merchants in Foreign Trade in the Eighteenth and Early Nineteenth Centuries." *Business History Review* 32 (Autumn 1958): 272-92.

Cesari, Gene S. "American Arms-Making Machine Tool Development, 1798-1855." Ph.D. dissertation, University of Pennsylvania, 1970.

Cochran, Thomas C. "The Paradox of American Economic Growth." *Journal of American History* 61 (March 1975): 925-42.

Davis, Lance E., and Legler, John. "The Government in the American Economy, 1815-1902: A Quantitative Study." *Journal of Economic History* 26 (December 1966): 514-52.

East, Robert A. "The Business Entrepreneur in a Changing Colonial Economy, 1763-1795." *Journal of Economic History*, supplement 6 (1946): 16-27.

Egnal, Marc. "The Economic Development of the Thirteen Continental Colonies, 1720-1775." *The William and Mary Quarterly* 32 (April 1975): 191-222.

——, and Ernst, Joseph A. "An Economic Interpretation of the American Revolution." *The William and Mary Quarterly* 29 (January 1972): 3-32.

Ferguson, E. James. "Business, Government, and Congressional Investigations in the Revolution." *The William and Mary Quarterly* 16 (July 1959): 293-318.

——. "The Nationalists of 1781–1783 and the Economic Interpretation of the Constitution." *The Journal of American History* 56 (September 1969): 241–61.

Handlin, Oscar, and Handlin, Mary F. "Revolutionary Economic Policy in Massachusetts." *The William and Mary Quarterly* 4 (January 1947): 3–26.

Hatzenbuchler, Ronald L. "Party Unity and the Decision for War in the House of Representatives, 1812." *The William and Mary Quarterly* 29 (July 1972): 367–90.

Lively, Robert A. "The American System." *Business History Review* 29 (1955): 81–96.

McKee, Marguerite M. "Service of Supply in the War of 1812." *Quartermaster Review* 6 (January 1927): 6–19; 6 (March 1927), 45–55; 6 (May 1927), 27–39; 7 (September 1927), 23–32.

Morton, Louis. "The Origins of American Military Policy." *Military Affairs* 22 (Summer 1958): 75–83.

Nash, Gary B. "The Transformation of Urban Politics, 1700–1765." *Journal of American History* 60 (December 1973): 605–32.

Price, Jacob M. "Economic Function and the Growth of American Port Towns in the Eighteenth Century." *Perspectives in American History* 8 (1974): 123–86.

Skelton, William B. "Professionalization in the U.S. Army Officer Corps During the Age of Jackson." *Armed Forces and Society* 1 (Summer 1975): 443–71.

Stagg, John C. A. "The Revolt Against Virginia: Republican Politics and the Commencement of the War of 1812." Ph.D. dissertation, Princeton University, 1973.

Ver Steeg, Clarence L. "The American Revolution Considered as an Economic Movement." *The Huntington Library Quarterly* 20 (August 1957): 361–72.

Wood, Gordon S. "Rhetoric and Reality in the American Revolution." *The William and Mary Quarterly* 23 (January 1966): 3–32.

Documents

Ferguson, E. James et al., eds. *The Papers of Robert Morris, 1781–1784.* 4 vols. Pittsburgh: University of Pittsburgh Press, 1973–78.

Nevins, Allan, ed. *Polk: The Diary of a President, 1845–1849.* 1929; reptd. New York: Longmans, Green, 1952.

U.S., Bureau of the Census. *Historical Statistics of the United States, Colonial Times to 1957.* Washington, D.C.: Government Printing Office, 1960.

CIVIL WAR TO EARLY TWENTIETH CENTURY

Books

Ambrose, Stephen E. *Halleck: Lincoln's Chief of Staff.* Baton Rouge: Louisiana State University Press, 1962.

——, ed. *Institutions in Modern America: Innovation in Structure and Process.* Baltimore: The Johns Hopkins Press, 1967.

American Iron and Steel Association. *History of the Manufacture of Armor Plate for the United States Navy.* Philadelphia: American Iron and Steel Association, 1899.

Anderson, Bern. *By Sea and By River: The Naval History of the Civil War.* New York: Alfred A. Knopf, 1962.

Bain, William E., ed. *B & O in the Civil War: From the Papers of Wm. Prescott Smith.* Denver: Sage, 1966.

Barney, William L. *Flawed Victory: A New Perspective on the Civil War.* New York: Praeger, 1975.

Bates, David H. *Lincoln in the Telegraph Office: Recollections of the United States Military Telegraph Corps during the Civil War.* 1907; reptd. New York: Appleton-Century, 1939.

Belden, Thomas G., and Belden, Marva R. *So Fell the Angels.* Boston: Little, Brown, 1956.

Berdahl, Clarence A. *War Powers of the Executive in the United States.* Urbana: University of Illinois, 1921.

Bishop, John L. *A History of American Manufactures from 1608 to 1860.* 3 vols. Philadelphia: Edward Young, 1866.

Blodgett, Geoffrey. *The Gentle Reformers: Massachusetts Democrats in the Cleveland Era.* Cambridge: Harvard University Press, 1966.

Bradley, Erwin S. *Simon Cameron, Lincoln's Secretary of War: A Political Biography.* Philadelphia: University of Pennsylvania Press, 1966.

Brock, William R. *Conflict and Transformation: The United States, 1844-1877.* Baltimore: Penguin, 1973.

Brodie, Bernard. *Sea Power in the Machine Age.* Princeton, N.J.: Princeton University Press, 1941.

Bruce, Robert V. *Lincoln and the Tools of War.* Indianapolis: Bobbs-Merrill, 1956.

Bunting, David. *Statistical View of the Trusts: A Manual of Large American Industrial and Mining Corporations Active Around 1900.* Westport, Conn.: Greenwood Press, 1974.

Carman, Harry J., and Luthin, Reinhard H. *Lincoln and the Patronage.* New York: Columbia University Press, 1943.

Carosso, Vincent P. *Investment Banking in America: A History.* Cambridge: Harvard University Press, 1970.

Carrison, Daniel J. *The Navy From Wood To Steel, 1860-1900.* New York: Franklin Watts, 1965.

——. *The United States Navy.* New York: Praeger, 1968.

Challener, Richard D. *Admirals, Generals, and American Foreign Policy, 1898-1914.* Princeton, N.J.: Princeton University Press, 1973.

Chandler, Alfred D., Jr. *Strategy and Structure: Chapters in the History of the Industrial Enterprise.* Cambridge, Mass.: MIT Press, 1962.

——, and Salsbury, Stephen. *Pierre S. Du Pont and the Making of the Modern Corporation.* New York: Harper & Row, 1971.

Church, William C. *The Life of John Ericsson.* 2 vols. New York: Charles Scribner's Sons, 1890.

Cochran, Thomas C., and Miller, William. *The Age of Enterprise: A Social History of Industrial America.* 2d ed. rev. New York: Harper & Row, 1961.

Cole, Arthur H. *The American Wool Manufacture.* 2 vols. Cambridge: Harvard University Press, 1926.

Cooling, Benjamin F. *Benjamin Franklin Tracy: Father of the Modern American Fighting Navy.* New York: The Free Press, 1968.

——, ed. *War, Business, and American Society: Historical Perspectives on the Military-Industrial Complex.* Port Washington, N.Y.: Kennikat Press, 1977.

Commons, John R., et al. *History of Labour in the United States.* 4 vols. New York: Macmillan, 1918-35.

Curry, Leonard P. *Blueprint for Modern America: Non-Military Legislation of the First Civil War Congress.* Nashville: Vanderbilt University Press, 1968.

Davis, Carl L. *Arming the Union: Small Arms in the Civil War.* Port Washington, N.Y.: Kennikat Press, 1973.

Davis, George T. *A Navy Second to None: The Development of Modern American Naval Policy.* New York: Harcourt, Brace, 1940.

Davis, Lance E., et al. *American Economic Growth: An Economist's History of the United States.* New York: Harper & Row, 1972.

Davis, Vincent. *The Admirals Lobby.* Chapel Hill: University of North Carolina Press, 1967.

Degler, Carl N. *The Age of the Economic Revolution, 1876-1900.* Glenview; Ill.: Scott, Foresman, 1967.

Deyrup, Felicia J. *Arms Making in the Connecticut Valley: A Regional Study of the Economic Development of the Small Arms Industry, 1798-1870.* 1949; reptd. York, Penn.: Shumway, 1970.

Diamond, Sigmund, ed. *The Nation Transformed: The Creation of an Industrial Society.* New York: George Braziller, 1963.

Dimock, Marshall E. *Congressional Investigating Committees.* Baltimore: The Johns Hopkins Press, 1929.

Donald, David H. *Liberty and Union.* Lexington, Mass.: D.C. Heath, 1978.

——, ed. *Why the North Won the Civil War.* Baton Rouge: Louisiana State University Press, 1960.

Dubofsky, Melvyn. *Industrialism and the American Worker, 1865-1920.* New York: Thomas Y. Crowell, 1975.

Evans, George H., Jr. *Business Incorporations in the United States, 1800-1943.* New York: Bureau of Economic Research, 1948.

Evans, Holden A. *One Man's Fight for a Better Navy.* New York: Dodd, Mead, 1940.

Evans, Robley D. *A Sailor's Log: Reflections of Forty Years of Navy Life.* New York: D. Appleton, 1907.

Falk, Edwin A. *Fighting Bob Evans.* New York: Jonathan Cape and Harrison Smith, 1931.

Faulkner, Harold U. *The Decline of Laissez Faire, 1897-1917.* New York: Rinehart, 1951.

Fine, Sidney. *Laissez Faire and the General-Welfare State: A Study of Conflict in American Thought, 1865-1901.* Ann Arbor: University of Michigan Press, 1956.

Fish, Carl R. *The American Civil War: An Interpretation.* New York: Longmans, Green, 1937.

Fiske, Bradley A. *From Midshipman to Rear-Admiral.* New York: Century, 1919.

Fite, Emerson D. *Social and Industrial Conditions in the North During the Civil War.* New York: Frederick Ungar, 1909.

Flower, Frank A. *Edwin McMasters Stanton: The Autocrat of Rebellion, Emancipation, and Reconstruction.* Akron: Saalfield, 1905.

Foner, Eric. *Free Soil, Free Labor, Free Men: The Ideology of the Republican Party Before the Civil War.* New York: Oxford University Press, 1970.

Foner, Philip S. *History of the Labor Movement in the United States.* 4 vols. New York: International, 1947-65.

Frederickson, George M. *The Inner Civil War: Northern Intellectuals and the Crisis of the Union.* New York: Harper & Row, 1965.

Friedman, Milton, and Schwartz, Anna J. *A Monetary History of the United States, 1867-1960*. Princeton, N.J.: Princeton University Press, 1963.

Frost, Holloway H. *We Build a Navy*. Annapolis: U.S. Naval Institute, 1929.

Furner, Mary O. *Advocacy and Objectivity: A Crisis in the Professionalization of American Social Science, 1865-1905*. Lexington: University Press of Kentucky, 1975.

Ganoe, William A. *The History of the United States Army*. New York: D. Appleton-Century, 1942.

Garraty, John A. *The New Commonwealth, 1877-1890*. New York: Harper & Row, 1968.

Gibb, George S. *The Whitesmiths of Taunton: A History of Reed and Barton, 1824-1943*. 1943; reptd. New York: Harper & Row, 1969.

Gilbert, James A. *Designing the Industrial State: The Intellectual Pursuit of Collectivism in America, 1880-1940*. Chicago: Quadrangle, 1972.

Gorham, George C. *Life and Public Services of Edwin M. Stanton*. 2 vols. Boston: Houghton Mifflin, 1899.

Gras, N. S. B., and Larson, Henrietta M. *Casebook in American Business History*. New York: Appleton-Century-Crofts, 1939.

Grob, Gerald N. *Workers and Utopia: A Study of Ideological Conflict in the American Labor Movement, 1865-1900*. Evanston: Northwestern University Press, 1961.

Hacker, Louis M. *The World of Andrew Carnegie, 1865-1901*. Philadelphia: Lippincott, 1968.

Hammond, Bray. *Sovereignty and an Empty Purse: Banks and Politics in the Civil War*. Princeton, N.J.: Princeton University Press, 1970.

Harper, Robert S. *Lincoln and the Press*. New York: McGraw-Hill, 1951.

Harris, Brayton. *The Age of the Battleship, 1890-1922*. New York: Franklin Watts, 1965.

Hart, Albert B. *Salmon Portland Chase*. Boston: Houghton Mifflin, 1899.

Hays, Samuel P. *The Response to Industrialism: 1885-1914*. Chicago: University of Chicago Press, 1957.

Hendrick, Burton J. *The Life of Andrew Carnegie*. New York: Doubleday, Doran, 1932.

——. *Lincoln's War Cabinet*, 1946; reptd. New York: Doubleday, 1961.

Herrick, Walter R., Jr. *The American Naval Revolution*. Baton Rouge: Louisiana State University Press, 1966.

Hewes, James E., Jr. *From Root to McNamara: Army Organization and Administration, 1900-1963*. Washington: Center of Military History, U.S. Army, 1975.

Hidy, Ralph W., and Hidy, Muriel E. *Pioneering in Big Business, 1882-1911.* New York: Harper, 1955.

Higgs, Robert. *The Transformation of the American Economy, 1865-1914: An Essay in Interpretation.* New York: John Wiley and Sons, 1971.

Hirsch, Mark D. *William C. Whitney: Modern Warwick.* New York: Dodd, Mead, 1948.

Hittle, J. D. *The Military Staff: Its History and Development.* 3d ed. Harrisburg, Penn.: Stackpole, 1961.

Hoogenboom, Ari. *Outlawing the Spoils: A History of the Civil Service Reform Movement, 1865-1883.* Urbana: University of Illinois Press, 1961.

Howe, George F. *Chester A. Arthur: A Quarter-Century of Machine Politics.* New York: Dodd, Mead, 1934.

Hunt, Thomas. *The Life of William H. Hunt.* Brattleboro, Vt.: E. L. Hildreth, 1922.

Israel, Jerry, ed. *Building the Organizational Society: Essays on Associational Activities in Modern America.* New York: Free Press, 1972.

Jaher, Frederick C., ed. *The Age of Industrialization in America: Essays in Social Structure and Cultural Values.* New York: Free Press, 1968.

Jaques, William H. *Modern Armor for National Defense.* New York: G. P. Putnam, 1886.

Jensen, Richard J. *The Winning of the Midwest: Social and Political Conflict, 1888-1896.* Chicago: University of Chicago Press, 1971.

Jessup, Philip C. *Elihu Root.* 2 vols. New York: Dodd, Mead, 1938.

Kamm, Samuel R. *The Civil War Career of Thomas A. Scott.* Philadelphia: University of Pennsylvania Press, 1940.

Karsten, Peter. *The Naval Aristocracy: The Golden Age of Annapolis and the Emergence of Modern American Navalism.* New York: Free Press, 1972.

Kirkland, Edward C. *Dream and Thought in the Business Community, 1860-1900.* Ithaca: Cornell University Press, 1956.

——. *Industry Comes of Age: Business, Labor, and Public Policy, 1860-1897.* New York: Holt, Rinehart and Winston, 1961.

Kleppner, Paul. *The Cross of Culture: A Social Analysis of Midwestern Politics, 1850-1900.* 2d ed. New York: Free Press, 1970.

Kolko, Gabriel. *Railroads and Regulation, 1877-1916.* Princeton, N.J.: Princeton University Press, 1965.

Krooss, Herman. *American Economic Development: The Progress of a Business Civilization.* 3d ed. Englewood Cliffs, N.J.: Prentice-Hall, 1974.

Larson, Henrietta M. *Jay Cooke: Private Banker*. Cambridge: Harvard University Press, 1936.

Lindsey, David. *Americans in Conflict: The Civil War and Reconstruction*. Boston: Houghton Mifflin, 1974.

Livesay, Harold C. *Andrew Carnegie and the Rise of Big Business*. Boston: Little, Brown, 1975.

Lockard, Duane. *The Politics of State and Local Government*. New York: Macmillan, 1963.

Long, Clarence D. *Wages and Earnings in the United States, 1860-1890*. Princeton, N.J.: Princeton University Press, 1960.

Long, John D. *The New American Navy*. New York: Outlook, 1903.

Macartney, Clarence E. *Lincoln and His Cabinet*. New York: Charles Scribner's Sons, 1931.

McSeveney, Samuel T. *The Politics of Depression: Political Behavior in the Northeast, 1893-1896*. New York: Oxford University Press, 1972.

Mahan, Alfred T. *Naval Administration and Warfare: Some General Principles*. London: Sampson Low, Marston, 1908.

Mann, Arthur. *Yankee Reformers in the Urban Age*. Cambridge: Harvard University Press, 1954.

Marcus, Robert D. *Grand Old Party, Political Structure in the Gilded Age, 1880-1896*. New York: Oxford University Press, 1971.

Martin, Albro. *Enterprise Denied: Origins of the Decline of American Railroads, 1897-1917*. New York: Columbia University Press, 1971.

Martin, Robert F. *National Income in the United States, 1799-1938*. New York: National Industrial Conference Board, 1939.

Meneely, Alexander H. *The War Department, 1861: A Study in Mobilization and Administration*. New York: Columbia University Press, 1928.

Miller, William, ed. *Men in Business: Essays in the History of Entrepreneurship*. Cambridge; Harvard University Press, 1952.

Mitchell, Donald W. *History of the Modern American Navy: From 1883 through Pearl Harbor*. London: John Murray, 1947.

Mitchell, Wesley C. *A History of the Greenbacks, with Special Reference to the Economic Consequences of Their Issue, 1862-65*. Chicago: University of Chicago Press, 1903.

Morgan, H. Wayne. *From Hayes to McKinley: National Party Politics, 1877-1896*. Syracuse: Syracuse University Press, 1969.

——, ed. *The Gilded Age*. Rev. and enlarged ed. Syracuse: Syracuse University Press, 1970.

Morison, Elting E. *Admiral Sims and the Modern American Navy.* Boston: Houghton Mifflin, 1942.

Munroe, John A. *Louis McLane: Federalist and Jacksonian.* New Brunswick, N.J.: Rutgers University Press, 1973.

Murdock, Eugene C. *One Million Men: The Civil War Draft in the North.* Madison: The State Historical Society of Wisconsin, 1971.

Nelson, Daniel. *Managers and Workers: Origins of the New Factory System in the United States, 1880-1920.* Madison: University of Wisconsin Press, 1975.

Nelson, Ralph L. *Merger Movements in American Industry, 1895-1956.* Princeton, N.J.: Princeton University Press, 1959.

Nelson, William H., ed. *Theory and Practice in American Politics.* Chicago: University of Chicago Press, 1964.

Nevins, Allan. *Grover Cleveland: A Study in Courage.* 1932; reptd. New York: Dodd, Mead, 1948.

———. *John D. Rockefeller: The Heroic Age of American Enterprise.* 2 vols. New York: Charles Scribner's Sons, 1940.

Nichols, Roy F. *The Disruption of American Democracy.* New York: Collier Books, 1948.

Niemi, Albert W., Jr. *State and Regional Patterns in American Manufacturing, 1860-1900.* Westport, Conn.: Greenwood Press, 1974.

Niven, John. *Gideon Welles: Lincoln's Secretary of the Navy.* New York: Oxford University Press, 1973.

Oates, Stephen B. *With Malice Toward None: The Life of Abraham Lincoln.* New York: Harper & Row, 1977.

Oberholtzer, Ellis P. *Jay Cooke: Financier of the Civil War.* 2 vols. Philadelphia: George W. Jacobs, 1907.

O'Gara, Gordon C. *Theodore Roosevelt and the Rise of the Modern Navy.* Princeton, N.J.: Princeton University Press, 1943.

Parish, Peter J. *The American Civil War.* New York: Holmes and Meier, 1975.

Perloff, Harvey S., et al. *Regions, Resources, and Economic Growth.* Baltimore: The Johns Hopkins Press, 1960.

Porter, Glenn. *The Rise of Big Business, 1860-1910.* Arlington Heights, Va.: AHM, 1973.

Potter, David M. *The Impending Crisis, 1848-1861.* Completed and edited by Don E. Fehrenbacher. New York: Harper & Row, 1976.

Pratt, Edwin A. *The Rise of Rail-Power in War and Conquest, 1833-1914.* London: P. S. King and Son, 1915.

Pratt, Fletcher. *Stanton: Lincoln's Secretary of War*. New York: W. W. Norton, 1953.

Randall, James G. *Constitutional Problems Under Lincoln*. Rev. ed. Urbana: University of Illinois Press, 1951.

——. *Lincoln, the President*. 4 vols; vol. 4 completed by Richard N. Current. New York: Dodd, Mead, 1945–55.

——, and David, Donald. *The Civil War and Reconstruction*. 2d ed. rev. Lexington, Mass.: D.C. Heath, 1969.

Rappaport, Armin. *The Navy League of the United States*. Detroit: Wayne State University Press, 1962.

Rawley, James W., ed. *Lincoln and Civil War Politics*. New York: Holt, Rinehart and Winston, 1969.

Redlich, Fritz. *The Molding of American Banking: Men and Ideas*. 2 vols. 1947–51; reptd. New York: Johnson Reprint, 1968.

Rein, Bert W. *An Analysis and Critique of the Union Financing of the Civil War*. Amherst: Amherst College Press, 1962.

Riddle, Albert G. *The Life of Benjamin F. Wade*. Cleveland: William W. Williams, 1886.

Ripley, Warren. *Artillery and Ammunition of the Civil War*. New York: Van Nostrand Reinhold, 1970.

Rosenberg, Nathan, ed. *The American System of Manufactures: The Report of the Committee on the Machinery of the United States 1855, and the Special Reports of George Wallis and Joseph Whitworth 1854*. Edinburgh: Edinburgh University Press, 1969.

Rothman, David J. *Politics and Power: The United States Senate, 1869–1901*. Cambridge; Harvard University Press, 1966.

Schlesinger, Arthur M. *Paths to the Present*. New York: Macmillan, 1949.

Schuckers, Jacob W. *The Life and Public Services of Salmon Portland Chase: United States Senator and Governor of Ohio; Secretary of the Treasury, and Chief Justice of the United States*. New York: D. Appleton, 1874.

Seager, H. R., and Gulick, Charles A., Jr. *Trust and Corporation Problems*. New York: Harper and Brothers, 1929.

Sharkey, Robert P. *Money, Class, and Party: An Economic Study of Civil War and Reconstruction*. Baltimore: The Johns Hopkins Press, 1959.

Silbey, Joel H., comp. *The Transformation of American Politics, 1840–1860*. Englewood Cliffs, N.J.: Prentice-Hall, 1967.

Smith, George W., and Judah, Charles. *Life in the North During the Civil War: A Source History*. Alburquerque: The University of New Mexico Press, 1966.

Sproat, John G. *The Best Men: Liberal Reformers in the Gilded Age.* New York: Oxford University Press, 1968.

Steigerwalt, Albert K. *The National Association of Manufacturers, 1895-1914: A Study in Business Leadership.* Ann Arbor: Bureau of Business Research, Graduate School of Business Administration, University of Michigan, 1964.

Stover, John F. *American Railroads.* Chicago: University of Chicago Press, 1961.

Summers, Festus P. *The Baltimore and Ohio in the Civil War.* New York: G.P. Putnam's Sons, 1939.

Taylor, George R., and Neu, Irene D. *The American Railroad Network, 1861-1890.* Cambridge: Harvard University Press, 1956.

Thomas, Benjamin P. *Abraham Lincoln.* New York: Alfred A. Knopf, 1952.

——, and Hyman, Harold M. *Stanton: The Life and Times of Lincoln's Secretary of War.* New York: Alfred A. Knopf, 1962.

Trefousse, Hans L. *Benjamin Franklin Wade: Radical Republican from Ohio.* New York: Tawyne, 1963.

——. *The Radical Republicans: Lincoln's Vanguard for Racial Justice.* New York: Alfred A. Knopf, 1969.

Turner, George E. *Victory Rode the Rails: The Strategic Place of the Railroads in the Civil War.* Indianapolis: Bobbs-Merrill, 1953.

Tyler, David B. *The American Clyde: A History of Iron and Steel Shipbuilding on the Deleware from 1840 to World War I.* Wilmington: University of Delaware Press, 1958.

Unger, Irwin. *The Greenback Era: A Social and Political History of American Finance, 1865-1879.* Princeton, N.J.: Princeton University Press, 1964.

Upton. Emory. *The Military Policy of the United States.* Washington, D.C.: Government Printing Office, 1904.

Vatter, Harold G. *The Drive to Industrial Maturity: The U.S. Economy, 1860-1914.* Westport, Conn.: Greenwood Press, 1975.

Wall, Joseph F. *Andrew Carnegie.* New York: Oxford University Press, 1970.

Ware, Norman. *The Industrial Worker, 1840-1860: The Reaction of American Industrial Society to the Advance of the Industrial Revolution.* Boston: Houghton Mifflin, 1924.

——. *The Labor Movement in the United States, 1860-1895: A Study in Democracy.* New York: D. Appleton, 1929.

Wasson, Robert G. *The Hall Carbine Affair: A Study in Contemporary Folklore.* Rev. ed. New York: Pandick Press, 1948.

Weber, Thomas. *The Northern Railroads in the Civil War, 1861-1865*. New York: King's Crown Press, 1952.

Weeden, William B. *War Government, Federal and State, in Massachusetts, New York, Pennsylvania and Indiana, 1861-1865*. Boston: Houghton Mifflin, 1906.

West, Richard S., Jr. *Gideon Welles: Lincoln's Navy Department*. Indianapolis: Bobbs-Merrill, 1943.

——. *Mr. Lincoln's Navy*. New York: Longmans, Green, 1957.

White, Leonard D. *The Republican Era: A Study in Administrative History—1869-1901*. New York: Macmillan, 1958.

White, William C., and White, Ruth. *Tin Can on a Shingle*. New York: E. P. Dutton, 1957.

Wiebe, Robert H. *The Search for Order, 1877-1920*. New York: Hill and Wang, 1967.

Williams, T. Harry. *Lincoln and His Generals*. New York: Alfred A. Knopf, 1952.

Williamson, Harold F., ed. *The Growth of the American Economy*. 2d ed. Englewood Cliffs, N.J.: Prentice-Hall, 1951.

Wilson, Edmund. *Patriotic Gore: Studies in the Literature of the American Civil War*. New York: Oxford University Press, 1966.

Yellowitz, Irwin. *Industrialization and the American Labor Movement, 1850-1900*. Port Washington, N.Y.: Kennikat Press, 1977.

Articles, Dissertations, and Theses

Allard, Dean. "The Influence of the U.S. Navy upon the American Steel Industry, 1880-1900." M.A. thesis, Georgetown University, 1959.

Chandler, Alfred D., Jr. "The Beginnings of 'Big Business' in American Industry." *Business History Review* 33 (Spring 1959): 1-31.

——, and Galambos, Louis. "The Development of Large-Scale Economic Organizations in Modern America." *Journal of Economic History* 30 (March 1970): 201-17.

Cooling, B. Franklin. "The Formative Years of the Naval-Industrial Complex: Their Meaning for Studies of Institutions Today." *Naval War College Review* 27 (March-April 1975): 53-61.

Elazar, Daniel. "Civil War and the Preservation of American Federalism." *Publius* 1 (Winter 1972): 39-58.

Everett, Edward G. "Pennsylvania Mobilization for War, 1860-1861." Ph.D. dissertation, University of Pittsburgh, 1954.

Farnham, Wallace D. "The Weakened Spring of Government: A Study in Nineteenth Century American History." *American Historical Review* 68 (April 1963): 662–80.

Galambos, Louis. "The Emerging Organizational Synthesis in Modern American History." *Business History Review* 44 (Autumn 1970): 279–90.

Ginsberg, Sanford J. "Corruption and Fraud in Government Contracts During the Civil War." M.A. thesis, Columbia University, 1940.

Jaques, W. H. "The Establishment of Steel Gun Factories in the United States." *Proceedings of the United States Naval Institute* 10 (1884): 527–909.

Kelley, Brooks M. "Fossildom, Old Fogeyism, and Red Tape." *The Pennsylvania Magazine of History of Biography* 90 (January 1966): 93–114.

MacDougall, Donald A. "The Federal Ordnance Bureau, 1861–1865." Ph.D. dissertation, University of California, Berkeley, 1951.

Poulson, Barry W. "Estimates of the Value of Manufacturing Output in the Early Nineteenth Century." *The Journal of Economic History* 29 (September 1969): 521–25.

Riker, William H. "The Senate and American Federalism." *The American Political Science Review* 49 (June 1955): 452–69.

Sexton, Donald J. "Forging the Sword: Congress and the American Naval Renaissance, 1880–1890." Ph.D. dissertation, University of Tennessee, 1976.

Simon, John Y. "Congress Under Lincoln, 1861–1863." Ph.D. dissertation, Harvard University, 1960.

Wacht, Richard F. "A Note on the Cochran Thesis and the Samll Arms Industry in the Civil War." *Explorations in Entrepreneurial History* 4 (1966): 57–62.

Wagner, Keith E. "Economic Development in Pennsylvania During the Civil War, 1861–1865." Ph.D. dissertation, Ohio State University, 1969.

Documents

Beale, Howard K., ed. *The Diary of Edward Bates, 1859–1866*. Washington, D.C.: Government Printing Office, 1933.

——. *Diary of Gideon Welles: Secretary of the Navy Under Lincoln and Johnson*. 3 vols. New York: W. W. Norton, 1960.

Dennett, Tyler, ed. *Lincoln and the Civil War in the Diaries and Letters of John Hay*. New York: Dodd, Mead, 1939.

Donald, David, ed. *Inside Lincoln's Cabinet: The Civil War Diaries of Salmon P. Chase*. New York: Longmans, Green, 1954.

"General M. C. Meigs on the Conduct of the Civil War." *American Historical Review* 26 (January 1921): 285–303.

Mayo, Lawrence S., ed. *American of Yesterday: As Reflected in the Journal of John Davis Long*. Boston: Atlantic Monthly Press, 1923.

Official Records of the Union and Confederate Navies in the War of the Rebellion. Series 2, vols, 1–3. Washington, D.C.: Government Printing Office, 1921–22.

Thompson, Robert M., and Wainwright, Richard, eds. *Confidential Correspondence of Gustavus Vasa Fox, Assistant Secretary of the Navy, 1861–1865*. 2 vols. New York: De Vinne Press, 1920.

Union Defence Committee of the City of New York. *Minutes, Reports, and Correspondence*. Historical introduction by John Austin Stevens. New York: Union Defence Committee, 1885.

U.S. Congress. *The New American State Papers: Agriculture*. 19 vols. Wilmington, Del.: Scholarly Resources, 1972.

——. *The New American State Papers: Explorations and Surveys*. 15 vols. Wilmington, Del.: Scholarly Resources, 1972.

——. *The New American State Papers: Labor and Slavery*. 7 vols. Wilmington, Del.: Scholarly Resources, 1973.

——. *The New American State Papers: Manufacturers*. 9 vols. Wilmington, Del.: Scholarly Resources, 1972.

——. *The New American State Papers: Public Finance*. 32 vols. Wilmington, Del.: Scholarly Resources, 1973.

——. *The New American State Papers: Social Policy*. 5 vols. Wilmington, Del.: Scholarly Resources, 1973.

——. *The New American State Papers: Transportation*. 7 vols. Wilmington, Del.: Scholarly Resources, 1973.

U.S. Congress. Joint Committee on the Conduct of the War. *Report*. 3 vols. 37th Cong., 3d sess., 1863, H. Rept. 108.

——. *Fort Pillow Massacre: Inquiry and Testimony*. 38th Cong., 1st sess., 1864, S. Rept. 63; with appended *Report on the Condition of the Returned Prisoners from Fort Pillow*. 38th Cong., 1st sess., 1864, S. Rept. 68.

——. *Report*. 3 vols. 38th Cong., 2d sess., 1865, S. Doc. 142.

——. *Supplemental Report*. 2 vols. Vols. 2–3 of Senate Reports, 39th Cong., 1st sess., 1866 (nos. 1241–42 of the congressional series).

U.S. Congress. House. *Annual Report of the Secretary of the Navy*. 37th Cong., 3d sess., 1862, H. Exec. Doc., no. 1, vol. 3.

——. *Annual Report of the Secretary of the Navy.* 38th Cong., 1st sess., 1863, H. Exec. Doc., no. 1, vol. 4.

——. *Annual Report of the Secretary of War.* 37th Cong., 3d sess., 1862, H. Exec. Doc., no. 1, vol. 4.

——. *Annual Report of the Secretary of War.* 38th Cong., 1 st sess., 1863, H. Exec. Doc., no. 1, vol. 5.

——. *Letter relating to contracts made by the Quartermaster's Department.* 2d sess., 1865, H. Exec. Doc., no. 84, vol. 14.

——. *Minority Report on Government Contracts,* 37th Cong., 3d sess., 1863, H. Rept. no. 50.

——. *Preliminary Report on the Eighth Census, 1860.* 37th Cong., 2d sess., 1862, Ex. Doc. 116.

——. *Report of the Secretary of the Navy.* 38th Cong., 2d sess., 1864, H. Exec. Doc., no. 1, vol. 6.

——. *Report of the Secretary of the Navy.* 39th Cong., 1st sess., 1865, H. Exec. Doc., no. 1, vol. 5.

——. *Report of the Secretary of the Navy.* 39th Cong., 2d sess., 1866, H. Exec. Doc., no. 1, vol. 4.

——. *Report of the Secretary of War.* 38th Cong., 2d sess., 1865, H. Exec. Doc., no. 83, vol. 14.

——. *Report of the Secretary of War.* 39th Cong., 1st sess., 1865, H. Exec. Doc., no. 1, vol. 3.

——. *Report of the Secretary of War.* 39th Cong., 2d sess., 1866, H. Exec. Doc., no. 1, vol. 3.

——. Committee on Naval Affairs. *Report, Government Armor-Plate Factory.* 64th Cong., 1st sess., 1916, H. Rept. 497.

——. *Report on a National Armory.* 37th Cong., 2d sess., 1862, H. Rept., no. 43, vol. 3.

——. *Report on Government Contracts.* 37th Cong., 2d sess., 1861, H. Rept. no. 2, vol. 1.

——. *Report on Government Contracts.* 37th Cong., 2d sess., 1861, H. Rept., no. 2, vol. 2.

——. *Report on Government Contracts.* 37th Cong., 3d sess., 1863, H. Rept., no. 49.

——. *Report on Manufactures.* 39th Cong., 1 st sess., 1866, H. Exec. Doc., no. 29, Vol. 7.

——. *Report on Navy Department Contracts.* 37th Cong., 2d sess., 1862, H. Exec. Doc., no. 150, vol. 10.

——. *Report on Ordnance and Gun Contracts.* 37th Cong., 2d sess., 1862, H. Exec. Doc., no. 151, vol. 10.

——. *Report on Ordnance and Ordnance Stores.* 39th Cong., 2d sess., 1866, H. Exec. Doc., no. 16, vol. 6.

——. *Report on Purchase of Navy Supplies.* 38th Cong., 1st sess., 1864, H. Exec. Doc., no. 40, vol. 9.

——. *Report on Purchase of Small Arms.* 37th Cong., 2d sess., 1862, H. Exec. Doc., no. 67, vol. 5.

——. *Report on War Department Contracts.* 37th Cong., 2d sess., 1861, H. Exec. Doc., no. 101, vol. 8.

U.S. Congress. Senate. *Annual Report of the Secretary of the Navy.* 37th Cong., 1st sess., 1861, S. Doc., no. 1.

——. *Annual Report of the Secretary of the Navy.* 37th Cong., 2d sess., 1861, S. Doc., no. 1, vol. 3.

——. *Annual Report of the Secretary of War.* 37th Cong., 1st sess., 1861, S. Doc., no. 1.

——. *Annual Report of the Secretary of War.* 37th Cong., 2d sess., 1861, S. Doc., no. 1, vol. 2.

——. *Letter of the Secretary of the Navy.* 37th Cong., 2d sess., 1862, S. Misc. Doc., no. 105.

——. Committee on Naval Affairs. *Methods of Conducting Business and Departmental Changes, Statement of Truman H. Newberry before the Committee.* 60th Cong., 2d sess., 1909, S. Doc. 693.

——. *Report on Contracts for Naval Supplies.* 38th Cong., 1st sess., 1864, S. Rept., no. 99.

——. *Report on Contracts for the Army.* 37th Cong., 2d sess., 1862, S. Exec. Doc., no. 17, vol. 4.

——. *Report on Contracts for War Vessels.* 39th Cong., 1st sess., 1866, S. Exec. Doc., no. 18, vol. 1.

——. *Report on Ordnance and Ordnance Stores.* 37th Cong., 2d sess., 1862, S. Doc., no. 72, vol. 6.

——. *Report on Payments for Military Transportation.* 38th Cong., 2d sess., 1865, S. Exec. Doc., no. 34, vol. 1.

——. *Report on Purchase of Vessels for the Government.* 37th Cong., 2d sess., 1862, S. Exec. Doc., no. 15, vol. 4.

——. *Report on Vessels Chartered for the War Department.* 37th Cong., 2d sess., 1862, S. Exec. Doc., no. 37, vol. 5.

The War of the Rebellion: A Compilation of the Official Records of the Union and Confederate Armies. Series 3, vols. 1–5. Washington, D.C.: Government Printing Office, 1899–1900.

INDEX

ABOUT THE AUTHOR
AND COMMENTATORS

PAUL A. C. KOISTINEN is professor of history at California State University, Northridge, California.

Dr. Koistinen has published *The Hammer and the Sword: Labor, the Military, and Industrial Mobilization, 1920-1945* (New York: Arno Press, 1979). He has also published in the areas of political, economic, and military history, and social problems. His articles and reviews have appeared in *The Journal of American History, Business History Review, Pacific Historical Review, Military Affairs, Labor History, Peace and Change: A Journal of Peace Research*, and *Ohio History*. Several of his articles have been included in numerous anthologies.

Dr. Koistinen has been the recipient of many fellowships and grants from the Foundation, California State University, Northridge, 1964 to the present. He was a Research Fellow of the American Council of Learned Societies and Harvard's Charles Warren Center for Studies in American History concurrently during 1974-75.

Dr. Koistinen holds a B.A., M.A., and Ph.D., from the University of California, Berkeley.

LES ASPIN is a member of the House of Representatives from the First Congressional District in Wisconsin. He has been a member of Congress since 1970. Congressman Aspin currently serves on the House Armed Services Committee and the Government Operations Committee, and is chairman of the Oversight Subcommittee of the House Select Committee on Intelligence.

Aspin has been active in government service and politics since 1960. He has held high and prestigious federal appointments, including a position in the office of the secretary of defense. From 1968-70 he was an assistant professor of economics at Marquette University. Congressman Aspin was an army officer from 1966-68, serving for a time in Vietnam.

Aspin received his B.A. from Yale University in 1960, his M.A. from Oxford University in 1962, and his Ph.D. from the Massachusetts Institute of Technology in 1965. His academic specialities include economics, politics, and philosophy.

ROBERT K. GRIFFITH, JR. is a major in the U.S. Army. From 1974-79 he was a member of the history department, United States Military Academy. In 1979 he was named a teaching fellow at the Combat Studies Institute of the U.S. Army Command and General Staff College.

Major Griffith is the author of "Quality not Quantity: The Volunteer Army During the Depression," which *Military Affairs* will publish, and "The Volunteer Army and American Society, 1919–1940" (Ph.D. diss., Brown University, 1979).

Major Griffith served with armored and armored cavalry units in the United States, Vietnam, and Germany. His military decorations include the Silver Star, Bronze Star, and Purple Heart.

Major Griffith graduated from West Point in 1967. He holds an M.A. and Ph.D. from Brown University.